Hospitality Innovation Management

HOSPITALITY INNOVATION MANAGEMENT

Ruchi Mehta

CENTRUM PRESS
NEW DELHI-110002 (INDIA)

CENTRUM PRESS
H.O.: 4360/4, Ansari Road, Daryaganj,
New Delhi-110002 (India)
Tel: 23278000, 23261597, 23255577, 23286875
B.O.: No. 1015, Ist Main Road, BSK IIIrd Stage,
IIIrd Phase, IIIrd Block, Bengaluru-560085 (INDIA)
Tel: 080-41723429
Email: centrumpress@gmail.com
Visit us at: www.centrumpress.com

Hospitality Innovation Management

First Edition, 2013

ISBN 978-93-81460-21-4

PRINTED IN INDIA

Printed at Balaji Offset, Delhi.

Contents

Preface

Innovation is at the heart of hospitality organizations' success because it allows them to improve the quality of products, increase efficiency, cut costs, meet the changing needs of customers, increase sales and profits, gain a greater market share and differentiate themselves from competitors. However, hospitality innovation is an understudied area. Ottenbacher and Gnoth suggested that due to the lack of such knowledge, "managers often rely on gut feeling, speculation, and their own limited experience about the keys to innovation success".

The importance of innovation as the key driver of sustained success has been well documented in the marketing and hospitality literature. In the past decade, several studies have investigated the success factors associated with service innovations. Few of these studies, however, have dealt with hospitality innovations. Executives from fast moving consumer goods companies have been attracted to the hospitality and leisure industry by the opportunity to transform businesses perceived as lagging behind in terms of brand development and innovation. Despite similarities between the hospitality and consumer goods sectors, those we spoke to referred to a marked distinction between how the sectors currently operate and future opportunities for growth. Asia Pacific, especially China, is expected to produce massive growth, as is Europe – still a fragmented sector due to the proliferation of family owned companies. Executives warn that businesses will have to decide whether they are top or bottom end niche players, since the middle ground is becoming increasingly commoditised with less room for growth.

The Internet has had a significant impact on what is otherwise still a fairly conservative industry, bringing more choice for consumers and affecting the marketing model. The sector currently tends to lack sophistication in consumer insight, innovation and marketing. More emphasis is needed on creating strategies based on consumer data and research to determine consumer needs and behaviour. With a shortage of talent in the sector, more resources need to be invested in developing existing people. Nevertheless, the industry will continue to bring in talent from outside and address the relatively low levels of compensation. As the sector matures, attracting great talent, particularly in marketing, should become easier.

There are three streams of hospitality innovation research. The first identifies critical procedures for developing hospitality innovation, the second focuses on developing a typology for hospitality innovation, and the third investigates factors that may enhance hospitality. One common thread among these lines of inquiry is that, to some extent, they all focus on the importance of HRM practices to hospitality innovation. For instance, in the first stream, various researchers have discussed how employees make a difference in the steps that lead to hospitality innovation. Jones found that many firms that were increasingly developing innovation did not have a formal R&D department; instead, they depended on creative personnel and developed an organizational culture that encouraged new idea formulation. Moosa and Panurach differentiated between centralized and decentralized innovation. The former type of innovation is usually generated by the marketing or R&D department, while the latter one is generated by front-line employees. They posited that the former type of innovation is "insufficient because centralized innovation will always be limited by the available talent, attention, insights and instincts of the managing group". Thus they suggested that organizations need to foster decentralized innovation because "front-line employees, those closest to the customers and the work of delivering products and services, have some of the freshest ideas and thoughts". Similarly, Ottenbacher and Harrington stressed the importance of human factors in hospitality innovation, noting that "because of the simultaneity of production and consumption and the importance of human factors in service delivery, employees play a more important role in fine dining innovation than in other product innovation situations".

This book has over all covered a new ideal in this subject so it is useful for students.

—*Author*

1

Strategies and Concepts for Innovation

The tourism consumer is the critical judge of successful marketing and public relations activities. In today's increasingly competitive marketing environment there has been a shift from traditional marketing techniques towards more aggressive and varied approaches to marketing and communication.

The change from transactional to relationship management in marketing over the past fifty years has been marked by improvements in consumer satisfaction and client recommendation of repeat purchase of products and services.

In the twenty first century informed and discerning clients dictate whether the brand and image are coherent and the recognition by organisations of the power of their brand and its image is a central theme to contextualise the marketing activity.

Today's brands are often built with effective PR campaigns and then maintained through a blend of marketing and PR tactics.

The impact of the Internet is having profound impact upon PR and Marketing practices enabling PR practitioners to conduct two way communications in order to maintain and enhance customer relationships.

Indicative Content

- Marketing strategies in the hospitality and tourism sector
- Creating and developing customer loyalty
- Network and relationship marketing

- Brand identity and strategy
- Strategic customer relations
- Viral and guerilla marketing
- Effectiveness of e-marketing.

Innovation Management – An Indian Experience

Innovation has been instrumental for technology upgradation leading to productivity, growth and international competitiveness of the industry. The technology development, its further adaptation and application have never been the straightforward process.

A successful technology innovation requires a strong interactive mechanism complete with the feedback loop for various stakeholders viz. industry, extraneous knowledge sources, inspection & certification agencies and most importantly, the users or the market. However, the problems become acute in rapidly changing technological and economic environment.

Technology innovation is key to the survival of small & medium enterprises (SMEs) in India. The SMEs play a crucial role in Indian industry. They constitute 15 million units, contribute 6-7% of total GDP and employ 30 million people.

More importantly, 40% of the industrial production in India comes from the SMEs. Finance is the key driver for innovation process for the SMEs and the cost of funds should be attractive enough for them for investing in projects involving technological risks. They are often beset by multi-faceted problems, which include the following :

- Availability of quality raw materials
- Inadequate infrastructure facilities
- Availability of skilled labour
- Access to market
- Development of in-house technical & managerial capabilities
- Long product development cycle
- Extraneous knowledge support
- Lack of standards & certification process in some cases their internal resistance to change....

In order to mitigate such problems and to effect a seamless technology development process for subsequent commercialization, the requirement of a well-defined strategy had strongly been felt by the Government. Four decades of planned development have elevated India to a stage, where the country can show some remarkable strength in modern technologies for achieving development goals.

There exists a chain of national laboratories, specialized R&D agencies in defence, atomic energy & space, Indian Institutes of Technology (IITs), universities & other academic institutions of higher learning, which are capable of providing world-class expertise, technically trained manpower and technology support to the industry.

The institutes have been pursuing application-oriented research, which led to amassing an excellent knowledge pool. However, the extent of knowledge flow from such centres of excellence to the industry for its actual exploitation for the prototype development and reaching out to market has been limited. Various policy interventions were directed and organizational structures along with the fiscal incentives were designed by the Government from time to time to bridge the gap.

Innovation Management Approaches

Keeping in view of the critical need for technology innovation, *Technology Information, Forecasting and Assessment Council (TIFAC)* was conceptualized as a unique knowledge networking institution in India for facilitating novel technology developments for the key sectors of economy. TIFAC was established as an autonomous organization under the aegis of Department of Science & Technology, Government of India.

As a follow-up of a detailed sectoral analysis coupled with the technology assessment exercise, composites were identified as an important performing material with a wide array of applications touching a large number of people from different walks of life.

The increasing demand for materials with higher strength-to-weight ratio has led to the cognizance of composites. The composite technology of a matrix reinforced with man-made fibres such as glass, Kevlar, carbon etc. after meeting the challenges of aerospace sector has cascaded down for catering to the industrial and domestic applications. Composite structures are becoming increasingly significant in a number of novel applications in engineering fields. They meet stringent requirement such as performance at high temperature, pressure, corrosive environment or high stress.

Due to their lightweight coupled with high strength, composites can replace wooden & heavy metallic parts in transportation (automobiles & railways) thus directly contributing to energy savings. The usage of composites for bio-medical applications can be a boon to the patients for reducing the drudgery of carrying heavy weight.

Assessing the status of composite industry in India, it was felt that there was an ardent need to boost the usage of composites through indigenous design capability, incorporation of advanced fabrication technologies, product development & testing.

Any major impact in the sector seemed unlikely unless it was taken up as a mission mode programme with commitment from the Government. The *Advanced Composites Mission*, initiated by TIFAC, aimed to promote various composite applications in components for railways & automobiles, construction materials, medical appliances, chemical & marine applications and others. Important strategic inputs and specific products were developed for commercialization under the mission mode programme.

In line with the above, setting up centres of excellence for assistance in design, prototype development, product evaluation and also for technology transfer & absorption by the Indian composite industry were identified as a priority areas. The Mission had set up two composite design & development centres viz. RV-TIFAC Composite Design Centre (CDC), Bangalore and Composite Technology Centre at IIT-Madras, Chennai. Manpower was recognized as another key factor for development of composite technology.

The Mission had launched a major project in partnership with the Central Institute of Plastics Engineering & Technology (CIPET), Chennai for developing courses & curricula for training persons in composite technology.

In view of the application potential of composites, a fast paced indigenous product development & its induction was felt necessary for important sectors. Other aspects such as usage of natural fibre (jute, sisal, pineapple, banana, coir...) in composites, development of new fibre & resin system, recyclability/reusability of composites and their effective disposal were also considered important thrust areas.

The Advanced Composites Mission had experimented with varied innovation management models for the aforesaid development of composite applications. They are explained hereunder:

Model - I : Laboratory Based Technology Development

Initially the projects were conceived by the Mission wherein the technology development activities would be undertaken by a national R&D lab. The projects would be financially supported by TIFAC and the participating industry; the funds were required to be released to the R&D lab working on the project. The industry partner was required to upscale the technology for commercialization once the product gets developed successfully.

Two projects were conceptualized in this mode in partnership with a defence research laboratory. The products targeted for development were high-technology applications warranting extremely critical testing & certification regime. In fact, the criticality of testing requirement was not assessed properly prior to project conceptualization.

The project evaluation & monitoring mechanism did not foresee any involvement of users or certification agencies. Thus the product development process distanced itself from the market and when the prototypes were developed successfully, their induction by the users was difficult.

The participating industry was not much inclined to the aforesaid mechanism, especially for providing funding support to the R&D lab. As the lab was the centre of all actions, the industry had perceived that they were extraneous to the entire development process. Moreover, all the assets were being created within the lab premises with the financial support from TIFAC and the industry– this was not an attractive proposition for the industry.

As the project involved very sophisticated level of technology development followed by critical testing procedures, the development cycle experienced many bottlenecks and delays. The industry partner lost interest in the project in due course as the project showed no promise for possibility of early commercialization.

Model – II : Lab Oriented Technology Development with Extraneous Industry Involvement

The experience of taking up the technology development activities at the R&D lab did not meet with much success as explained above. This prompted the Mission to involve the user agencies more proactively in the project to the extent of sharing the financial assistance along with TIFAC. In this new approach, the financial support was still extended to the national R&D labs and the industry partners were not directly involved in the project.

The knowledge partner (R&D lab), identified for the project, had sufficient expertise in product design & development, selection of raw materials and necessary product testing. The user agency had identified the product to be developed under the project and shown keen interest in participating in TIFAC mode of project implementation.

They took a very active part in the project by extending financial assistance to the R&D lab to the tune of 50% of the total project cost.

The user agency helped in finalizing the design approach, carrying out necessary in-house testing & field trials for prototype approval. Such an involvement by the user agency was expected to play a catalytic role for early induction of the product. On successful technology development and transfer of technology licensing rights to the user agency, they also ensured repayment of funds to facilitating agency, TIFAC.

As technology facilitator, TIFAC had extended financial support to the tune of 50% of the total project cost to the R&D lab for undertaking developmental project.

This technology innovation approach was followed in *development of FRP sleepers* for railway girder bridges. The Research & Development Establishment (Engineers), Pune was identified as the R&D lab and Research, Design & Standards Organization (RDSO), Lucknow acted on behalf of the user agency (Indian Railways) for the project.

Composite sleepers were designed to replace the existing wooden and steel channel sleepers on girder bridges. The sleepers were successfully tested at RDSO & Structural Engineering Research Centre (SERC), Chennai and finally accepted by the Indian Railways due to excellent vibration absorption, extended life cycle, considerable weight saving and improved maintainability.

However, there was no direct involvement of the industry in the entire development process. While the R&D lab designed the product and finalized its fabrication process, they could not develop the prototype for lack of advanced fabrication equipment. Hence, the technology was required to be transferred to competent composite fabricators with good technical capabilities for prototype development and its large-scale replication in case of commercial induction.

Though industries were identified at later stage for the prototype development, they were not fully geared to adopt and absorb the technology from the R&D lab. This led to delay in entire product development cycle.

Model – III : Industry Centric Innovation

Based on earlier experiences of mixed successes, a new strategy was adopted and the Mission policies were reoriented considerably for ensuring an active involvement of the industry in the entire process of technology development. It was realized that successful technology development model should be industry centric, keeping the industry as the centre of all the actions namely, product conceptualization & design, assets creation for prototype development, testing and finally large-scale replication for wider induction. This called for extraneous knowledge support from the leading centres of excellence across the country and brought the industries closer for technology absorption, development & dissemination. The knowledge partner provided design support to the industry in terms of engineering drawings, preparation of data sheets, reports and advice on raw material selection, fabrication process, testing etc. for successful development of the prototype composite product. The programme involved faculty members from the renowned institutes such as IITs.

In order to reduce technology development cycle, the Mission started involving key persons from the user groups, certifying agencies etc. in the project monitoring committees for effective project management, technology support, product evaluation etc.

The Committee provided a right mix of expertise on design, process, machine/equipment, testing & quality assurance. Such user oriented project monitoring has been the cornerstone of project management and it has greatly helped in improving the market reach of composite products and their acceptance in the shortest possible time. Thus, the projects were more focused with clear time bound objectives and most of them were completed with successful product development and user acceptance.

With the modified Mission priorities, the Technology Development Assistance was extended directly by TIFAC to the industries on repayable basis. The major thrust was on generating market-driven projects with potential applications in sectors such as railways, telecom, building & construction, biomedical etc. With this change in focus, industry's participation was intensified & many new projects with novel composite applications were initiated.

Supported by the Technology Development Assistance from TIFAC, the industries had set up advanced fabrication system in-house and testing & quality control facilities for manufacturing composite products meeting the international standards & quality norms. This has contributed significantly to the up gradation of composite technology for a wide array of applications. This greatly contributed to the capability improvement for the industry and generated confidence among the users in product acceptance.

Achievement Highlights

The Advanced Composites Mission made substantial contribution towards development and growth of indigenous composite products. With the evolution of optimally workable technology innovation mechanism, a large number of projects was initiated in partnership with the Indian composite industry and academia.

The composite technology originally developed for the aviation and space sectors has started reaching common market in a cost-effective manner.

The Mission was successful in bringing a culture of technology development towards commercialization especially for the technology starved SMEs. In view of the achievements and successes of the Advanced Composites Mission, the Advanced Composites Programme was taken up by TIFAC as a regular activity. Some of the products developed under the programme for different sectors are highlighted as follows:

- Composites in transportation – gear-case for diesel locomotives, energy efficient axial flow radiator cooling fans for diesel locomotive,
- modular toilets for railway coaches, main & sliding doors for railway passenger coaches,
- interiors for drivers' cabin in diesel locomotive for railways, interiors for railway passenger coaches,
- Sky bus coach for Konkan Railway,
- bracket assembly for overhead railway electric traction,
- houseboat, components for high-end passenger buses, filament wound road tankers,
- high speed boats Industrial composite products – double-wall vessels for chemical storage, axial flow fans (for cooling towers, textile mill dehumidifiers, air heat exchangers, mine ventilation), pressure vessels, filament wound pipes & pipe-fittings, filament wound venturi scrubber, CNG cylinders for automobiles, grids/gratings for chemical industry,
- modular acoustic enclosures for DG sets o Building & infrastructure
- multi-purpose modular housing system o Biomedical application
- below knew artificial limbs for physically handicapped, carbon fibre external ring fixator as an orthopaedic appliance o Natural fibre composites
- jute-coir boards as wood substitutes, bamboo laminates for flooring tiles and shutters, jute composite components for footwear.

Select Case Studies

The Advanced Composites programme has proven itself as an efficient delivery mechanism imparting excellent economic advantage in terms of creating material with superior properties, substituting scarce materials, developing value-added applications and most importantly business volume generation.

The industry partners for the programme have achieved strong and profitable growth (+10% to 30% of sales increase per year generating 10% to 40% of return on capital employed). The following section discusses select case studies concerning technology development projects with the details on the need for developing such products, process of development and the outcomes.

Composite Modular Toilets for Railway Passenger Coaches

Indian Railways have been striving to improve passenger comfort and amenities with better reliability. It was felt that the toilets at the passenger coaches needed gross improvement in aesthetics and functionality.

The toilets, presently built integral with the coaches, are not at all aesthetically appealing. The toilet floors are provided with faulty gradient and thus they are prone to water accumulation and heavy leakages.

The leakage from the toilet floors corrodes the undercarriage structural elements. All these called for frequent maintenance and expensive repairs especially for the undercarriage. In such a scenario, the toilets made of composites with a moulded floor could be the right step for preventing the leakage and corrosion. This has been the collective view of the Carriage Directorate of RDSO-Lucknow and ICF-Chennai of Indian Railways.

In view of the above, the development of composite modular toilet units of improved aesthetics and maintainability was identified as one of the priority projects for Indian Railways. In line with the identified requirement, the project was launched by TIFAC in partnership with *Hindustan Fibre Glass Works, Vadodara* with technology support from *IIT-Bombay*.

Apart from the involvement of Industrial Design Centre (IDC) of IIT-Bombay for improved aesthetics, ergonomics and usability, support from Department of Aerospace Engineering was also sought in terms of structural design of composite toilets, reinforcement lay-up, mould design & fabrication, selection of suitable raw materials, testing & mechanical characterization and quality assurance norms for fabrication.

In order to bring in the right expertise and assistance for performance evaluation & guidance, the Advanced Composites Programme involved experts from various units of railways such as Railway Board, RDSO, RCF, ICF etc in the project evaluation committee.

The composite modular toilet unit was developed with four parts: the flooring trough, one L-shaped sidewall, one C-shaped sidewall & roof. All these composite components were fabricated by resin transfer moulding (RTM) process; such large components were fabricated by RTM for the first time in India.

The modularity in construction for the toilet helped in taking its each part inside the compartment through the main door and they could be assembled in situ within a short time. The composite toilet unit has been light in weight, corrosion resistant, fire retardant; it has longer life with easy maintainability. Salient features of the toilets are as follows:

- Composite sandwich door, lipped with pultruded composite frame on all four sides of the door
- Ventilation provided in the toilet on the side-wall and at the lower part of the door
- Sacrificial PVC flooring with improved anti-skid and anti-abrasion properties used above the composite trough
- Concealed type Ki-tech flexible conduits with aluminium core encased within two HDPE layers for longer life with virtually no maintenance and required contours during fixing
- Light-weight 110 V DC fan, one CFL light (110 V), push type flush valve, longer vertical handle for support on right side of the pan etc. incorporated in the Indian style toilet unit.

Various other features such as space for toiletries, mug space & its mounting arrangement, taps for washbasin & near pan, wall protector, mirror positions etc. were finalized for the composite toilet unit.

Four toilet units were fitted into an AC-II tier coach of Mumbai-Delhi Rajdhani Express. The coach with composite toilets was inaugurated by Dr. R Chidambaram, Chairman-TIFAC, on October 20, 2001, at Carriage Repair Workshop of Western Railway, Mumbai, in the presence of a galaxy of senior officials from Indian Railways.

Based on the initial field trials, composite toilets were inducted by the Indian Railways for many important trains. The project bagged the Certificate of Merit under the National Award for Excellence in Consultancy Services–2001 awarded to IDC/IIT-Bombay by the Consultancy Development Centre of DSIR, Govt. of India. The technology for composite toilet units was licensed to nine composite fabricators due to its large demand by the Indian Railways.

Composite Interiors for Driver's Cabin in Diesel Locomotive

There are two driver seats along with the consoles as mirror images at two ends of the driver's cabin for diesel locomotives. The driver's cabin accommodates the tool kit, almirah, panels for various instruments & control etc. The cabin in its present design is too cramped for free movement & comfort for the operators.

The consoles appear cluttered with not so well designed placement of several dials & gauges. The Indian Railways have been seriously contemplating ways and means for an ergonomic improvement of driver's cabin interiors for diesel locomotives along with an improved aesthetic appeal.

In view of the long felt needs by the Indian Railways for modernizing the driver's cabin interiors, the project was launched with *M/s. Black Burn Co. Pvt. Ltd., Kolkata* with technology support from *IIT-Bombay*. The project aimed at developing the driver's cabin interiors for diesel locomotives using composite components thereby improving the aesthetics and ergonomics for improved user comfort.

The Industrial Design Centre (IDC) of IIT-Bombay helped in prototype design & development, preparation of various design drawings, fabrication of full-scale prototype etc. For a user oriented development approach, the experts from Railway Board, RDSO, DLW, DLMW and Western Railway were inducted in the project review & monitoring activities.

The new design of the cabin as evolved has addressed appropriate paneling, comfortable seats, clear visibility while operating the locomotive, proper arrangement of gauges, provision of space for tools & kits etc. The problems of heat & sound insulation were also addressed while developing the cabin interiors.

In addition, the safety features such as increase in roof height inside the cabin, scientific illumination of the cabin, ergonomically correct placement of various instruments, indication regarding driver's attentiveness were all addressed in the driver's cabin. The modifications as suggested by the users were incorporated at various stages.

The design of interiors comprising wall & roof panels, flooring, console panel etc. was carried out based on human body clearances, space requirement for ingress & outgress, tool box dimensions, minimum space for drivers' belongings etc. The side panels & console panels were given an off-white granular granite finish. The roof panels were painted white to improve the interior light condition.

A cupboard was provided at the short-hood side to accommodate tools and other accessories. The space between the consoles was increased considerably to facilitate free movement of personnel and height adjusted to ensure eyeball contact between driver & assistant.

Openable hatches were provided below the console desk for access to the cables, gauges & other mountings. The roof comprised of two arched panels on either side and a central panel to accommodate lighting fixtures with shadow light. The set of wires/ cables feeding the two console panels were laid below the floor.

The floor of the cabin was made in three-piece modular composite panels for accessing underneath. Wide openable hatches were provided at the long-hood side for access to various MCBs/ switches/knobs, gauges and other accessories. The existing metal door was cladded with composite panels inside and a standard lock was provided.

On approval of the full-scale mock-up of driver's cabin, the drivers' cabins of two diesel locomotives (WDM-2A) were furnished with composite interiors at Ratlam loco-shed of Western Railway by Black Burn & Co. The users' feedback from the field trials of the diesel locomotives furnished with composite interiors has been quite encouraging.

The diesel loco maintenance unit from Ratlam loco-shed had

inferred that the newly furnished diesel loco driver's cabin has created quite a conducive workspace. STR covering the technical specifications, design drawings, fabrication process and testing requirements for the newly developed composite interiors has been finalized by RDSO and efforts are underway in inducting them on large-scale by Indian Railways.

Composite Houseboat for Tourism

Originally known as 'kettuvallom' and used for carrying rice & other grains in the villages dotting along the backwaters of Kerala, houseboat is a rather recent innovation positioned as the unique attraction for an already thriving tourism industry in the state. A houseboat can be the ultimate statement in luxury.

The tour operators in Kerala have experimented with many variants of the houseboat. While the standard houseboat is equipped with two or three bedrooms, some have been made into a honeymooner's haven with one large bedroom.

Some have also been designed with a double-deck configuration with top deck being used for conference and the lower one serving as the dining hall.

Conceptualized around 10 years ago, houseboat in the backwaters of Kerala has become quiet a rage with a current population of around 250 and about 15-20 boats being built every year for catering to an ever rising demand, houseboat is traditionally made of resinous wood and it takes 8-10 trees (70-80 years old) to build one.

Apart from denuding the forest cover, building a traditional houseboat is extremely manpower intensive and nearly 40 man months of skilled labour are required to shape it up.

The wooden hull is highly prone to decay due to its continuous contact with water calling for regular tarring of the hull and frequent outages of the houseboat. The superstructure outer surface thatched with woven bamboo mat requires replacement every year due to an excessive fungal attack in a moist environment.

Thus the cost of maintenance becomes quite prohibitive for the houseboat and for the tourists to enjoy that 'ultimate in luxury' the cost of occupancy rises!

The introduction of diesel engines into houseboats has made

them economical to operate, but it has become uncomfortable due to noise and vibrations. All these made houseboat a good candidate to be developed in composite for corrosion resistance, ease in fabrication and maintenance free service.

The development of *composite houseboat* for tourism was taken up as a project under the Advanced Composites Programme of TIFAC for improved aesthetics, boat stability, comfort level and maintainability.

The project was launched in partnership with *M/s. Samudra Shipyard Pvt. Ltd., Aroor near Cochin*. A multi-agency approach was adopted for seeking expertise in hull design, testing, fabrication assistance, design of superstructure, interiors, amenities etc. *NGN Composites-Chennai,* a consulting agency working in composites technology development, had assisted in mechanical design & fabrication of hull, deck & superstructure.

The technology support from NGN Composites included design and development of patterns and moulds for boat hull & superstructure and quality control during fabrication process. The Dept. of Ocean Engineering of IIT-Madras had provided hydrodynamic design of boat hull, bulkheads, ballasts and conducted the necessary tests for boat stability.

The *Industrial Design Centre (IDC) of IIT-Bombay* had extended design support for developing a superstructure with improved space utilization of the available envelop, aesthetics and ergonomics of the living area with the detailed design of bedrooms, toilets, dining area, lounge, kitchen etc. including design of panels, partitions & other interiors. The important milestone of IDC's contribution has been modular design approach of the entire superstructure.

The scaled down (1:17) version of composite hull was designed & fabricated by IIT-Madras and tested for its hydrodynamic stability in their towing tank. The model hull behaviour was studied at various speeds and the hull profile was determined for scaling up.

Finally the full-scale hull size measuring 26 m long x 4.50 m wide x 1.50 m deep was firmed up. IIT-Madras has also designed the propeller profile, shaft & the drive mechanism for the propulsion system.

The sandwich hull with polyurethane foam core was fabricated in composite. The decking for the houseboat has always been a problem area with a whole lot of wooden planks being used in the conventional ones. This problem was addressed by using moulded resin infused composite gratings, developed under another TIFAC project. The gratings were vertically supported along the centre line of the hull.

For superstructure, efforts were made to retain the traditional look with curved wall profiles and pagoda type roofing. The entire superstructure was made into five modular parts requiring only three moulds for fabricating the half modules.

The pagoda style roofing with flat false ceiling inside the bedrooms provides good thermal insulation due to the available air gap. The superstructure was configured to accommodate two bedrooms each measuring 4.00 m x 3.50 m with large windows, attached toilets, a 1.0-m wide passage, living room with open deck, kitchen, crew toilet etc.

Hard wood like bamboo composite flooring tiles, developed under a TIFAC project, were used in the bedrooms. The houseboat components such as the hull, deck and the superstructure consumed about 19.20 tons of composites, thus making the houseboat one of the largest composite products in the country.

A 104 HP Cummins diesel engine, used for the propulsion system, was housed inside the hull with anti-vibration mountings. An acoustic barrier in the form of high resilience foam was used in the engine enclosure for a noise free operation.

A 10-KVA DG set was installed inside the hull for the power back-up when the engine is not in operation as the boat is anchored during the night. Polymer concrete ballasts weighing 1.50 tons were added inside the hull to improve boat stability.

Three bulkheads were provided in the hull to isolate the hull puncture and water leakage. The composite houseboat has been operational in the backwaters of Kerala and its services are being enjoyed by the tourists on regular basis.

The composite houseboat has been a small step in technology development but this would go a long way in saving the environment. Involvement of the multi-agency expertise and a user-oriented approach have been instrumental in reducing the product development cycle limiting the entire exercise to under one year. While boat building in India has been a traditional activity, it is now important to introduce new materials such as composites and processes such as vacuum infusion technique. With very long coast lines along the peninsula, large natural inland water bodies and long rivers, development of composite boats of various forms & functions in India would certainly assume importance and attract investment in the near future.

Jute-Coir Composites as Wood Substitute

Natural fibre composites have gained interest in the last decade, especially in the housing & construction sector. In view of the indigenous wood supply for plywood industry having been stopped virtually and with increasing landed cost of imported plywood veneers, the natural fibre composite boards were required to be developed without compromising any properties and simultaneously offering good value to the customers. Value-added composites from natural fibre could be excellent revenue generation proposition for the farmers.

Keeping in view the aforesaid objectives, the project was launched in collaboration with *M/s. Natura Fibretech Pvt. Ltd., Bangalore* for the development of jute-coir composite boards with face veneer (oriented jute) and coir/rubber wood veneers inside. A thin layer of jute fibres impregnated with phenolic resin was used as the face veneer for improved aesthetics and to impart a wood like finish.

The orientation & uniformity of jute fibre improved with carding and this also helped in better penetration of resin into the fibre. As colour of face veneer is important for appearance, a mixture of brown & bleached jute would resemble the natural wood. The thin jute face veneer, supported by a craft paper sheet, serves as an impervious layer resulting in reduced consumption of paints while finishing the board.

For inside veneers, needle felted coir mat was impregnated with specially formulated coir compatible phenol-formaldehyde resin with reasonably fast curing properties. The waste rubber wood veneers were also impregnated with phenolic resin.

For the boards containing rubber wood, the resin impregnated wood veneers are arranged as intermediate layers during assembly. The assembling is carried out by placing oriented jute layer at two outer faces with semi-cured coir felt sheets inside. The number of coir and rubber wood layers to be used as inside veneers depends on desired thickness of the finished board. The assembly of various layers is compression moulded and cured in multi-plated hydraulic press with continuous monitoring of temperature, pressure & time.

In the project, 80% of the material used in the composite were renewable natural fibres such as jute and coir. The coir fibre contains 46 % lignin as against 39% in teakwood.

Therefore, it has improved resistance against rotting under wet and dry conditions and has better tensile strength. Similarly lower cellulose content in coir (43%) as against 63% in wood makes it more durable than teakwood. Several applications were identified for jute-coir composite boards: building & construction, furniture industry, transportation etc.

The project evaluation committee was constituted considering the product acceptance, usage & induction by involving experts from BMTPC, CPWD, RDSO, IJIRA. The characteristics of natural fibre composite boards are as follows:

- Attractive natural look; it can be painted, polished or laminated at will
- Water proof with minimum surface absorption Economical
- Strong and rigid
- Fire retardant
- Environment-friendly
- Can be nailed, screwed and cut sharply.

The product range developed under the project, comprises coirply (jute+coir+rubber wood waste) boards as plywood substitute and *natural fibre reinforced panel* (jute+coir composites) as MDF substitute. The jute-coir boards as MDF & plywood substitutes was tested satisfactorily at IPIRTI-Bangalore as per relevant IS codes. The performance of jute-coir composite boards has proven superior to plywood & MDF boards.

Typical MDF boards do not prove well on the grounds of moisture absorption & screw holding strength. Detailed evaluation of the jute-coir board samples was also carried out by RDSO & ICF for their applications as berth backings in railway coaches; the results conformed to the railways' requirements. In fact, with sustained efforts by the Programme Scientists & the industry partner, the Indian Railways had approved the product for coach interiors. Indian Railways inducted the jute-coir boards (8 ft. x 4 ft. x 6 mm thick) on large-scale for berth backing at ICF-Chennai.

The Bureau of Indian Standards (BIS) has brought out the relevant standards (IS 14842 : 2000) for coir veneer boards and the product developed under the project conforms to the codes.

These natural materials have all the properties required for a general purpose board and can be used in place of plywood or MDF boards for partitioning, false ceiling, surface panelling, roofing, furniture, cupboards, wardrobes etc.

With active pursuance of the Advanced Composites Programme, the product made excellent in-roads to railways, CPWD, BSNL, Govt. of Karnataka and others.

Apart from the domestic market, the product also enjoys very good technology transfer possibilities in the international arena especially in the coir producing countries in Africa and South-East Asia. As the product is derived from fast renewable natural resources, the project does serve its basic objective of saving forest.

Development of Artificial Limbs for Physically Handicapped

Artificial limbs can be quite effective in restoring the normal movement for victims of trauma, accidents and other amputees. In addition to replacing lost functions, artificial limbs can result in cosmetic improvements for the patient and help build the self-confidence.

The artificial limb developed initially in the world has been an exoskeleton, which was more of a cosmetic replacement rather than a functional one. Though these appear like natural limbs, they cannot impart normal gait to a person.

The conventional exoskeleton types of artificial limbs are heavy in weight and are not at all comfortable for the patients. Subsequently efforts were directed internationally to develop endoskeleton type of artificial limbs. Modern artificial limbs have come a long way from the old wooden exoskeleton type of artificial leg. The endoskeleton replicates the functionality of bones for load bearing and involves proper mechanical joints for normal gait. Advanced endoskeleton type artificial limbs are now made from modern lightweight materials and often-incorporate electronic & pneumatic mechanisms.

In India, commonly used artificial legs are exoskeleton type made of high-density polyethylene. Though the imported endoskeleton types of limbs are available in India, they are very expensive.

As physical deformities aggravate the economic woes of the victims in our country, it called for an indigenous development to restore the functional normalcy of physically challenged people at an affordable price.

On assessing the present scenario towards improving design, functional needs & aesthetics of the artificial limbs in India to cater to societal needs a project on developing '*composite artificial limbs for physically handicapped*' was launched in collaboration with *Mohana Orthotics & Prosthetic Centre, Chennai* with technology support from *IIT-Madras* and *Madras Institute of Technology, Chennai* in terms of design, prototype development and complete testing of composite limbs.

The below-the-knee endoskeleton artificial limbs developed under the project were lighter in weight and better appearance than ever before with improved gait for the patients.

This below-the-knee endoskeleton limb consists of five parts: a composite tubular structure fabricated by filament winding of glass fibre in epoxy matrix, top & bottom connectors made by injection moulding of glass filled nylon, a polyurethane foot with composite keel embedded in it and a polypropylene socket to accommodate the amputee stump.

The socket is patient specific and does not create any problems like pressure sores even for diabetic patients. All the five parts and the socket are adjustable to meet individual requirements and to take care of static & dynamic alignment patterns.

A very innovative design approach was adopted for designing the composite keel, fabricated by compression moulding, for providing improved strength & flexibility in the foot piece. Provision was made to take care of the alignment when they were fitted to the patient.

The new polyurethane foot allowed a foot to press and spring on the ground very much like a real foot. 3-D modelling of the endoskeleton with all the embedded components considering actual properties of various materials was carried out. A simulated endurance test was conducted for 5-year service life of the artificial limb considering average stance duration of 0.5 seconds for normal gait and three hours walking time per day thus testing the limb for around 40 million cycles.

The indigenously developed artificial limb has high modulus, long-term dimensional stability, high fatigue resistance, long-term bio-stability excellent abrasion resistance and bio-compatibility. They look like a natural foot, it is sturdy, durable, waterproof and made of locally available material.

The unique design of this composite limb permits walking, cycling, climbing and even driving a vehicle by a person physically challenged otherwise. A whole lot of innovative technology inputs from MIT was instrumental in developing a user friendly & world-class artificial limb with excellent market potential in India and abroad.

Such indigenously developed below-knee artificial limb cost maximum Rs.3,500/- only as against Rs.40,000/- for the imported ones. The endoskeleton type below-knee artificial limb developed by Mohana Orthotics was awarded the prestigious *National R&D Award 2001* by the Department of Scientific & Industrial Research (DSIR), Govt. of India.

The Advanced Composites Programme has been a truly successful experiment in innovation management in Indian context. Each of the earlier described innovation management approaches as adopted under the programme had their efficacies in specific cases. The first approach of laboratory based technology development exercise was typically suitable for the composite applications involving cutting edge technologies.

The expertise as well as the facilities for application development were available only at a defence lab and such projects could not be initiated by an industry on its own. In the second approach for the technology development, the prototypes were developed and tested successfully.

This was due to the financial stake of the user agencies and their complete involvement in the project especially for facilitating the testing & product certification. The entire technology development exercise could have been faster if the industry were involved right from the early stages of the project and not only for the prototype development.

Building on the experiences of earlier approaches of innovation management practices, the optimal mechanism of industry centric innovation had emerged with the promise of near-term deliverables. Around 30 projects were conceptualized following this approach and a large majority of them were concluded successfully with the products reaching out to the users.

The attributes such as attractive scheme of financial assistance, technological risk sharing and knowledge-based project monitoring by experts coupled with the market intervention by reaching to the user agencies had all helped the programme to record its achievements in a short span. The programme had roped in a good number of academicians with excellent expertise in product design & fabrication and effectively utilized their knowledge in realizing the applications.

The networking by the programme among the academia/ research institutions, standards & certifying agencies as well as the experts from the actual users has gone a long way in reducing the product development cycles.

Different Dimensions of Indian Tourism Industry

The tourism industry has two major aspects:

1. Tourism
2. Travel.

Tourism includes various types, like medical tourism, health tourism, spiritual tourism and rural tourism. The travel segment includes various tour operators and other travel agencies. There are a number or emerging dimensions of tourism. These include:

1. Medical Tourism: Indian tourism is aiming to promote its allopathic treatment as a tourist attraction. Medical tourism tends to provide world-class treatment at low price and is gaining worldwide acceptance. Doctors and other medical experts are organizing health camps and other general awareness programs. The vast array of health care services includes ayurveda, yoga, naturopathy, meditation, spas and many more.

2. Spiritual Tourism: India has a rich heritage of cultures and religions. Hinduism, Buddhism, Christianity, Islam, Jainism have lived here for centuries. There is so much mental pressure and disturbance all over the world that people are looking forward to find solace. India is being represented as a destination for spiritual tourism. Spiritual tourism includes all the religions, religious places associated with them, and emotional attachment and beliefs attached to these centres. Thus, through religious tourism there is a sincere effort to bring better understanding among various communities, nations and thus foster global unity.
3. Rural Tourism: Real India is rural India. Almost 74% of the population is in rural areas. For the development of rural India, government is promoting rural tourism. Rural tourism showcases the rural life in India, the art, culture and heritage, the nature and wild life and various other aspects of rural India. The rural India has a great potential to attract foreign tourists. The rural tourism helps in improving lives of rural people and maintaining the quality of environment.
4. Adventurous Tourism: India is an incredible destination for adventures. The snow capped Himalayas, erratic streams, safaris, etc all add to its natural glory. Water sports, elephant safari, mountaineering, skiing, gliding, trekking, river rafting, etc are breath-taking opportunities for adventurous people. Ladakh, the Garwal hills, the Himachal hills, Darjeeling, Goa, Lakshadweep, Andaman and Nicobar Islands, are some of the places that offer adventure tourism.
5. MICE Tourism: MICE (meetings, incentives, conferences and exhibitions) is associated with business travelers. It caters to various forms of business meetings, international conferences and conventions, events and exhibitions. India is gaining pace to become an ideal MICE destination due to the flourishing business here. The MICE industry converts the annual business meetings and conferences into a glamorous and enjoyable event for the delegates and attendants. To develop business tourism in

India, some renowned MICE centres are already established. The Ashok (New Delhi), Hyderabad International Convention Centre (Hyderabad), Le Meridien (Cochin), Delhi International Expo Centre (Noida) are some of them.

6. Eco Tourism: People are visiting India to unravel the secrets of nature. Eco tourism (also known as nature tourism) relates to nature and its attractiveness so that the visitors experience it in its pristine settings. Eco tourism attracts domestic as well as international tourists towards the magnificent ancient cities, hill stations, remote villages, desert areas and wildlife centuries and parks in India. It is the fastest growing sector of Indian tourism comprising 40 to 60 percent of all international tourism.

The travel segment includes various travel agencies and tour operators who organize the tours and trips for domestic as well as international visitors. There are various associations that control the activities of travel agents and tour operators. These include:

1. Travel Agents Association of India
2. Pacific Asia Travel Association
3. Travel Agents Federation of India
4. Indian Association of Tour Operators.

Hurdles of Tourism Industry

Socio Political Barrier to Tourism Marketing in South Asia

Tourism is the second largest growing business area after information technology in the global economy. Many of the economies are successful in marketing their country and destinations and generating a substantial amount of foreign exchange from tourism Sector.

Even countries with poor level of infrastructure and facilities are able to attract investors to invest money in their country for tourism promotion. Tourism promotion like other forms of marketing largely depends on the customer traffic.

If there is a growing customer traffic trend then more and more money shall flow to an economy in the form of gross revenue earnings and also as foreign direct investments for tourism destination marketing. The product marketing does not involve much complexity like tourism marketing.

Tourism marketing is a very complex phenomenon because the number of uncontrollable factors is more than the number of marketing mix variables. Though the conventional marketing wisdom says that the larger social and political factors affect the marketing offer in product marketing but it is more prominent in the case of tourism marketing.

The political upspring, terrorism, religious fundamentalism, level of crime perception by the foreign tourist affects the prospects of a destination. The South Asian nations are facing a down turn in the tourism business due to the above reasons.

The factors of low per capita tourist investment sustained effort for tourism marketing by the developing countries have become secondary today. The tourism business is largely governed by the non marketing factors than pure business propositions in South Asia. The geo political developments and the kind of social background has largely affected the perception of the foreign tourists negatively for which the inbound traffic is in a down turn. The decision to establish or maintain a direct investment position abroad necessitates addressing the issue of risk that confronts multinational firms. In the examination of any foreign direct or indirect investment opportunity, the environment encompasses numerous areas of concern for the investing firm.

One of the main functions of risk analysis is to determine when and how economic and non- economic factors can affect the foreign investment climate in a particular country, given that risk is a direct outcome of the political and non-political realities faced by international business. Furthermore, this activity is even more crucial in the current global marketplace, given the increasingly complex and uncertain environmental conditions faced by international tourism promoters, particularly to developing countries.

Socio Political Risk

The business literature speaks about socio political risk in many ways. For example, Weston and Sorge have posited that risk arising from actions of governments or political forces which interfere with or prevent foreign business transactions, or change the terms of agreements, or cause the confiscation of wholly or partially foreign owned business property are called sociopolitical risks. These arise from the uncertainty of social and political events that affect business, rather than with the events themselves. Friedmann and Kim define it as business risk brought by non economic and broad social factors to the business.

A sociopolitical risk event is any outcome in the host country which if it occurs, would have a negative impact on the success of the venture and investment flow. So we can summarize the sociopolitical risk as foreign investors' risk or probability of occurrence of some social and political event (s) that will negatively change the prospect for the profitability of a given investment in the host country. Socio Political Risk and Tourism Promotion Socio-Political risk always plays a negative role to reduce the availability of factors and opportunities of tourism promotion.

Investment in destination promotion, infrastructure development to connect the destination, accommodation facilities, food service, transportation services and retail investments will be discouraged, as the risk of capital loss will tend to rise, primarily because social, political and economic rules governing investments are likely to fluctuate, thereby increasing the uncertainty in the future net return associated with investment projects.

Such increased risks would also raise the cost of capital, as the likelihood of loan defaults would go high and the period of completion of various projects will also rise. Both domestic and international inbound tourism would be discouraged due to such risks. Indeed, capital flight and leakage might be additional outcomes as well.

As sociopolitical risk introduces additional elements of uncertainty into the rules governing tourism investment projects, the risk of capital loss is raised for longer- term projects. Hence, overall productivity in an economy is likely to be lowered via a shift in the marginal efficiency of investment schedule. Sociopolitical risk also negatively influences the timing and pricing of the tourism production process.

For example, the tourism destination planned and promoted with an expected period of launching will not work due to delay in the process of completion of the facilities. So the huge capital invested by intermediaries in promoting destinations in international market will go hay wire due to this problem. The traffic planning of the airlines will also be largely affected by this process. Tourism marketing is a circuitry exercise where multiple sectors are dependant on each other. In a combination they build up a whole tourism product. The increased expectations of changes and uncertainties in the rules of operation of airlines diminish reliability, but they would also produce erratic stops and starts in other tourism investment projects. The economy as a whole would therefore experience a lack of optimal growth path. Thus, it can be argued that political risk increases the uncertainty of the environment in which successful foreign tourism promotion should take place, and hence decrease the incentive to save and invest in tourism by an individual tourist to a particular country destination.

Travel Intermediaries and Tourism Promotion

Travel intermediaries are defined as members in the distribution chain in the tourism marketing channel. They include retail travel agents, tour packagers, incentive marketers, tour wholesalers. They provide lodging, transportation and other travel products and services demanded by domestic and foreign tourists. The ability of travel intermediaries to combine travel products and offer them to customers as a package at a price generally lower than those available to individuals provides travel economy and convenience for a significant segment of tourists.

Travel intermediaries have considerable influence in the decision making process of the tourist. They serve as an opinion leader and expert for taking a travel decision process. They play the role of influencers for many of their loyal customers.

This implies that they are of greater importance to both the tourist and the destination marketer particularly in the cases of destinations with far greater distance from the point of origin. Mclellan and Noe identified them as gatekeepers of information, since they provide information about destinations even if travellers do not choose to use their services. Hawkins and Hudman are of the opinion that the distribution sector of tourism is much stronger and travel intermediaries have far greater power to influence and affect tourist demand when compared to their counterparts in other industries.

The Problem

Despite its variety and immense tourism potential, South Asia's share of the total global tourist arrivals and revenue receipts is meager. This small proportion is concentrated in a few countries particularly India, Nepal and a few parts of Srilanka. One of the most important factors responsible for this poor growth is the phenomenon of sociopolitical risk events.

Since tourism is an extremely fragile industry a crucial consideration in a potential traveller's decision to visit a foreign destination is that country's political stability, social coherence and other real or perceived barriers like service quality, poor infrastructure and health issues. Given the spate of sociopolitical risk events in many counties in South-Asia since the late 1980s, little published research in the tourism literature to date has addressed this problem in any comprehensive manner. The purpose of the study is to examine the effects of touristic attractiveness, channel power and sociopolitical risk on the performance of tourism promotion firms and on travel intermediaries. The two broad purposes of this study are to assess empirically the perceived impact of selected sociopolitical risk variables and to identify other perceived environmental barriers and threats to tourism promotion in South Asia.

Review of Literature

In the tourism literature, few researchers have examined the issue of political risk in South Asian countries and its effects on tourism promotion. Authors have cited sociopolitical risk, lack of investment capital and distance from major tourist- generating markets as barriers to tourism promotions in South-Asia in general. Negative images, lack of foreign exchange for tourism development, lack of skilled manpower, weak institutional frameworks for tourism planning, political instability caused by communal violence, civil war conflicts are inhibitors to tourism development.

However, little is known about how international tourism firms perceive sociopolitical risks and other general barriers and threats to tourism promotion in South Asia.

As stated above, the major source of knowledge upon which this research drew for the delineation of sociopolitical risk factors for tourism is from sociopolitical risk variables existing in general business. The general business literature describes social political risk with illustrations such as civil war, labour conflict, foreign exchange control, production quotas and import-export restrictions. Simon's typology is used for this study.

Methodology

A five point scale with 5 as the most significant negative effect and 1 as very insignificant negative effect was used. The respondents were asked to list different kinds of barriers and threats as they perceive, were of concern to them in doing business in their respective South Asian destinations through a series of open ended questions in the designed instrument. An attempt was made to gain insights into both the qualitative and quantitative aspects of the travel intermediaries' perceptions.

Sampling Procedure and Data Collection

Data for this study were collected between October 2000 and January 2001 which happens to be the main tourist season in various parts of South Asia. Members of Indian Association of Tour operators (IATO) and Indian Association of Travel Agents (IATA) were contacted to supplement the research with a list of clientele of international travel intermediaries operating from various European nations and American states for the survey. These organizations were selected because they provided a membership listing of firms that can be consistently and practically identified as tour operators, destination marketing firms and travel agents whose revenues are derived from packaging and selling tours to South Asian countries.

A sample for the study was drawn using the proportional stratified systematic random sampling method. The sample size was determined to be 230. Of the 230 questionnaires mailed, 27 had undeliverable addresses. After a follow- up, 169 questionnaires were returned, with 129 usable, representing a response rate of 28.6 percent. Although low, such a response rate is typical of mail questionnaire studies that involve business enterprises, in contrast to survey research that involves individuals. The business owners and managers of the organizations selected for the study often face severe time constraints as a result of their work activities and are often inundated with paperwork, meetings and travel making the process to go slow as per their convenience.

Data Analysis

Descriptive statistics were calculated for all variables comprising the scaled sociopolitical risk variables. Factor Analysis through Principal Component Analysis of the seventeen risk variables was conducted to examine the relationship among the interrelated variables. This procedure resulted in two factors. Only factors with eigenvalues greater than 1.0 were included in the final analysis. The extracted factors were rotated using the varimax orthogonal rotation method. A variable was considered to load on a given factor if the factor loading was 0.40 or greater for that factor and less than 0.4 for the other. The reliability of the factors was determined using Cronbach's coefficient alpha test.

The main criterion for inclusion in a particular region is if a respondent indicated sending at least two states or districts in a country then he is included in the region. Those who indicated at least two countries in South Asian region, they were classified into the multiple region categories.

This is done due to the possibility of within country variability in responses to the perceived risk for a country due to the travel intermediary's business link with that country for promoting tourism. The researcher also tried to investigate the relationships between the underlying sociopolitical risk factors and respondents' particular country of tourism promotion in South Asia. Perception towards socio political barriers and threats to tourism promotion is obtained using an open- ended format of the survey instrument.

The researcher conducted content analysis for all open- ended questions in which groupings were made for similar responses into categories and assigning names to the common correlated elements. Content analysis is a research method that uses a set of procedures to make valid inferences from text. The central idea is that many of the words of the text are classified into much fewer content categories. Words, phrases or other units of text classified in the same category are presumed to have similar meanings. This similarity may be based on the precise meaning of the word, or on words sharing similar connotations. This paper has adopted a similar procedure to group several words implying a concern with concept of perceived barriers and threats in South Asia in an attempt to make valid inferences from the open- ended responses.

Blue Print to Success for Indian Tourism Industry

One of the dynamic sectors that contributes significantly to a country's economy is tourism. For many countries such as China, Malaysia and Thailand, tourism contributes as much as 5% of their GDP. The fast pace of technological changes and the interplay among a host of sub-sectors like hospitality and infrastructure make travel and tourism a complex area to study. Moreover, the process of creating a desired image in the minds of potential tourists for a destination involves manipulating both tangible and intangible features associated with a place.

As tourists' lifestyles evolve and expectations expand, marketers of destinations face a difficult task in fulfilling their wishes and aligning the messages with the tourists' lifestyle. Managing the marketing mix effectively in itself is a major task, as interdependence among different elements has to be effectively handled. To top it all, sporadic external events such as outbreak of SARS, attack on WTC and subsequent terrorist attacks cast their shadow.

Variety, they say, is the spice of life. Tourists are always on the lookout for interesting places to visit and absorb the pleasures, luxuries and variety around the world. Attracting first-time tourists and providing service so as to entice repeat visits is naturally the endeavor of different countries.

Besides the traditional tours to natural locales and heritage sites, new segments such as medical tourism and sports tourism are emerging strongly. Cheaper treatment costs in developing countries are drawing patients, who club visits to nearby places of interest post-recuperation. Major sporting events across the world have traditionally attracted sports enthusiasts. Of late, aggressive marketing of sports events is pulling in more and more sports enthusiasts. South Africa, which hosted 2003 Cricket World Cup, attracted 20,000 foreign cricket fans to the country during the event.

Technology is also playing a big role in the changing dynamics of travel and tourism. Internet has enabled worldwide reach for a host of facilitators, and enabled rise of new segments such as FIT (Free Independent Travelers), who shun mass tourism packages and set out to explore on their own.

Internet's absorption by travel and tourism businesses has meant that such travelers can be flexible in their travel plans and arrange for these on the Internet itself. Fewer tourists are opting for prepackaged tours and are arranging themselves travel and accommodation plans through the Internet. This 'dynamic packaging' has been labeled 'the most radical change in the tourism industry in half a century' by The Economist. Jupiter Research estimates that online travel bookings would catapult from $28 billion in 2002 to $53 billion by 2008.

An interesting offshoot of technology for the tourism industry has been the opening of space travel as the last frontier for the obscenely rich. Businessweek, in its February 02, 2004 issue reported, "Getting astronauts and tourists into space on the cheap is the notion behind a privately sponsored race with a $20 million reward. Announced in 1996 by entrepreneur Peter H Diamandis, the X Prize is modelled after the $25,000 Orteig Prize that enticed Charles A Lindbergh to fly solo across the Atlantic in 1927.

To win the X Prize, a privately developed spacecraft capable of carrying three people must soar to 62 miles, then pull-off a repeat within two weeks. That would show the plane's ability to operate like an airliner – and potentially make space travel almost as routine as air travel has become since Lindbergh's feat."

How are marketers positioning their countries so as to reach out to a globally dispersed audience? What challenges are staring at the travel and tourism sector? What are the developments in India? What have been the initiatives and responses of some of the global players in expanding their markets and facing challenges? The book attempts to answer these and other related questions.

Section One – Positioning Destinations

The articles in this section cover the basics of positioning and innovations in marketing of destinations. Travel and tourism is all about journeying to a particular choice of destination. The choice for tourists is so abundant that a good part of one's lifetime would have to be dedicated to cover all the desirable places of visit. Whether one is interested in natural scenic locations, adventure sports, biodiversity, heritage or places of religious importance, there are enough destinations to choose from within the country or overseas.

Countries are increasingly realizing the contribution of tourism to their economies. Many economies are even centred around tourism. Identifying places of interest for potential tourists and creating a positive attitude and perception among them are becoming common practices among national tourism boards. Wide choice for tourists and aggressive marketing by destinations demand a cohesive and focused approach by tourism marketers.

In fact, this is what is leading destination marketers towards devising positioning strategies. For example, Malaysia wants to usurp an Asian experience with its slogan 'Malaysia. Truly Asia.'. India, on the other hand desires to impress with a wide range of experiences, through its campaign 'Incredible India'. Such clear-cut positioning planks demand a good deal of coordination and cooperation among the various stakeholders in the tourism industry.

The first article, "Positioning Tourism Destinations", highlights the importance of taking a proper positioning stance when it comes to marketing of destinations. Hardly, any country enjoys a unique natural competitive advantage, unmatched by other countries in providing a similar experience. Realizing the importance of tourism to their economies, policy makers across countries are putting in place the systems to facilitate growth in tourist arrivals. Tourism marketers are also quite aggressive in promoting different destinations.

While operating in competitive markets, countries need to differentiate their features and offerings in the minds of potential tourists. The image that is cultivated thus must be unique and constantly reinforced.

The author provides guidelines on developing an appropriate positioning plank. These include taking a target audience perspective and combining objective and subjective elements. He also stresses on the need to apply the positioning statement as a guide for maintaining consistency in providing the overall service experience to tourists. It is pointed out that the tests of positioning are to ensure that it should be believable and delivered.

The next article, "Marketing and Destination Growth", discusses the challenges in marketing destinations. While the need to clearly divide the responsibilities between public and private sector agencies is one challenge, managing the interplay among domestic and international elements is another. Moreover, destinations have to be marketed both on the demand side and the supply side. Brand building depends on the nature and extent of relationship among the different stakeholders – National Tourism Offices (NTOs), State Tourism Offices (STOs), Local Government Authorities (LGAs) and Destination Marketing Organizations (DMOs).

Section Two – Tourism: Challenges

Aspects covered in the four articles of this section are – a blueprint for New Tourism, sustainability of tourism in the 21st century, the state of service quality in Indian tourism and challenges of ecotourism.

Travel and tourism have been transformed over the last few decades globally. More and more destination choices are emerging, options that appeal to a wide cross-section of people are increasing, networking across sectors is on the rise and innovations are the order of the day. In the midst of this transformation, it is time that the industry takes a close look at the challenges facing it.

Aggressive pursuit of tourists and their unrestricted access is putting under strain the ecology of the places where mass tourism prevails. Transport, stay and visit of tourists – all are contributing to the erosion of nature in its pristine form. A callous attitude towards preserving the ecological balance on the part of tourism boards and irreverence of visitors to the local ecosystem are to be blamed. Aggressive pursuit of short-term numbers in terms of more tourists is preventing a long-term perspective on the sustainability of mass tourism in sensitive places.

Besides the threat to ecosystems, the present state of service quality is another major challenge. Consumers across product categories are getting savvier and more demanding. Service aspects considered as add-ons earlier are taken for granted now. Though tourism is one area where loyalty or repeat visits are relatively less important for marketers, it cannot be ignored that as affluence rises, people tend to visit not only more places but also revisit their favourite destinations. Unsatisfactory service anywhere in the chain (travel, accommodation or food) is likely to create bad publicity, which can have a debilitating affect in a category where word-of-mouth publicity plays a major role. India has seen a slight jump in international tourist arrivals, up from 2.48 million in 1999 to 2.80 million in 20034.

States such as Goa, Rajasthan and Kerala are already well-entrenched as attractive destinations within the country, specially for foreign tourists. Other states such as Maharashtra and Andhra Pradesh are also taking proactive approaches, with the launch of luxury Deccan Queen rail package by the former and opening of Andhra Pradesh Tourism Information Counter in London by the latter. An opportunity has opened up in the form of NRIs, eager to explore their Indian roots – bringing forth a new segment, Culture Tourism. Even as its global campaign 'Incredible India' promises to change positively the image of the country among international tourists, a great deal needs to be done on the domestic tourism front. As against international standards of 10:1 ratio between domestic and international tourism, India has a corresponding ratio of just 3:1. Opportunity does exist, waiting to be exploited.

The first article in this section, "Blueprint for New Tourism", is a clarion call from The World Travel and Tourism Council (WTTC). The article contends that there is a need for adopting a unified approach on the part of governments and the industry. A new sense of partnership between public authorities and private sector is advocated. New Tourism, according to WTTC, focuses on benefits not only for people who travel, but also for people in the communities they visit, and for their respective natural, social and cultural environment.

Governments must not only coordinate infrastructure development but also guarantee respect for local environments. Industry, on the other hand, must recognize that long-term sustainability of the sector can be ensured by respecting local communities. The article drives home the importance of partnership between public and private sector. Collaborations in developing the human resources and sharing informations are suggested.

"Tourism and Sustainability in the 21st Century", the next article, is sourced from International Friends of Nature. They assert that by shrinking areas of unspoilt nature at destinations, tourism jeopardizes that which it depends on. Thanks to ecotourism, communal management of local resources is under increasing threat. Twenty-first century tourism faces several challenges, such as preserving the nature and culture of destinations; curbing consumption of natural resources; putting in place a professional code of conduct for tour operators and hotels; and devising tourism policies aimed at sustainable destination management.

The next article, "Tourism in India: State of Service Quality", traces the growth in contribution of services sector to India's GDP, discusses the perceptions about customer service and debunks some of the myths associated with customer service in tourism. It is pointed out that when a person moves from being a 'prospect' to a 'tourist', he encounters compromises in service standards.

Some of the myths associated with quality customer service are – having a large workforce translates into better service; training alone takes care of service; being obsequious is what customer service is all about; and providing high salaries ensures better customer service. The author points out that treating employees well and creating satisfied internal customers would help in getting satisfied external customers.

The last article in this section, "Challenges of Ecotourism", discusses the implications of unfettered growth in ecotourism. Author, John N Shores, a consultant, opines that ecotourism has become an all-inclusive term, with multiple definitions abounding. Considering the susceptibility of various ecosystems to the impact of tourism, he advocates a cooperative effort involving travelers, tour operators, local communities and environmentalists to preserve them.

He proposes a six level scale to classify nature-based travel. EL 0, the first level, involves exposing the travelers to and making them aware of the fragility of the ecosystems they visit. EL 1 involves taking monetary support from tourists, to maintain the visited ecosystems. EL 2 is participatory, in that the visitors plant trees or clear litter and make a personal contribution to the preservation efforts.

EL 3 is for certifying that the tour system is benign to the environment. EL 4 is all about demonstrating the net positive effect of travelers, reflected through lower energy consumption and recycling. EL 5 makes the entire system environmentally sound, that encapsulates transport, stay and treatment of residual products.

Section Three – Cases

Over the last two years, global travel and tourism sector has faced multiple challenges in different pockets. Acts of terrorism (9/11 attack on WTO and bomb explosions in Bali, Indonesia) and outbreak of SARS in Far East Asia dampened the spirits to a great extent.

Several airlines had to bear the consequences of reduced air travel, hotels faced drastic reductions in their occupancy rates and tourism-dependent economies experienced a negative growth. Experiences of different players in this sector are compiled in this section. The way the crises were handled by those affected and also the initiatives behind kickstarting growth in tourism, in areas unaffected by the crises, are captured.

The first case, on "United Airlines", discusses its attempt to cope with the dynamic external business environment. Its flexible responses to the severe challenges it faced made its assets more productive. Besides offering convenient scheduling throughout its domestic and international routes, it attracted and retained high-yielding customers.

All airlines operate under the influences of technological, political, social, regulatory and economic forces. By devising a route structure that offered maximum nonstop flights from the Pacific Rim to the US and developing the Star Alliance that brought together 15 carriers, it is in a position to put the days of bankruptcy filing in 2002 behind and emerge out of its problems in 2004.

The next case, "InterContinental Resort Bali", traces the impact of the bomb explosions in Bali, Indonesia and the response shown, in the face of adversity by InterContinental Resort, a premium destination for international tourists. The region enjoys good tourist arrivals from Australia and has a rich history. The InterContinental Resort provides several amenities, such as adventure sports, spa and even a helipad.

The explosions had a devastating short-term impact, with occupancy falling by more than 50 percent. The resort had to shut down half of its blocks and re-deploy employees. The management of the resort swung into action immediately on getting news of the blast and enhanced security for its guests. It had even designed attractive packages to lure domestic tourists. Employees' concerns were also well handled. SARS (Severe Acute Respiratory Syndrome) ravaged the fortunes of several travel and tourism players in 2003. The case, "SARS – The Industry Responds", is sourced from Deloitte and Touche and captures the effect of the dreaded disease and different responses of regional players in Asia. Many regional airlines had to suspend 50 percent of their flights and hotels saw huge fall in occupancy rates. Government and industry got together in Hong Kong in a campaign called 'We Love HK' to counter the negative impact of SARS. Attractive price-led incentives for travel, hotel stay and shopping were devised and local tourism was promoted in a very big way. Capacity-driven free offers were extended to lure new customers. Employees of Cathay Pacific were given special leave, to avoid job cuts and save money.

"Malaysia – Destination for Business Travellers", the next case focuses on Malaysia's rise as a favourite spot for Meetings, Incentives, Conferences and Exhibition (MICE) travel. The country's share of MICE arrivals tripled between 1999 and 2002. The case analyses this growth and lists out the facilities available; and also highlights the efforts of the country in adding to its strengths. It provides world-class convention centres (upto 35,000 square metres of exhibition space, with some centres having capacity to accommodate as many as 2,000 delegates); hotels adjoining convention centres; customized conference settings; and entertainment options within convention centres. New centres keep cropping up, publicity support is extended by mentioning in the events calendar and familiarization trips for travel organizers are regularly conducted.

Regional cooperation is picking up in travel and tourism sector. The next case, "Regional Networking in Asia", points out how networking is increasing among national tourism organizations in Asia. Impact of SARS seems to have accentuated this development, with international arrivals in Asia dropping by a whopping 80 percent in the immediate aftermath of its detection. Pacific Asia Travel Association (PATA) worked with global media to stimulate travel to the region, as part of its 'Project Phoenix'. Association of South East Asian Nations (ASEAN) set up ASEAN Tourism Fund, to promote the region as a single destination. Tourism Malaysia and Singapore Airlines joined together, to offer a common package tour that covered both Malaysia and Singapore. 'Asia Now' and 'Together in Asia' were the joint promotions undertaken by Hong Kong, Singapore and Thailand in the US and UK respectively.

The next case, "Branding India", is sourced from Swagat magazine and captures the successful efforts of India Tourism Board to reposition India as a premium destination for upscale tourists. As part of the 'Incredible India' campaign executed globally, commercials were released on worldwide television channels, print ads placed in leading travel publications, online banner ads placed on leading portals, newsletters were sent to global travel agents and media meets arranged with travel writers. Thanks to the extensive media coverage, international tourist arrivals picked up significantly and India is able to differentiate itself.

"Branding Kerala", the last case, highlights the success of Kerala in becoming one of the preferred Indian destinations for tourists. A proactive approach of the state administration has resulted in a scenario where tourism has become a major revenue source for the state's economy. Its successful 'God's Own Country' promotional campaign played a major role in the state standing apart from other competing destinations and distinguishing itself. Moreover, popularizing Ayurveda's positive health impact evened out the seasonal trends in tourist arrivals. Its achievement: being named among the ten hot spots for the millennium by Emirates.

Marketing of Tourism Services in India

A Study With Special Reference to Orissa their workers, have contributed a lot in infusing interest to look around to a place for an annual or biannual visit with family members. Even though India has a very meager share amounting to 0.38 percent of tourists and 0.51 percent of the amount of world tourism trade in 2001, it has the hope for attracting more and more foreign tourists by exploiting her unexploited tourist spots of the country. Mostly tourists from North America, Central and South America, Africa, Australia, Western Europe, Eastern Europe, West Asia, South Asia, South East Asia and East Asia are visiting India as foreign tourists.

Out of these the share of North America, Western Europe, West and South Asia occupies a major share in increasing Indian tourism trade. India accounts for four out of five tourists to South Asia. Another healthy trend in the foreign tourism in India since 1991 is the conspicuous increase in business travels with its spin off effects in up-gradation of accommodation and introduction of new technology in communications and other services. On an average, a foreign tourist stays for about 27 days in India which is an important indicator of increase of the foreign exchange earned by the country.

Tourism in India has vast employment potential, much of which still awaits exploitation. At present about 8.5 million persons are directly employed by hospitality services. This is about 2.4 percent of the total work force of the country. In addition, the industry provides indirect employment to about 30 million persons. Further it is interesting to note that the employment generation in proportion to investment is very high in tourism industry. According to an estimate, an investment of Rs.10 lakh creates 89 jobs in hotels and restaurants sector as against 44.7 jobs in agriculture and 12.6 in manufacturing industry.

Another important aspect of employment in tourism is that it employs a large number of women in hotels, airlines services, travel agencies, handicrafts making and marketing and cultural activity centres. As per 1983-84 indices the employment output ratio in tourism was 71, whereas in leather 51, textiles 27, electricity 14, beverages 12 and cement 6.

Generally the visit of a foreign tourist to India provides employment to one person and 6.5 domestic tourists generate one job. Hotel sector is the key segment of tourism industry to earn foreign exchange. Realising the importance of hotel segment the government has taken initiatives to encourage hotel industry by providing tax benefits and other incentives. Foreign investment and collaboration are now facilitated under new economic policy. The hotel industry has shown a spectacular growth during the last one and half decades. The number of hotel rooms has increased from 30200 in 1986 to 57386 in 1995 and to 62000 in 1996 and to 68000 in 2001. In the approved list of Department of Tourism the classified hotels are 125 in One Star, 286 Two Star, 274 Three Star, 73 Four Star, 56 Five Star, 42 Five Star Deluxe, and 41 of heritage hotel category. Inspite of rapid strides made by the hotel industry since last one decade or so, the hotel accommodation falls short of the requirement of growing inflow of the tourists. Assuming a modest growth rate of 7 to 8 percent per annum, the requirement to hotel rooms is expected to rise to 91,000 by 2002-03 and to 1.125 lakh rooms by 2005. Besides a large number of budget hotels will be required for about 200 million strong middle class Indian tourists also. Places of tourist interest are so numerous and of varied nature that it is not easy to describe these places comprehensively.

These include mostly the Himalayan Region, the great plain of north India, the peninsular plateau and coastal plains. In general the tourist spots are counted more like Buddhist sites, Shrines, Forts, places of historical importance, hot springs, Jain monasteries, lakes and birds, sanctuaries, religious centres, science spots, sea beaches, summer resorts, water falls and wild lives etc. In this context, a reference can be drawn for Orissa that all above kinds of spots are richly available to attract more and more foreign as well as domestic tourists.

About 25 lakh of domestic tourists and 30000 foreign tourists visit Orissa annually. The share for South Orissa is 30 percent of the total tourist arrival to Orissa. Orissa has several important nationally and internationally famous tourists' centres like Puri, Bhubaneswar, Konark, Cuttack, Chilika Lake, Chandipur, Gopalpur, Beach etc.

The other places are Baripada, Khiching, Baud, Koraput, Bolangir, Jeypore and Udayagiri etc. The area remains unexplored because of want of infrastructural development, more comfortable modes of transport, accommodation etc. Although India has progressed a lot since the fifties with respect to tourism, she is still way behind the developed, even the developing countries. India earns one seventh of China, one fourth of Indonesia and less than half of Philippines from tourism in comparison. The development of tourism depends upon the development of an integrated infrastructure of national and international highways, railways, ports, civil aviation, telecommunication, hotel accommodation and allied services. Inadequacies of such infrastructural facilities adversely affect tourism. The sluggish growth of Indian tourism arises from India's inability to sell effectively her rich tourist potential. India should market itself as a value added tourism destination stressing its variety and cost effectiveness. Satisfaction of the tourist should be the top priority of the tourist industry. Apart from infrastructural development, tourism requires an environment of peace and stability where the tourist is sure of his safety and security. Political unrest and fear of violence is a death knell to tourist industry. Unfortunately, one part or the other of the country is hit by *bandhs*, strikes, ethnic clashes and insurgency which adversely affect our tourism service marketing. Epidemics, such as plague, AIDS and dengue fever are also detrimental to the growth of tourism.

It is surprising that some small countries like Malaysia, Indonesia, Hongkong and get Singapore have been able to attract more tourists and better receipts than India. Even in terms of quality, the diminutives like Maldives and Bhutan present an appreciable model of sustainable tourism.

In this context, in order to give a philip to the tourism trade the Central Government as well as the State Government should come forward to develop some of the newly unexploited and selected tourist places, diversify some of the culture oriented tourism to holiday and leisure tourism, develop trekking, winter sports, wild life, beach resorts tourism, launching, key markets near tourist centres, provide inexpensive accommodation and to improve service efficiency.

India still hopes better to improve the tourism marketing services and to take an equal and more challenging steps with her competitors in the field more vigoursly.

Promoting Private Sector of Tourism in Jammu and Kashmir

Tourism is considered to be the largest export industry in the world. However, this industry can have an impact on the economy only when it has the motivational force of the Private Sector. Being a service oriented industry it requires professionalism and dedication which are generally lacking in the Public Sector especially in our part of the world.

In the initial stages when tourism was just picking up, the state had to intervene. Private capital would be hesitant in investing without being sure of returns. To give a push to the activity it was essential for the government to go for infrastructure development. A lead was given to the industry and the public sector activities were in fact started totally as part of the department of tourism. It was like facilitating and motivating the private entrepreneurs to take up this activity.

The annual expenditure on maintenance of various establishments run by the government in the shape of huts and tourist bungalows was over Rs.1.50 crores but the total revenue generated was hardly Rs.30 lakhs per year. These establishments were also run as a healthy competition to private sector to keep the prices of these services in check.

The greatest mistake was turning over all these establishments in one go to state run tourism development corporation. In almost all major tourist destinations, the infrastructure for accommodation, food, transport, and recreation is run by the private sector. The government has only to take care of the very basic infrastructure such as road connectivity, power, water, and communications. It has been proved everywhere that any commercial venture run by the government invariably ends in the red.

There are many reasons for this. Firstly, the government service is taken more or less as social security. Employees cannot be fired even if their contribution is zero. The hire and fire system cannot be enforced in government due to a number of reasons. On the contrary in the private sector one has more flexibility both in the selection of the professional staff and policy of hire and fire can be enforced with some minimum guarantees. Apart from tourism, almost all other government corporations are in red. If we have to aim for development of international tourism, we have to promote private sector in a big way. In fact, the state sector organisations should also be gradually disinvested. To begin with some of the lucrative properties should be put up for joint ventures.

Many attempts have been made in the past in this regard but most of these have failed as only loss making properties were offered for joint ventures or outright disinvestment. In addition, the procedures were made so complicated that every enterprising investor got fed up and ran away. The government has to take a conscious decision and plan it properly. Something like a golden handshake has to be worked out for the staff and their consent obtained.

Any ad hoc measure is bound to recoil. These days specialist agencies are available for such jobs. Once it has been sincerely decided that the private sector has to be promoted, a number of substantive incentives have to be provided to attract investment. The present incentive rules initiated in mid nineties do not come up to the mark. At the time of declaring these incentives the main motive was to accede to the popular demand of declaring tourism as an industry. This was done with least financial commitment in view of the bad financial position of the state at that time.

Even though tourism was declared to be a priority industry yet the important incentives such as on power were not made available to this sector. It was declared an industry in name only.

The first requirement would be to revise these incentive rules and make investment in tourism related infrastructure most attractive for both local as well as international investors. Not many people know that there are already a host of incentives available as part of the central industrial policy for various tourism projects. Most of the incentives are for Eco-Tourism projects, which is the most suitable activity for our state having a fragile environment. Lack of knowledge among the members of the trade as well as the administrators is making the local entrepreneurs lose these incentives by default! All tourism ventures should be given a complete tax holiday at least for ten years to motivate the private sector. There should be no bar on the location of these units provided these are in conformity with all local laws. Preference should be given to joint ventures involving local entrepreneurs and also ensuring substantial local employment in such projects. One often hears about single window clearance but it is never implemented on ground.

People coming for investments in any field have to spend months and sometimes years to obtain various clearances. The ideal situation can be setting up of a Tourism Investment Board with private/public sector participation to ensure clearance of projects at an accelerated pace. The areas for investment are extensive. To begin with is the world class accommodation in the major cities like Srinagar and Jammu. Many global hotel chains can be motivated for giving local franchise with government facilitation and if necessary, a counter guarantee in view of the prevailing circumstances.

In fact, totally new resorts can be developed by professional developers and made available for sale among locals who have enough resources for making sizeable investments in this field. Next comes transport. We are nowhere near the minimum world standards. Avis and other rent a car brands which are already in some metros have yet to arrive here. We do not have luxury cars and coaches for sight seeing. Even though over last couple of years locals have taken some initiatives in regard to cars, yet the coaches of the Volvo brand are missing from Kashmir.

There has always been a persistent complaint about lack of recreational and entertainment facilities. We need not always go for night clubs and casinos but there are plenty of other recreational facilities which are missing. These could include bowling alleys, indoor ice and roller skating rinks, amusement parks, cable cars with mountain top panoramic restaurants, theatres, standard art galleries, and museums. There are umpteen other possibilities for decent avenues of entertainment. Unfortunately, instead of promoting private investment, the government is itself venturing into these projects thereby creating some more liabilities for future. It is the right time for both the industry as well as the government to wake up and prepare jointly a comprehensive tourism policy especially in regard to participation of private sector. The only involvement of the government apart from facilitation and motivation should be monitoring and regulation. We need very strong and upright set ups involving a panel of experts from various related fields of hospitality industry to over see all these developments in regard to tourism. They should adopt international standards and ensure adherence to these by all concerned.

There should also be a fool proof redressal mechanism. It is possible to have these things under the existing legislation in the tourism field by incorporating amendments keeping in view global standards. In addition, various players in the industry need to streamline their own organisations by establishing some sort of ethics committees and setting up reasonable standards of service with continued adherence for allowing membership to these bodies. Defaulters should be automatically thrown out to maintain credibility of standards. Given all the above inputs our motto for future development in tourism should be, "Private Sector, Private Sector, and Only Private Sector"!

2

Innovation in Space Tourism

"We have proved rocket propulsion practicable for space travel... This 3rd day of October, 1942, is the first of a new era in transportation, that of space travel."-Walter Dornberger, having achieved controlled space flight for the first time.

If the German engineers developing rocket-propelled vehicles had continued in peacetime as Dornberger hoped, the V2 (of which a winged version was flown to Mach 4) and the Me163 piloted rocket-plane projects would between them have surely led to the start of suborbital passenger space flights by 1950. In this case, orbital passenger space travel services would presumably have started by the mid-1960s. Instead, rocket development was "highjacked" by the cold war competition between the USA and USSR, so that launch vehicles were derived from long-range missiles, rather than being designed ab initio as passenger vehicles. Government space agencies have continued to develop expendable rockets, of which the safety and cost/passenger are inevitably much closer to those of missiles than to passenger vehicles. (The space shuttle, as well as being partly expendable, was designed primarily to fulfill a military requirement, not to achieve low-cost space travel.)

Suborbital passenger space flight services are due to start in 2010. There has thus been more than a half-century delay in developing passenger space travel. To understand the implications of this delay, and the cost to society, it is useful to note that the world population when space travel could have started was 1/2 what it is today, while the use of energy and other resources, and the production of pollution were all 1/4 of what they are today.

Air travel safety was 100 times lower than today, and the general public were correspondingly less risk-averse in general. Thus, in many respects it would have been easier to develop space tourism at that time than it is today. On the other hand, cumulative engineering capabilities and experience are far greater in every field today, and there is also great pent-up demand for passenger space travel. Consequently, when this industry finally starts, it can in principle grow much faster today than it would have during the 1950s.

Considering the question how different would world conditions be today if passenger space travel services had started as early as they could have during the 1950s, the answer depends on the scale to which passenger space travel might have grown by today. Cost estimates by the Japanese Rocket Society, Bristol Spaceplanes, Bekey and others, corroborated by the very low cost of "Space Ship One", indicate that once space travel grows to 1 million passengers/year, prices could fall to 5,000 Euros for Suborbital flights, and 20,000 Euros for orbital flights. The latter is approximately 200 Euros/kg or about 1% of launch costs today. We can estimate that if Suborbital passenger travel had started in 1950, orbital travel could have grown to perhaps several million passengers/year by 2000.

Cost estimates for the development of low-cost orbital passenger transportation systems are of the order of 10 billion Euros. Even 10 times this amount would be less than 5 years of space agencies' current budgets.

The economic benefits would greatly outweigh such a cost, due to the much larger commercial markets that would be created as a result, in contrast to the very small markets created with 1 trillion Euro-equivalents invested in satellite and launch vehicle manufacturing to date.

Starting from today, in order to achieve the scale of activity, over the next 30 years, government funding equivalent to about 10% of space agencies' budgets, or some 2 billion Euros/year would probably suffice to stimulate private investment in reusable orbital passenger vehicle manufacturing and operations. Thereafter most of the funding could come from private companies, just as airlines and hotel chains today finance their own growth.

Implications of Launch Cost Reduction

Reducing the cost of space travel to 1% of existing launch vehicles' costs, in combination with the growth of a new consumer service market in space, would greatly aid the growth of many commercial space activities, thereby creating numerous new business opportunities both on Earth and in space. This process is already at work on a small scale in relation to Suborbital flight services: in addition to a large number of travel companies acting as agents for Suborbital flights (including JTB, the largest travel company in Japan), Zero-G Corporation supplies parabolic flight services, Bigelow Aerospace is developing the first space hotel, Spaceport Associates advises on spaceport design, Orbital Outfitters Inc supplies customised flight suits, and so on. All of this activity is occurring some years before the first high-priced services even start, so a much wider range of different space travel-related businesses are sure to grow in future.

In the case of orbital services there will be an even wider range of companies with much larger revenues, including companies supplying various services to orbiting hotels. These will include services which terrestrial hotels purchase today, plus such additional services as space-based window maintenance services, air supply, solar-generated electricity, water supply, waste disposal services and others.

As activities in orbit expand progressively, they could grow to include use of materials extracted from the Moon and near-Earth asteroids and cometoids, of which the potential has been researched for decades. Due to the much higher cost of activities in orbit than on the surface of the Earth, the first market for non-terrestrial materials like ice, water, oxygen and hydrogen, is likely to be orbital hotels, as discussed in.

Another potentially major space-based industry, which has been held back for 40 years by high launch costs, is the supply of space-based solar power (SSP) to Earth. Although the potential of this system was recognised in studies by the US Department of Energy in the late 1970s, and confirmed in the 1990s, total funding has remained minimal. However, progress could be rapid once launch costs fall to a few percent of ELV costs. Hence, as passenger space travel activities expand to large scale, a growing range of manufacturing activities in Earth orbit, on the lunar surface and elsewhere, are likely to develop spontaneously. These will open the door to large-scale activities in space, as described in.

The growth of orbital passenger space travel to several million passengers/year within a few decades would represent a direct commercial turnover of some 100 billion Euros/year. In such a scenario of rapid growth, annual investment in new facilities, research and development might add the same amount again. Indeed, having reached such a scale, there would be no foreseeable limit to further growth-in particular it need not be constrained, like terrestrial activities, by environmental or social stresses. Quite apart from the numerous opportunities which such a scenario offers for growth of the space industry, it also offers great potential benefits for humanity, in several different fields, as discussed in turn in the following.

Employment

In most countries, most of the population do not have economically significant land holdings, and so employment is the economic basis of social life, providing income and enabling people to have stable family lives. The high level of unemployment in most countries today is therefore not only wasteful, it also causes widespread poverty and unhappiness, and is socially damaging, creating further problems for the future. One reason for investing in the development of passenger space travel, therefore, is that it could create major new fields of employment, capable of growing as far into the future as we can see.

The passenger air travel industry, including airlines, airports, hotels and other tourism-related work enabled by air travel, employs about 20 times the number of people employed in aircraft manufacturing alone, about 50 million people today. Likewise, passenger space travel could create employment many times that of expendable launch vehicles-in vehicle operations and maintenance, at spaceports, in orbiting accommodation, in many companies supplying these, in services such as staff training, certification and insurance, and in a growing range of related businesses.

This is important because high unemployment, both in richer and poorer countries, has been the major economic problem throughout the world for decades. Consequently the growth of such a major new market for advanced aerospace technology and services is highly desirable. By contrast, in recent years employment in the traditional space industry in USA and Europe has been shrinking fast: a 2003 report by the US Federal Aviation Administration stated that employment in launch vehicle manufacturing and services fell from 28,617 in 1999 to 4,828 in 2002, while employment in satellite manufacturing fell from 57,372 to 31,262. Likewise, European space industry employment fell by 20% from 1995 to 2005; the major space engineering company Astrium cut 3,300 staff from 2003 through 2006; and in 2005 alone, European prime contractors cut 13.5% of their staff or some 2,400 people. Unfortunately, the probability of space industry employment recovering soon is low, because satellite manufacturing and launch services face both low demand and rapidly growing competition from India and China where costs are significantly lower.

It is therefore positively bizarre that government policy makers have declined to even discuss the subject of investing in the development of passenger space travel services, and have permitted no significant investment to date out of the nearly 20 billion Euro-equivalents which space agencies spend every year! This is despite the very positive 1998 Nasa report "General Public Space Travel and Tourism", and a 2002 Nasa-funded study which concluded that Suborbital travel services in the USA alone might grow several times larger than the commercial satellite industry.

In the capitalist system, companies compete to reduce costs since this directly increases their profits. However, reducing the number of employees through improving productivity raises unemployment, except to the extent that new jobs are created in new and growing industries. In an economy with a lack of *new industries,* increasing so-called "economic efficiency" creates unemployment, which is a social cost. In this situation, under governments concerned for public welfare, either the rate of creation of new industries must be increased, and/or the reduction of jobs should be slowed, at least until the growth of new industries revives, or other desirable social arrangements are introduced. These include more leisure time, job-sharing, and other policies designed to prevent the growth of a permanent "under-class" of unemployed and "working poor" – a development which would pose a major threat to western civilisation.

One of the many ill effects of high unemployment is that it weakens governments against pressure from corporate interests. For example, increased restrictions on such activities as arms exports, unfair trade, environmental damage, corporate tax evasion, business concentration, advertising targeted at children, and antisocial corporate-drafted legislation such as the "codex alimentarus" and "tort reform" are socially desirable. However, when unemployment is high, corporations' arguments that government intervention would "increase unemployment" have greater influence on governments.

As outlined above, the opening of near-Earth space to large-scale economic development promises to create millions of jobs, with no obvious limits to future growth. At a time when high unemployment is the most serious economic problem throughout the world, developing this family of new industries as fast as possible should be a priority for employment policy. To continue economic "rationalisation" and "globalisation" while not developing space travel is self-contradictory, and is both economically and socially extremely damaging.

Economic Growth

The continuation of human civilisation requires a growing world economy, with access to increasing resources. This is because competing groups in society can all improve their situation and reasonable fairness can be achieved, enabling social ethics to survive, only if the overall "economic pie" is growing. Unfortunately, societies are much less robust if the "pie" is shrinking, when ethical growth becomes nearly impossible, as competing groups try to improve their own situation at the expense of other groups. Continued growth of civilisation requires continual ethical evolution, but this will be possible only if resources are sufficient to assure comfort, health, education and fair employment for all members of society.

The world economy is under great stress recently for a number of reasons, a fundamental one being the lack of opportunities for profitable investment-as exemplified by Japan's unprecedented decade of zero interest-rates. This lack of productive investment opportunities has led a large amount of funds in the rich countries to "churn" around in the world economy, causing ever greater financial instability, thereby further harming economic growth and widening the gap between rich and poor. Increasing the opportunities for profitable, stable investment requires continual creation of new industries. Governments today typically express expectations for employment growth in such fields as information technology, energy, robotics, medical services, tourism and leisure. However, there are also sceptical voices pointing out that many of these activities too are already being outsourced to low-cost countries. Most of the net new jobs created in the USA during the 21st century so far have been low-paid service work, while the number of US manufacturing jobs has shrunk rapidly. The decades-long delay in developing space travel has contributed greatly to this lack of new industries. The rapid economic development of China and India offers great promise, but creates a serious challenge for the already rich countries which need to accelerate the growth of new industries if they are to benefit from these countries' lower costs without creating an impoverished underclass in their own societies-the long-term cost of which would greatly outweigh the short-term benefits of low-cost imports. The development of India and China also creates dangers because the demands of 6 billion people are now approaching the limits of the resources of planet Earth. As these limits are approached, governments become increasingly repressive, thereby adding major social costs to the direct costs of environmental damage. Consequently the decades-long delay in starting to use the resources of the solar system has caused heavy, self-inflicted damage to our economic development, and must be urgently overcome.

Popular Demand is the Basis of Economic Growth

The continuing heavy dependence of the space industry on taxpayer funding, despite cumulative investment to date of some 1 trillion Euro-equivalents, is due to the simple fact that those directing the industry have chosen not to supply services which large numbers of the general public wish to buy. Yet it is elementary that only by doing this can the space industry grow into a normal commercial activity. Doing this will create a new industry which raises private investment to develop newer and larger facilities in order to sell better services to more customers-in the familiar "virtuous circle" of business growth. Eventually this activity may even reach a scale sufficient to repay the public investment to date.

In successful companies, investment is skillfully judged so as to produce goods and services for which there will be large commercial (i.e. non-governmental) demand. If this earns sufficient profits, then the activity will continue to grow spontaneously for decades or more, like manufacturing of cars or airliners. If, instead, funds intended for investment are spent on developing non-commercial products, such as surveillance satellites or a space station for which the only significant customer is government, then clearly the space industry is doomed to remain forever a small, taxpayer-funded activity-a hindrance rather than a help to economic growth.

Economic policy makers responsible for deciding the public budget for space development must no longer rely on the advice of the space industry itself, which ever since its origin has had different objectives than the economic benefit of the general public. That is, economic policy makers, who are responsible for trillions of Euros of activity, must take the initiative and fund the development of passenger space travel systems as soon as possible-a policy level well above what is called "space policy", which is responsible for less than 1% of this. Among other steps, this will require the important institutional innovation of collaboration between civil aviation and civil space activities. Since, even with today's knowledge, researchers foresee the possibility of economic development in space growing to a scale similar to terrestrial industry, it must be considered as having the potential to become a major new axis for economic growth-but with minimal environmental impact, as discussed below-and therefore deserving of the most serious and urgent attention by economic policy makers.

Environmental Protection

Economic development in space based on low launch costs could contribute greatly, even definitively, to solving world environmental problems. As a first step, substantially reducing the cost of space travel will reduce the cost of environment-monitoring satellites, improving climate research and environmental policy making.

Space-based Solar Power Supply

A second possibility, which has been researched for several decades but has not yet received a budget to enable testing in orbit, is the delivery of continuous solar-generated power from space to Earth. Researchers believe that such space-based solar power (SSP) could supply clean, low-cost energy on a large scale, which is a prerequisite for economic development of poorer countries while avoiding damaging pollution and climate change. However, realisation of SSP requires much lower launch costs; which only passenger space travel could achieve. Hence the development of orbital tourism could provide the key to realising SSP economically.

Carbon-neutral Space Travel

Clean energy produced by SSP could eliminate the environmental impact of space travel, and even make it "carbon neutral" if this is considered desirable. Moreover, SSP has a much shorter energy payback time than terrestrial solar energy, due to the almost continuous supply of power which it can generate, rather than only in daytime during clear weather. Some critics claim that Suborbital space travel will become a significant environmental burden. However, while superficially correct in the short term, this is the opposite of the truth over the longer term. It would be a dangerous error to prevent the growth of space tourism in order to avoid its initial, minor environmental impact, since this would prevent a range of major benefits in the future, including the supply of low-cost, carbon-neutral SSP, and other space-based industry.

Space-based Industry

If orbital travel grows to a scale of millions of passengers/year-as it could by the 2030s, with vigorous investment-it will stimulate the spontaneous growth of numerous businesses in space. These will grow progressively from simple activities such as maintenance of orbiting hotels, to industrial use of asteroidal minerals. For example, the development of SSP would lead to a range of industrial processes using the advantages of space, including low-cost electricity, high vacuum, weightlessness and minerals in shallow gravitational wells.

If SSP grows to supply a significant share of the terrestrial energy market, more and more industry would operate outside the Earth's ecological system. While most industries cause growing damage to the Earth's environment as they grow in scale, industrial activities which are outside the Earth's ecosystem need not cause any such damage. Hence the growth of space-based industry to large scale offers the longer-term possibility of decoupling economic growth from the limits of the terrestrial environment. Indeed, it has been argued that only the use of space resources, including especially SSP, offers the possibility of protecting the Earth's environment while enabling sufficient economic growth to preserve civilised society.

Global Cooling

As a measure of the uncertainty about climate change there is a significant group of climatologists who, while acknowledging the physical mechanism of the "greenhouse effect", argue that it is outweighed by other natural influences, including the global cooling trend which is heading towards the next Ice Age. With a period of tens of thousands of years, the last Ice Age saw much of Northern Europe covered by ice 1 kilometre deep!

In the face of such a threat, it is notable that SSP satellites with area of tens of square kilometres, whether transmitting microwave power or sunlight reflected with large orbiting mirrors, could uniquely help to counteract Ice Age cooling by melting snow and ice over large areas. This could prevent the vicious circle of accelerating cooling due to increased reflection of sunlight from snow-covered areas. Direct weather modification is a new field with many uncertainties, but it may be the only way to prevent the destruction of civilisation by the next Ice Age. Thus, from the point of view of risk management, it is a major attraction of SSP that it could help to mitigate climate change, whether due to global warming, as CO2-free electric power supply, or global cooling, by directly warming the Earth's surface.

Ethical Consumption

Passenger space travel and its numerous spin-off activities have the important potential to escape the limitations of the "consumerism" which governments in the rich countries have encouraged in recent decades in order to stimulate economic growth, defined as GDP. This is resulting in "excess consumption" which causes unnecessary environmental damage, while reducing rather than increasing public satisfaction. "First world" citizens are increasingly trapped in a culturally impoverished "consumer" lifestyle which reduces social capital, social cohesion and happiness. By contrast, expenditure on the unique experience of space travel promises to play a more positive role in the economy and society, enriching customers culturally without requiring mass production of consumer goods.

Education

The educational value of space activities is well known: children and young people find the subject of space and space travel uniquely fascinating. A number of space-based, science-fiction films and television series have achieved extraordinary popularity, extending over decades. As a result, various organisations have created space-related educational programmes involving satellite design, small rockets and simulation of space flights. Unfortunately, while these activities are popular with the participants, it has to be recognised that they are not effective in increasing young people's scientific education overall, which continues to decline in most countries. That is, children who enjoy science classes find satellite projects inspiring, but these classes do not prevent the "flight from science" seen in rich countries, which is so dangerous for the successful continuation of civilisation.

However, the possibility of being able to travel to space oneself is of much greater interest to young people than watching videos of other people travelling to space, or than simulating travelling to space. Hence the start of low-cost passenger space travel services holds unique promise for education in fields related to space travel. In particular, the expectation that the price of a Suborbital flight could fall as low as 5,000 Euros as the service grows to millions of passengers/year offers the possibility of almost all children being able to take a flight sometime.

Culture

The history and artefacts of the European Renaissance are still the subject of worldwide admiration today. One reason for this unique flowering-such as in 14th century to 16th century Firenze-was that there was a social ethic whereby the successful and wealthy had a sufficiently strong sense of civic duty that they used part of their wealth to enrich the community, particularly by building inspiring civic spaces-libraries, galleries, palazzi and other buildings-and by commissioning works of art and scholarship, with results which still inspire us 600 years later. Such an ethic requires that those who are materially successful, however "self-made" and praiseworthy they may be, recognise that they are also all beneficiaries of good fortune-to have been born in a country, an era, a locale, and a family in which they have opportunities to learn language and manners, to accumulate formative experiences, to obtain useful knowledge, and then opportunities to exercise their talents and grow into a great career. In a successful society, people who are blessed with such good fortune accept that they have a social duty to repay this-by creating a similarly nurturing environment for future generations. The enduring popularity of the achievements of the Renaissance surely illustrates the enormous value of such an ethical sense in society.

Need for a New Worldwide Renaissance

By contrast, as societies became richer over the following centuries, they were increasingly disfigured by becoming more materialistic, a trend accompanied by more and more brutal and destructive wars, including the horrific "world wars" and communist revolutions. This trend has continued with the recent shocking decline in ethics of the US and UK governments openly flouting national and international law-and even the Geneva Conventions, once seen as a bulwark of European civilisation (by making war less inhumane through banning torture and the killing of civilians).

The way of thinking of Renaissance leaders is strikingly different from today when the wealthy are encouraged to follow the rubric: "If you've got it, flaunt it", or appear to follow the frankly psychopathic: "Everything for us-and nothing for anyone else." The futility of such an attitude is well-known throughout the ages, as expressed in such sayings as: "You cannot take it with you when you die," or "There are no pockets in a shroud". The great universalist religions of Buddhism, Christianity and Islam are in agreement that material wealth is transient and acquisitiveness is not the path to happiness: to the contrary, having gratitude for good fortune, and making efforts to help others less fortunate than oneself are extolled. The reason why these teachings have lasted for millenia is because they help people to live satisfying lives, to raise healthy children, and to maintain stable, resilient societies. They are the basis of humane culture and true civilisation.

Thus it is clear that, while societies have grown far richer since the Renaissance, the way of thinking of the rich today is far poorer. Despite almost unlimited opportunities for creativity and cultural contribution, most of the rich today leave behind little or nothing worth remembering. At best they typically use their money to buy large numbers of possessions, which are redistributed on their death. Of course many people, including the wealthy, give to charitable organizations, many of which do very good work. However, much of this work does little more than offset some of the worst effects of the policies followed by the rich countries which widen the gap between rich and poor worldwide.

We can judge this behaviour: the great benefactors of the Renaissance were more admirable human beings. Unless corrected soon, this futile materialism will destroy civilisation. Yet under "neo-liberal" or "neo-con" dogma, instead of using the opportunity provided by wealth to contribute culturally to society, the already rich exert pressure on governments to reduce their taxes further, to remove remaining restraints on monopolies and illegal surveillance of the general public, while falsely blaming already deteriorating welfare systems for government's fiscal crisis. The lack of new industries described above weakens governments against such pressures. Such psychopathic greed and dishonesty among the upper levels of a society are the prelude to its destruction, and represent the most serious challenge to western civilisation. A new, worldwide Renaissance is urgently needed.

"The Earth is Not Sick – She's Pregnant"

Healthy societies can revitalise themselves. An interesting explanation of the potential of space travel and its offshoots to revitalise human civilisation is expressed in the idea that "The Earth is not sick: she's pregnant". Although this idea may seem strange at first hearing, it is a surpisingly useful analogy for understanding humans' current predicament. According to the "Pregnant Earth" analogy, the darkening prospect before humanity is due to humans' terrestrial civilisation being "pregnant"-and indeed dangerously overdue-with an extra-terrestrial offspring. Once humans' space civilisation is safely born, the current stresses within the mother civilisation will be cured, and the new life may eventually even surpass it's parent. This idea not only illuminates many aspects of humans' present problems, it also provides detailed directions for how to solve these problems, and explains convincingly how successfully aiding this birth will lead to a far better condition than before the pregnancy. A young couple may be happy in each other's company, but their joy is increased by the birth of children and life with them, from which many new possibilities arise.

Likewise, the birth of humans' coming extra-terrestrial civilisation will lead to a wide range of activities outside our planet's precious eco-system. This evolution will solve not only humans' material problems, by making the vast resources of near-Earth space accessible, but it will also help to cure the emptiness of so-called "modern" commercial culture – including the "dumbing down" by monopolistic media, the falling educational standards, passification by television, obesity, ever-growing consumption of alcohol, decline in public morality, narcotics, pornography, falling social capital, rising divorce rates, and youths' lack of challenge and lack of "dreams". It will do this by raising humans' sights to the stars, and showing that the door to them is unlocked, and has been for decades-we have only to make a small effort to push it open forever.

Re-opening a true geographical frontier, with all its challenges, will in itself be of inestimable value for the cultural growth of modern civilisation. The widespread sense that we live in a closed world which is getting more and more crowded will be replaced by an open-ended, optimistic vision of an unlimited future. Access to the cornucopia of space resources that await humans' exploitation can clearly make a unique contribution to this. To the extent that leaders of major industries are motivated by ambition in business competition, they will welcome this opportunity to extend their activities to new fields in the far wider arena of space; to the extent that they are motivated by the attempt to achieve monopolistic control and profits, they may try to hinder development in space, even at the cost of preventing its wide benefits, since this will be more profitable to them. However, implementing the "Pregnant Earth" agenda can stop this cultural regression and start a true worldwide Renaissance, an unprecedented flowering of civilisation of which human culture has been in need ever since the inspiration of the Italian Renaissance was followed by a decline into progressive materialism and war-mongering.

World Peace and Preservation of Human Civilisation

The major source of social friction, including international friction, has surely always been unequal access to resources. People fight to control the valuable resources on and under the land, and in and under the sea. The natural resources of Earth are limited in quantity, and economically accessible resources even more so. As the population grows, and demand grows for a higher material standard of living, industrial activity grows exponentially. The threat of resources becoming scarce has led to the concept of "Resource Wars". Having begun long ago with wars to control the gold and diamonds of Africa and South America, and oil in the Middle East, the current phase is at centre stage of world events today.

A particular danger of "resource wars" is that, if the general public can be persuaded to support them, they may become impossible to stop as resources become increasingly scarce. Many commentators have noted the similarity of the language of US and UK government advocates of "war on terror" to the language of the novel "1984" which describes a dystopian future of endless, fraudulent war in which citizens are reduced to slaves.

Expansion into near-Earth Space is the Only Alternative to Endless "Resource Wars"

As an alternative to the "resource wars" already devastating many countries today, opening access to the unlimited resources of near-Earth space could clearly facilitate world peace and security. This is acknowledged by the U.S. National Space Security Office, which started its 2007 report on the potential of space-based solar power: "Expanding human populations and declining natural resources are potential sources of local and strategic conflict in the 21st Century, and many see energy as the foremost threat to national security". It ended the report: "Considering the timescales that are involved, and the exponential growth of population and resource pressures within that same strategic period, it is imperative that this work for "drilling up" vs. drilling down for energy security begins immediately".

Although the use of extra-terrestrial resources on a substantial scale may still be some decades away, it is important to recognise that simply acknowledging its feasibility using known technology is the surest way of ending the threat of resource wars. That is, if it is assumed that the resources available for human use are limited to those on Earth, then it can be argued that resource wars are inescapable. If, by contrast, it is assumed that the resources of space are economically accessible, this not only eliminates the need for resource wars, it can also preserve the benefits of civilisation which are being eroded today by "resource war-mongers", most notably the governments of the "Anglo-Saxon" countries and their "neo-con" advisers. It is also worth noting that the $1 trillion that these have already committed to the Iraq war is *far more* than the investment needed to access space resources.

Industrial and financial groups which profit from monopolistic control of terrestrial supplies of various natural resources, like those which profit from wars, have an economic interest in protecting their profitable situation. However, these groups' continuing profits are justified neither by capitalism nor by democracy: they could be preserved only by maintaining the pretence that use of space resources is not feasible, and by preventing the development of low-cost space travel.

Once the feasibility of low-cost space travel is understood, "resource wars" are clearly idiotic as well as tragic. A visiting extra-terrestrial would be pityingly amused at the foolish antics of homo sapiens using long-range rockets to fight each other over dwindling terrestrial resources-rather than using the same rockets to travel in space and have all the resources they need!

High Return in Safety from Extra-terrestrial Settlement

Investment in orbital access and other space infrastructure will facilitate the establishment of settlements on the Moon, Mars, asteroids and in man-made space structures. In the first phase, development of new regulatory infrastructure in various Earth orbits, including property/usufruct rights, real estate, mortgage financing and insurance, traffic management, plotting, policing and other services will enable the population living in Earth orbits to grow very large. Such activities aimed at making near-Earth space habitable are the logical extension of humans' historical spread over the surface of the Earth. As trade spreads through near-Earth space, settlements are sure to follow, of which the inhabitants will add to the wealth of different cultures which humans have created in the many different environments in which they live.

The success of such extra-terrestrial settlements will have the additional benefit of reducing the danger of human extinction due to planet-wide or cosmic accidents. These horrors include both man-made disasters such as nuclear war, plagues or climate change, and natural disasters such as super-volcanoes or asteroid impact.

It is hard to think of any objective that is more important than preserving peace. Weapons developed in recent decades are so destructive, and have such horrific, long-term side-effects that their use should be discouraged as strongly as possible by the international community. Hence, reducing the incentive to use weapons by rapidly developing the ability to use space-based resources on a large scale is surely equally important. The achievement of this depends on the low space travel costs which, at the present time, appear to be achievable only through the development of a vigorous space tourism industry.

Summary

As discussed above, if space travel services had started during the 1950s when they first could, the space industry would be enormously more developed than it is today. Hence the failure to develop passenger space travel has seriously distorted the path taken by humans' technological and economic development since WW2, away from the path which would have been followed if capitalism and democracy operated as intended. Technological know-how which could have been used to supply services which are known to be very popular with a large proportion of the general public has not been used for that purpose, while suffering due to the unemployment and environmental damage caused by the resulting lack of new industries have increased.

In response, policies should be implemented urgently to correct this error, and to catch up with the possibilities for industrial and economic growth that have been ignored for so long. This policy renewal is urgent because of the growing danger of unemployment, economic stagnation, climate change, educational and cultural decline, resource wars and loss of civil liberties which face civilisation today. In order to achieve the necessary progress there is a particular need for collaboration between those working in the two fields of civil aviation and civil space. Although the word "aerospace" is widely used, it is largely a misnomer since these two fields are in practice quite separate. True "aerospace" collaboration to realise passenger space travel will develop the wonderful profusion of possibilities outlined above.

Humans' Urgent Choice: Heaven or Hell on Earth?

As discussed above, the claim that resources are running out can be used to justify wars which may never end: present-day rhetoric about "the long war" or "100 years war" in Iraq are current examples. If political leaders do not change their viewpoint, the recent aggression by the rich, "Anglo-Saxon" countries and their cutting back of traditional civil liberties are ominous for the future. However, this "hellish" vision of endless war is based on an assumption about a single number – the future cost of travel to orbit – about which a different assumption leads to a literally "heavenly" vision of peace and ever-rising living standards for everyone forever. If this cost stays above 10,000 Euros/kg, where it has been unchanged for nearly 50 years, the prospects for humanity are bleak. But if humans make the necessary effort, and use the tiny amount of resources needed to develop passenger space vehicles, then this cost will fall to 100 Euros/kg, the use of extra-terrestrial resources will become economic, and arguments for resource wars will evaporate entirely. This is not a decision for the far future or the 22nd Century. It has to be made very soon if humans are to have a reasonable future.

The main reason why this step has not been taken yet seems to be lack of understanding by investors and policy-makers of the myriad opportunities that space travel will create. Now that the potential to catch up half a century's delay in the growth of space travel is becoming understood, continuing to spend 20 billion Euro equivalents/year on government space activities while continuing to invest nothing in developing passenger space travel would be a gross failure of economic policy, and strongly contrary to the economic and social interests of the public. As this policy error is corrected, and investment in profitable space projects grows rapidly in coming years, we can look forward to a growing worldwide boom. Viewed as a whole, humans' industrial growth has been seriously underperforming for decades, due to the failure to exploit these immensely promising fields of activity. The tens of thousands of unemployed space engineers in Russia, America and Europe alone are a huge waste. The millions of disappointed young people who have been taught that they cannot travel in space are another enormous wasted resource. The potential manpower in rapidly developing India and China is clearly vast. Correcting this error, even after such a costly delay, is going to ameliorate many problems in the world today.

We do not know for certain when the above scenario will be realised. However, it could have such enormous value that considerable expenditure is justified in order to study its feasibility in detail. At the very least, vigorous investment by both private and public sectors in a range of different suborbital passenger vehicle projects and related businesses is highly desirable. Fortunately, the ambitious and rapid investment by the Indian and Chinese governments in growing space capabilities may finally jolt the space industries of Russia, America, Europe and even Japan out of their long economic stagnation, and induce them to apply their accumulated know-how to economically valuable activities – notably supplying widely popular travel services to the general public

General Public Space Travel and Tourism

The travel and tourism business is among the largest in the world. In the United States alone, travel and tourism generate sales of more than $400 billion per year. This translates into jobs: the travel and tourism business is the second largest employer in the U.S.

Recently, the idea of extending travel and tourism beyond the surface of the Earth has been increasingly suggested – trips by ordinary people to space, not as scientists or technologists, but for personal reasons including adventure, recreation and business. This idea is not a new one; it has been examined several times in the past 30 years and some initial abortive attempts to commence actual travel and tourism businesses took place in the U.S. a dozen years ago. Early in this decade the Japanese Rocket Society encouraged the conduct of broad space tourism studies, including market studies. In 1994, the (then) six major U.S. aerospace firms concluded in their Commercial Space Transportation Study (CSTS) that general public space travel and tourism had the potential to become a very large market if space transportation safety and reliability could be sharply increased, and per passenger costs could be reduced, substantially.

The latest professional space travel and tourism market survey – one conducted in the United States by non-space interests – clearly suggests that very many (tens of millions) "average" American adults can envision themselves taking a trip to space (as they imagine, today, what such a future trip would be like) and, altogether, paying a great sum to do so.

However, substantial obstacles remain that prevent the immediate creation of a large scale business.

Today, the cost of access to space for people using currently operational vehicles remains very high; a half-dozen astronauts can accompany the delivery of payloads to space on Shuttle trips that cost some $400 million each. In addition, the safety and reliability of operational space transportation vehicles is presently far too low: a risk of some 1-in-100 of failure involving fatalities may be acceptable today for government missions and for a few adventure travellers, but not for airline-like general public passenger-carrying operations which will have to be safer by several factors of ten.

Finally, there has been a persistent lack of credibility because now it is generally thought that only NASA and the Russian government can send people to space and that they must be highly trained professional astronauts. This so-called giggle factor is especially prevalent among some experienced aerospace systems engineers unfamiliar with potential new capabilities that are inherent in recent technological advances and the increased insistence of the Congress that public spending in space result in greater economic growth, especially in the human spaceflight area. And they may not recall the enormous strides made in commercial aviation over just a few decades. The general public is actually more accepting of the idea of public space travel than these engineers.

Fortunately, critical advances have been made during the past decade in many of the technologies that can enable non-astronaut human space travel to become both technically and economically feasible, and more are foreseen. As a result, the potential exists for the creation, in the next very few decades, of a $10-20 billion... per year "general public space travel and tourism" business.

Too, initial steps can be taken at the surface, then in the atmosphere and later in space so that early profitability and experience, and credibility-creating activities, can begin prior to full orbital trips and long-term stays there.

During 1996-1997, the Space Transportation Association (STA) and the National Aeronautics and Space Administration (NASA) have, through a cooperative Space Act agreement, conducted a study of the potential for future general public space travel and tourism businesses. Several important findings were made. In their light, suggestions concerning what must be done to surmount the barriers to this business creation have been formulated.

Although several significant issues were identified, consensus grew within this study that the aerospace industry and travel and tourism interests, working in partnership with each other and with the Federal government where appropriate, could overcome all identified obstacles and that a viable, and potentially very large, general public space travel and tourism business could begin to be created over the next decade or so.

The basic objective of the NASA-STA study was to determine the feasibility of a commercially viable, general public space travel and tourism business being created in the U.S. through private initiatives with private resources, along with government encouragement, cooperation, and key scientific research and technology development investments.

As indicated, it is believed that such a business could grow to have great benefits for the U.S. economy while, at the same time, substantially increasing public interest in space activities generally. For, once the sharply increased safety and reliability, and sharply decreased unit costs required for large scale space tourism businesses to succeed have been achieved, many other things could then be done in space using such markedly advanced space capabilities.

A General Public Space Travel and Tourism National Steering Group for the NASA-STA study was formed in the Fall of 1996.

This Group conducted a preliminary assessment of the opportunities and problems faced by those who could be interested in forming space travel and tourism businesses, and it found that the former are inviting and, in principle, the latter are tractable. The Steering Group outlined a framework for a General Public Space Travel and Tourism Workshop, and many of its members participated personally therein. Finally, a draft of this Report was provided to the Steering Group by the STA- NASA study leaders and members of the Steering Group participated in its editing.

The General Public Space Travel and Tourism

To develop the concept of general public space travel and tourism further, and to bring together representatives from our space-related government and university interests, the travel and tourism business, the financial community and the aerospace industry, a Workshop was held during February 19-21, 1997. The primary purpose of this Workshop, which was held at the Georgetown University's Thomas and Dorothy Leavey Center, was to define what must be done in order to allow this new and potentially large space-related market to develop and to generate preliminary strategic concepts, milestones and organizational constructs toward that end. The Workshop was planned to have a relaxed, working atmosphere to encourage the flow of ideas.

Participants worked in teams to discuss the following topics:

* Space Transportation and Destination Facilities
* Passengers, Crew, Life Support and Insurance Considerations
* Regulation, Certification, Legislation, Policy and Environmental Issues
* Financial, Economic, Business Planning and Market Considerations
* Initial Ground Facilities, Space Tourism Theme Parks and other Orbital Trip "Precursor" Considerations
* Research and Technology Development Requirements, and Use of Existing Space Assets

Participants included:

* Travel and tourism business leaders

* Hotel architect, airline and business leaders
* Insurance interests
* Aerospace entrepreneurs
* Aerospace technical experts
* Space health and medical experts

The objectives of each of the several working sessions were: (a) to develop a detailed statement of the topic, (b) to identify key issues associated with general public space travel and tourism, (c) to identify opportunities to eliminate barriers, and (d) to make recommendations for future action. By the end of the Workshop, each of the teams formulated a series of findings which were captured in both a presentation to the Workshop as a whole and in white papers provided to the NASA-STA study leaders. These results were integrated with other information sources by these leaders to form the kernel of this NASA-STA study final Report.

The strong consensus view of the Workshop was that there is a very real potential for a large, profitable, commercially-driven general public space travel and tourism business to begin to develop beginning a very few years from now.

The Prospects for General Public Space Travel and Tourism

Space Transportation and Destination Facilities Considerations

Getting into and back from space safely and reliably, and for an acceptable price and in reasonable comfort, and having somewhere to go there, are fundamental to the concept of general public space travel and tourism. Areas for consideration are far-ranging, and include space transportation vehicles and their operation (both opportunities to use existing vehicles and the development of specialized transports) and space "habitats" and other facilities in space which will eventually serve as destinations. Some kinds of initial space transportation vehicles would likely also serve as habitats in short duration trips, while space residences would eventually develop to support longer term stays, much as in earthbound travel. Appropriate passenger-carrying Earth-Orbit transport vehicles are clearly essential. These may well be feasible in the relatively near future but, depending upon their size and the overall length and sophistication of the trips, required investment costs could be high — in extreme cases, very high. At present, there are several Federal government-aerospace industry and several purely private sector programs underway that, to various extents, can be visualized as providing some initial space travel and tourism capability. Dramatic advances in propulsion systems and structures are needed to see the lowest unit cost vehicle and largest service market develop. The probable costs to develop these systems will be high and government R&D co-investments are needed.

Validation of the real market for general public space travel and tourism is going to be an essential step. A central issue will be: is it possible to get that validation with current vehicles? In principle, the Shuttle fleet and small-scale trips using vehicles now under development could explore the market incrementally.

A notional — but not at all improbable — concurrent market and system-service development sequence might follow a path such as:

* enlarged terrestrial space-related travel and tourism businesses
* increasingly higher altitude adventure tourist suborbital trips
* global suborbital space plane package delivery and passenger-carrying services
* short duration adventure tourist orbital trips
* longer duration orbital trips, including stays at Low Earth Orbit destinations

Eventually, supra- LEO trips would be taken, but this study is limited to the consideration of trips to no higher altitudes than LEO.

Although services could be initiated with passengers living in the transport vehicle (as current astronauts do in the Space Shuttle), destination residential facilities will eventually have to be developed. In both cases zero-gravity "sickness" problems must be solved, generally, or artificial gravity provided. Fortunately, there is much attention being paid to the former and studies have shown that the latter is possible.

LEO residential facilities will be sophisticated and expensive undertakings compared to those on the surface. Ultimately, providing levels of comfort and privacy that are comparable to very large and successful terrestrial ocean cruise lines will be a very strong driver for the acquisition of improved in-space infrastructure.

As is often the case in the creation of a new kind of business, issues and arguments tend to be circular: both markets and financing are dependent on each other already being in place. Some use of such government facilities as the Shuttle and the U.S. portion of the International Space Station (ISS) is very highly desirable inasmuch as (a) general public passenger R&D is required, (b) key technologies and subsystems operations must be demonstrated, and (c) general public merchandising demonstrations would be invaluable. Too, having the ISS close by and cooperating with early residential facility use could be comforting to architects, builders, operators and guests.

Passengers, Crew, Life Support and Insurance Considerations

The "human" issues and problems associated with public space travel and tourism are no less important than the technological challenges of getting them to/from space. There is the need to identify the accommodations that will be required to support the general public; the need for experienced crew and attendants and their likely functions; the need for life support equipment that will be required in passenger vehicles and habitats; space sickness, its effects, and its countermeasures and their implications; flight and hull insurance — all, hopefully, at an early moment. Numerous issues must be resolved and actions taken before safe, large scale, comfortable and routine general public space travel and tourism can begin.

There appear to be a variety of options called for beyond terrestrial, and lower atmosphere space travel and tourism, including varying costs, accommodations, and levels of preparedness and acceptable risk-taking by various kinds of future passengers.

There could include:

* suborbital trips (lasting less than 1 hr; all in the space transportation vehicle)

* three orbit trips (lasting up to 5 hours; all in the space transportation vehicle)
* three day trips (possibly including a LEO facility)
* resort packages (with stays of 1-2 weeks at a LEO facility and possibly even extra-facility activities)

For any of these cases, the transport vehicle and any in-space facility must provide accommodations with certain minimal personal and social standards. These include: safety, privacy, baggage handling, entertainment, training and exercise facilities, and easy to operate toilets, showers, eating-drinking facilities, and medical capabilities (in situ plus telemedicine). For instance, gravity loads during launch and re-entry should be limited to some 2 times that of surface gravity.

One of the major issues concerning general public space travel and tourism (especially during early, relatively short duration trips) is the prevention and/or the amelioration of space sickness in "zero gravity". Nearly half of all people who have gone into space have experienced nausea and become ill because of the lack of gravity. Untreated, nausea and other effects can last for period ranging from a few hours to several days.

However, there are steps that can be taken. First, medication exists which will help almost all individual travellers. Although this medication is inappropriate for a Space Shuttle pilot because of its side effect of drowsiness, there is no present reason to believe that it cannot provide relief to many/most passengers. In addition, for longer term stays, techniques exist by which artificial gravity could be created which would prevent essentially all space sickness. For the latter case, technological- operational approaches range from spinning centrifuges or turntables operating inside an otherwise "zero-gravity" habitat for short stays, all the way to large-scale rotating habitats that could provide as much as Earth-normal gravity on long stays.

Overall, the issue of accommodations, life support and other amenities provided for the paying clients of a space travel and tourism business requires careful consideration. These can be expected to vary in scale and type depending upon the character and expectations of the travellers (especially the ones who could be identified as "adventure tourists") and on the duration of an individual's stay in space. Another important consideration will be the size and skills of the crew providing support and personal services to the passengers. (Reflecting upon the early days of commercial aviation's passenger service accommodations could be helpful.)

In order to assure confidence in comfort and safety a relatively large crew will probably be needed. Members of such crews will need exceptional people skills to handle the situations that are bound to arise in such an "alien" situation — informing without alarming, and calming without isolating when there are problems. Some or all crew members must also have appropriate medical training. In addition, adequate medical facilities must be provided locally, commensurate with the duration of the particular services being provided. Also, for longer duration trips and where a greater degree of physical exertion may be expected (such as in-space sports) an appropriately trained and experienced physician must be available.

Appropriate and thorough passenger preparation will be essential. This may very well include specialized training in some cases. For example, a working familiarity with the systems on board the residential facility might be a useful aspect of assuring health and safety. Rather than being a burden, it may well prove that preparation activities are a valued part of the overall public space travel and tourism experience (perhaps like attending a space camp). Broad experience in the preparation process itself could well become a terrestrial revenue-generating element of an overall general public space travel and tourism business.

Even after the technologies needed to make travel and tourism service affordable have matured and the systems have been developed, tested and deployed, uncertainties and risks will remain.

This will be true for in-space facilities, but it will be especially true for EO transports. Passenger, crew and vehicle insurance could become available, but would be expensive until transports are proven to be reliable by repeated usage over time. The "third party" liability issue must be addressed by both the vehicle developers and operators, and the Federal government, and this matter is now receiving increased attention. Practices similar to those employed on other so-called "adventure travel" trips, such as mountain climbing in the Himalayas where tourists sign a waiver of liability and proceed at their own risk, may be applicable in this case as well.

Again, both transports and hotels must be designed, developed and operated with basic general public physical, psychological and social considerations in mind.

Regulation, Certification, Legislation, Policy and Environmental Considerations

A myriad of legal and regulatory aspects of public space travel and tourism must be resolved before viable large scale businesses can emerge. This is especially true of those public agencies with the responsibility to regulate in the interest of public safety. This includes identification of public policies and/or laws that exist or must be enacted to enable business formation, licensing, certification and approval processes for both passengers and vehicles, clearance and over-flight considerations, and environmental and safety issues including atmospheric pollution, solar radiation (flares) and orbital debris.

National and international regulatory issues will affect general public space travel and tourism significantly. It will be crucial to assure both the Congress and the general public that this new business is considered to be safe by reasonable standards and acceptable by those who would take space trips. For example, it might be reasonable to expect that the earliest services will be safe by the standards of sky-diving, but not by the standards of today's commercial aviation; recall that the latter required improvement over decades to reach its present high level. Whatever standards are applied, it will be important to streamline regulatory processes and to establish uniformity in those standards and their application.

The ability to start viable businesses that offer diverse services of various scales and prices will be the ultimate test for the realization of the concept of general public space travel and tourism. Financial planning, capital needs and sources, and the creation of viable business plans are fundamental to creating a sound new business area.

This study is not recommending any specific ventures inasmuch as these remain the purview of the private sector and its judgment regarding business opportunities, but it does identify general issues and classes of opportunities.

For instance, the early years of space tourism flights should be in vehicles whose operations are licensed under the existing authority of the Associate Administrator for Commercial Space Transportation in the FAA-DOT. This office already licenses space cargo launches, and has the statutory authority to closely monitor the safety related policies, procedures, and operations and equipment of launch operators.

After some years of experience with various vehicle types and potential failure modes, the Federal government then could formulate standards for certification of passenger spaceships. This evolution to certification would free spaceship operators of the need for specific approval for each trip that is required under the licensing regime.

Major uncertainties that will affect the initiation of general public space travel and tourism business startups include: market demand and elasticity; transport vehicle acquisition and O&M costs; trip price; trip safety, reliability and comfort; and insurance and regulatory burdens. Notional business models suggest that profitability of eventually truly large scale service operation will depend on per orbital trip costs of not more than about $1-2 Million (roughly 100 times less than Space Shuttle costs and 10 times less than today's Reusable Launch Vehicle program goal). In addition, an overall safety of 0.9999+ (roughly 100 times better than Shuttle) will be needed. Vehicles should be designed able to return to Earth and land safely if required by any space trip emergency. Finally, high utilization of the space transportation vehicles will be critical — including turnaround times of some 24 hours (roughly 100 times shorter than today's individual Shuttle experience).

As these technical-operational goals are achieved, the price per ticket could drop below $50,000 per passenger, and might eventually reach the range of $10,000-$20,000. (By that time, if U.S. economic growth continues at the same rate as the past decade, in effect prices, in 1997 dollars, could be reduced by a factor of some 1.5X, and over 10 million households could have incomes, in 1997 dollars, of over $100,000 per year.) Market forecasts all suggest large real markets, but vary significantly in their predictions of market elasticity. However, with ticket prices well below $50,000, it is believed that there could be the order of 500,000 space trip passengers/year. (Transporting these many people/year would require the carrying to/from space of hundreds of millions of pounds of payload per year – roughly 1,000 times more than today's total U.S. civil, commercial and industry annual space trip payload, but still many factors of ten less than is carried by commercial airlines.)

Some notional business models that have been constructed suggest that, then, high annual internal rates of return may be achievable. However, it is recognized that such results are crucially dependent upon market elasticity surveys and space transportation service cost estimates that are at early stages of development. They each have major uncertainties and the general public's present trip expectations could change over a decade's time; therefore, such economic feasibility projections could be in substantial error and they should be updated every few years.

As a part of the business start-up process, incremental business formation involving niche markets will be vital. For example, poll data indicate that some people would go on very expensive "space adventure trips" now – even at prices approaching $1 million per ticket and with substantial physical risk. As part of this process, a carefully planned public relations and merchandising campaign is needed to improve public awareness of this opportunity and to change public perceptions of risks and viability. This is essential not just from the standpoint of informing eventual clients, but also from that of satisfying the concerns of potential investors.

The perceived level of risk and uncertainty in a general public space travel and tourism venture will, of course, have a direct bearing on the availability and cost of money for that venture.

Overall, the assessment to date suggests that if EO transportation system-services can be developed that demonstrate acceptable safety, reliability, comfort and affordability, and are sized to serve large enough markets, financially viable general public space travel and tourism businesses can be created by the private sector. And it is judged that, once public in-space trips of any character commence and continue with regularity, today's terrestrial space tourism businesses would flourish.

Initial Ground Facilities, Space Tourism Theme Parks and Other Orbital Trip "Precursor" Considerations. A variety of ground facilities and activities may be called into play to support successful formation of general public space travel and tourism enterprises, especially including businesses that are formed to exploit the latent market demand even before actual in-space trips are available to the public. These facilities could include theme parks, trip training facilities, and other such public quasi-entertainment facilities that could develop around future general public space travel and tourism launch/recovery sites, and whose function it would be both to prepare the public for the space experience and simultaneously to profit from the undertaking. The success of these businesses could be crucial in raising both public awareness and large amounts of capital for the actual public in-space travel and tourism to follow. Again, these activities would also serve as transition activities for the present terrestrial travel and tourism businesses.

As noted above, Earth-based space travel and tourism already exists and is flourishing. However, to serve as an effective "precursor" to public in-space travel, terrestrial space travel and tourism must enlarge its marketing focus from children and adolescents of the "Star Wars" approach so as to emphasize average, typically very successful, professional adults. Private business may make a lot of money on these types of facilities and entertainment activities, including those around a future commercial spaceport, as well as through training camps, space camps, theme parks, space-related merchandise, etc. Such activities may begin well before actual in-space trips occur, and they could continue growing once in-space trips become available.

A variety of information-oriented "precursor" activities will probably be needed to engender the rapid creation of a general public space travel and tourism business. For example, greatly expanded communications efforts are needed to develop space travel and tourism groups and to promote entertainment in such related applications as movies, prizes, CDs, and books. In addition, using motion picture and/or other media personalities to promote public space trips may be a sound strategy. Private, non-profit, organizations (such as the newly created Space Tourism Society) could lead these information-oriented activities and assist in the building of a consensus on various issues. This would be an important step. For instance, a virtual reality experience could be offered — one in which, on the surface, a person led by an astronaut could experience to some degree the characteristics of human spaceflight. Such experiences can be expected to whet the general public's appetite for "the real thing".

Too, it is now time for a few senior Federal officials who have responsibility for our civil and private sector space interests to consider taking trips to orbit. Their fundamental domain of responsibility is space itself, not the Earth's surface, and their doing so could be a graphic signal to the Country that space trips are no longer to be confined to astronauts. Certainly their personal participation in opening up space to the general public is as important as sending probes throughout the solar system. In so doing, they would simply replicate the trips of such Federal officials as the President and the Secretaries of Defense and State, who oftentimes visit dangerous areas around the globe to ensure that our Country's interests are well understood and supported.

Finally, it will be important that "precursor" activities provide early revenues to nascent general public space travel and tourism businesses and create a new public understanding that human spaceflight activities can be separate and distinct from those of NASA's.

Research and Technology Development Requirements, and Use of Existing Space Assets

There are several appropriate research and technology development activities that the Federal Government should undertake to allow the future creation of privately-funded general public space travel and tourism businesses. These include any technology developments or demonstrations that are too risky or too long term for the private sector to undertake under novel market circumstances, and any research programs, such as in life sciences — all of which are traditional government undertakings. The Government's role in advancing our satellite communications and remote sensing business interests continues to be a useful precedent. Government-owned space assets, such as the Space Shuttle and the U.S. segment of the International Space Station should be used for the conduct of scientific, technological and operational inquiries and, as well, for market-stimulation and initial private citizen trips. National policy regarding Shuttle fleet operations should be examined in anticipation of the desirability of allowing this latter use. The privatization of the Shuttle is proceeding well with initial operations now being conducted by the private sector – the United Space Alliance. Analogous privatization of ISS operations should also be seriously studied.

EO transport vehicles based on current technologies and operating methods are not sufficiently safe or reliable for widespread general public transport, and they cost too much to operate. For example, a space travel and tourism business that used a current NASA Space Shuttle configured to carry 50 people would have to charge some $10 million per ticket just to cover operations and maintenance costs. In the relatively near term, improvements to the Shuttle vehicles and their enlarged operations might enable a 2-4 times reduction in these levels. At such prices, it might be possible to start a business, but it would be one which could only accommodate a few people each year at best.

To ensure that the use of costly public assets are used in a fundamentally egalitarian fashion, private sector interests could explore the use of a national lottery and/or auction with government cooperation.

A lottery would provide funds needed to work out the procedures for training and supporting non-professional space travellers. The purpose of an auction would be to determine at what price private trip services might be able to sell their initial tickets; the answer would significantly reduce the uncertainty about the initial market for space tourism, and thus improve the ability of commercial space travel companies to secure financing for private spaceships.

The lottery and auction would be conducted only twice each, with a lottery and auction for Shuttle trips and again for combined Shuttle-Space Station trips. After these tests, space tourism would be conducted solely by private entities. It should be noted that the Department of State's Immigration and Naturalization Service now conducts an international visa lottery and the Federal Communications Commission (FCC) has auctioned off use of portions of the electromagnetic spectrum – interesting and encouraging precedents.

In general, the Space Shuttle is suitable for R&D purposes, modest initial "adventure travel" public uses, and fundamental educational and merchandising activities. While some additional R&D could be conducted on the International Space Station its capability should be augmented by a private sector tourist module. Access to these systems would be very helpful in the development of general public space travel and tourism businesses.

R&D programs are underway to reduce the unit cost of space access. For example, the NASA/Lockheed Martin X-33 technology development and demonstration project – a part of the Reusable Launch Vehicle (RLV) program– is investing in both new technologies and operations approaches. This investment could enable the beginning of more businesses by driving the cost per ticket down to the order of $100,000 each. However, this level is still too high for the development of a truly "mass market". Perhaps a lower "loss leader" price could be charged for Shuttle and/or RLV trips with an acceptable overall profit being obtained by including that from trip-related surface business activities.

Through the Advanced Space Transportation (AST) program NASA is also pursuing the development of technologies which, eventually, could reduce ticket prices to under $50,000.

The program includes:

* Highly reusable engines and vehicles
* Combination and/or combined cycle propulsion
* Off-board energy for launch assist or elimination of most propellants
* Advanced manufacturing, operations (including automation and robotics), and thrust augmentation systems (including upper stages)
* Advanced operations that enable further, dramatic, reductions in the number of ground and trip personnel

The validation of these technologies should be pursued in future successors to the X-33 technology demonstration program.

Staying at an orbital residence for as little as a week would increase the cost of this kind of general public space travel and tourism significantly. Acceptable unit costs would require more advanced technology and operating concepts than those being used for the International Space Station, and the government should initiate R&D activities to lower such infrastructure costs.

Summary of Findings and Recommendations

The opening of the frontier of space — not just to government missions and astronauts, but now to private individuals and private sector businesses — is a space challenge of overarching importance. It is especially important for the democratic United States of America.

This study should play an important role in beginning, in earnest, the process of United States government and business interests recognizing and overcoming the barriers to large-scale general public access to space in the early years of the next century. This fundamentally new human experience could be much closer to being realized than most people now imagine.

The following are the specific Findings and Recommendations of the study that are expected to help make this happen.

Findings

The NASA-STA study found that:

* Professional space tourism studies have been conducted in the United Kingdom, Germany and, especially, Japan. Japanese studies have included conceptual designs for vehicles that would carry large numbers of tourists.
* In a very real sense, "space tourism" already exists in the United States. It exists in the form of millions of visitors each year to space-oriented museums, to space launch/recovery sites and space research and development centres, to a space camp, and in space-related activities generally. And zero-gravity aircraft trips are becoming available.
* Polls consistently find that public interest in actually going to space continues to be large, real and widespread. However, very few realize that it is possible (given appropriate actions) that soon ordinary people, not just highly-trained and government-paid astronauts, could be able to take a space trip — as only a very few have since the beginning of the space age.
* Immediate steps can and should be taken to enlarge today's terrestrial space travel and tourism businesses. In addition, small scale enterprises may be able to get started using very near-term vehicles and/or technologies.

* For instance, two new companies have announced publicly that they are organized to provide space-related terrestrial and atmospheric trips and to position themselves to offer 100 kilometer altitude trips within 5 years; other companies are known to be considering offering similar space tourism services.
* Public communications and merchandising can make a significant difference in raising the level of this awareness. High profile public figures and senior space-responsible Federal officials could play a very effective role in promotion and education campaigns relating to general public space travel and tourism.
* Economic return on investment could be sufficiently high to attract capital for large-scale ventures. But the initial problems to be solved focus upon creating profitable businesses that serve small markets at high prices. As business moves to do so are successful, and if major issues are satisfactorily addressed, then the creation of financially viable high volume-low price businesses could commence.
* As a result, general public space travel and tourism has the potential to emerge as a large and growing commercial business in the early decades of the next century. Our positive economic experience in the large and rapidly growing private sector satellite communications, navigation/position-fixing and remote sensing business areas should encourage this prospect.
* The cost of a Shuttle trip to/from orbit for a half-dozen people (and upwards of 40,000 pounds of cargo) now approximates $400 million, the individual Shuttle trip turn-around time is about a half-year, and the possibility of a fatal accident about 1%. These spaceflight characteristics can be reduced by roughly a factor of ten times with a next generation of technology, and roughly another factor of ten times in a following generation, i.e., following the pattern that underlies the success of commercial aviation.
* However, to enable the development of broadly-accessible, "mass markets" for public space travel and tourism, new,

much lower-cost and much higher safety/reliability transport vehicles are needed, and relatively large-scale and continuing space industry and government programs will be needed to acquire them.

* The DOD-NASA DC-X/"Clipper Graham" technology development and maturation programs, and the ongoing cooperative private sector/Federal government X-33 and X-34 programs, are most encouraging steps forward.
* NASA's 1998 Strategic Plan (NASA Policy Directive (NPD-1000-1000.1)) moves in the correct direction when it asks in its " Administrator's Strategic Outlook" section: "How can we enable revolutionary technological advances to provide... space travel for anyone, anytime...?"
* We must learn how to reduce, if not eliminate, general public passenger space sickness discomfort.
* Very many more rocket launches will heighten concern about launch site noise and atmospheric pollution, and heighten concern regarding space debris collisions. These concerns must be realistically addressed.
* And recent Mir experience emphasizes the need for space hotel fire detection and suppression characteristics among other safety enhancement needs.
* The $ multi-billion per year NASA and DoD space transportation market should be looked to, as well as the satellite communications market, in considering the required rapid and confident amortization of acquisition costs of new passenger-carrying vehicle-fleets.
* Limiting the in-space experience to the transportation vehicle is acceptable for initial business. In this vein, early suborbital trips should become initial stepping stones to later orbital flights.
* However, to enable large-scale market expansion, orbital residential facilities will be needed. The technologies being developed today represent a good starting point, but clearly more work is needed to reduce the cost of human habitation in space by a large factor.

* Regulatory, policy, legislative/statutory and insurance questions must be addressed with an eye toward balancing public safety with making higher risk adventure travel start-up businesses possible. These discussions should include several organizations within the government.
* Creation of the United Space Alliance to operate the Shuttle fleet, which should lead to the fleet's use for private as well as public use, is an important and positive institutional change. It could well become the precursor, in the human spaceflight area, of our aerospace industry looking, entrepreneurially, to the private sector marketplace as well as the Federal government, for the large new human spaceflight business opportunities.
* Long distance, very high speed suborbital passenger and cargo transport prospects are also emerging, and would be enhanced by any conceptually related Defense vehicle and operations development programs. These could well furnish the earliest means for expansion into large-scale space travel.
* Both existing and new non-profit organizations outside the government could play important roles in enabling public space access to develop as a major new business activity.
* It should be appreciated by all civil space leaders that a large-scale private sector space travel and tourism business would strengthen the general public constituency for the conduct of civil space science and exploration activities, which otherwise will continue to be increasingly constrained by eroding general public financial support.
* It must be appreciated that widespread space tourism services will become available only as the marketplace is positively judged by our free enterprise business community, not our Federal government, and it should also be appreciated that the realization of a large general public travel and tourism business could take longer than otherwise if one or more of the following happen(s):

a. Another Challenger-like space accident involving loss of life;

b. A marked and prolonged turndown in our Country's economic circumstances;

and/or

c. Insufficient appreciation of the true economic dimension of the business by related aerospace, travel and tourism, and government interests.

Recommendations

In order to facilitate the development of a general public space travel and tourism business, the following steps are recommended:

* Our national space policy should be examined with an eye toward actively encouraging the creation of a large general public space travel and tourism business.
* In the near term, expansion of our terrestrial space travel and tourism businesses should be encouraged; theme and virtual reality space parks; space camps; training, production and launch recovery facilities; and other money-making "precursors" to in-space trips should be considered.
* Space industry companies, space-related financing and insurance interests, theme park developers, airline and cruise ship operators, hotel architects and operators, adventure tour operators,..., all should begin to inform themselves of general public space travel and tourism business prospects to determine their self interests therein.
* In pursuing these recommendations, it is now most important that a complete spectrum of people and businesses become engaged: financial, airline, cruise, hotel, terrestrial tourism and travel, and aerospace. Encouraging the involvement of small businesses and entrepreneurs is especially important.
* The assistance of existing and/or the creation of new not-for profit, non-government, organizations (such as a Space Travel and Tourism Association) should be sought to play a role in the needed communications efforts.

* The Aerospace Industries Association (AIA), the American Institute of Aeronautics and Astronautics (AIAA), the Institute of Electrical and Electronics Engineers (IEEE) and the Travel Industry Association of America (TIAA) should now begin to give increased business and professional attention to space travel and tourism.
* Universities that offer travel and tourism educational programs should now begin to consider terrestrial, in-atmosphere and in-space, trips and businesses.
* The Department of Commerce should focus upon coordinating general public space travel and tourism matters with those of the Departments of Transportation and Defense, NASA, and our presently evolving space travel and tourism businesses, so that the Federal civil space program will adequately encourage and support travel and tourism business interests. The Departments and NASA should also consider how to address this new and potentially large space business prospect.
* The Federal government's role should be that of cooperating closely with our private sector to reduce the latter's initial technological, operational and market risk, much as it has, with laudable success, in aviation, satellite communications and space remote sensing business development. It should:
    a. As it does now for our private sector aviation interests, develop and demonstrate technology that would increase space trip safety, reliability and comfort, and decrease unit costs — all by factors of ten; learn how to deal with high rocket launch rate noise, atmospheric pollution and debris collision concerns; learn how to provide low cost human habilitation facilities in orbit; and learn how to ameliorate general public passenger space sickness discomfort;
    b. Following on to the NASA Reduced Gravity Student Flight Opportunity Program precedent (in which college students performed experiments under microgravity conditions aboard a NASA KC-135 aircraft) allow the use of such public space assets as

the Shuttle fleet and the U.S. portion of the International Space Station (augmented by a private module) to conduct general public tourist R&D and initial fundamental "demonstration" merchandising activities — much as it continues to do, effectively, for the satellite communications business area;

c. Use its own space transportation needs, costing $ multi-billions per year, imaginatively, as a market to assist the private sector to amortize, confidently, its large initial vehicle-fleet acquisition costs;

d. inform the general public about space travel and tourism possibilities; such communications should focus on the idea that ordinary people— not just astronauts — should be able to go on a space trip in the relatively near future as a result of government-private sector cooperation;

e. See senior Federal officials responsible for our civil and business space interests consider taking the lead in "opening up space to the general public" by taking trips to space themselves;

f. balance, prudently, between regulating for public safety and encouraging business success under novel operational circumstances; and

g. Cooperate in holding an annual General Public Space Travel and Tourism Conference.

Government-sponsored R&D investments should specifically address:

a. Driving the per flight costs of space transportation down by 10-100 times in order to allow lower trip prices to be charged, in particular by developing and maturing technologies — including particularly rocket engines — that would be needed for low cost and high safety, reliability and comfortable transport vehicles;

b. Driving down the costs of longer duration visits to LEO dramatically, i.e., for human space habitation, by developing and maturing high safety, low cost and high reliability technologies;

c. Demonstrating ways to reduce the effects of space sickness to levels acceptable to the general public;

d. Assuring that high quality, high reliability, "human support" capabilities (such as emergency rescue and in-space health care) can become available; and

e. Environmental concerns, generally.

* Our X-33 and X-34 cooperative space industry-NASA program leaders should give specific attention to the prospects of general public space travel and tourism, as should the private sector space transportation activities of such companies as AeroAstro, Boeing, Kelly Space, Kistler, Lockheed Martin, Pioneer Rocketplane, Rotary Rocket, Vela Technology, and others.

* Private sector interests should consider the possibility of using lotteries and/or auctions to see that early R&D and merchandising trips involving the general public, especially those that use public assets, are conducted in an egalitarian fashion and paid for with the private funds that it/they could provide.

A Final Observation

In addressing, seriously, the possibility of our private sector providing space travel and tourism systems and services to the general public we should all appreciate that what is being discussed here is nothing less than a fundamental challenge to our views of, and participation in, extra-earth activities.

It is not unreasonable to characterize this challenge as politically, socially and economically revolutionary.

We now see the opportunity of opening up space to the general public — a "sea change" in our half-century sense that people in space would continue to be very few in number, would be limited to highly trained professionals who, at personal physical risk, would conduct mostly taxpayer supported scientific and technical activities there under government purview.

Now the dream of very many of us during the Apollo era that we could someday take a trip to space for our own personal reasons is finally approaching realization.

But bringing this about will require fundamental changes in the way that scientists, engineers, system-service operators, government officials, investment houses, business people, industry leaders, entrepreneurs...., go about creating space-related infrastructure and offering space-related services.

It is hoped that this report will draw wide attention to a fundamentally new human dimension of space that can and should be created, and to suggest ways by which many of us can help to see this come about responsibly and at a relatively early moment.

3

Innovation Portfolio of Hospitality

Case Study

General Information

Location: The Philippines is an archipelago consisting of about 7,100 islands. The country is divided into three major island groups: Luzon, Visayas and Mindanao. It is bounded on the north by the Bashi Channel, on the west by the South China Sea, on the South by the Sulu and Celebes Seas, and on the east by the Pacific Ocean.

Its northernmost islands, the Batanes, are approximately 240 kilometers south of Taiwan, while the southernmost islands, the Sulu group, lie approximately 24 kilometers from the Borneo coast. Situated between the Pacific and Indian Oceans, and between Australia and mainland Asia, the Philippines is at the crossroads of international travel routes.

Land Area. The total land area is approximately 300,000 square kilometers. The archipelago stretches out for about 1,800 kilometers from north to south, and for about 1,050 kilometers from east to west.

Topography. The Philippines has an irregular configuration of extensive coastline, vast extent of mountainous country lying close to the sea, narrow and interrupted coastal plains, and a generally north-south trend of inland water bodies.

Population. As of 1995, the population was estimated at 70 million with persons 15 years old and above considered the productive segment of the economy, comprising 63 per cent. The population density is about 234 persons per square kilometer of land.

Updates on the Philippine Economy

The economic turn around that began in 1992 continued to gain momentum in 1995 with the real growth in gross national product (GNP) accelerating at 5.7 per cent, an improvement on the previous year's 5.3 per cent. On the production side, industry and services expanded significantly, accounting for about 96 per cent of increase in aggregate domestic production during the year which offset the weak showing of agriculture which was hit by typhoons and other natural disasters. Meanwhile, strong exports and personal consumption expenditures accounted for growth in the demand side, the highest so far since 1992. Inflation was at single digit levels as of end 1995 and is expected to attain the same level by year end 1996.

The bright economic picture can be attributed to a number of factors, foremost of which were measures to maintain a stable macroeconomic environment and reforms to create a liberalized environment for business. Furthermore, the necessary conditions for growth such as political unity, peace and order, and infrastructure support were attended to by the government. The government recognized that physical infrastructure development must keep in step with economic growth.

The huge cost to the economy of under-investment in infrastructure was witnessed in 1992-1993, at the height of the power crisis. Cognizant of the huge investment requirement in infrastructure and the insufficiency of public funds to bridge this investment gap, the government instituted policies that encouraged private sector participation. The decision to mobilize private sector involvement in power generation proved to be fruitful as the crisis was resolved in 1994.

The government has adopted reforms and initiatives towards easing the entry of foreign and local investors into industries. Industries whose growth were previously hampered by government regulations like telecommunications and inter-island shipping were deregulated. The efficiency gains are visible. In telecommunications, for example, waiting time for a telephone connection has been drastically reduced while charges for overseas calls declined. As a result, markets are getting integrated both domestically and internationally, and mutually beneficial transactions are being realized in the process. The liberalization of the shipping industry, on the other hand, opened up domestic routes to other firms.

The noteworthy performance of the economy over the period 1993-95 is no reason to be complacent. The development strategy that has been embraced has opened up the economy to global competition.

This means that policies supportive of long-term growth must continue. Raising agricultural productivity, in particular, is a major challenge, given the inclusion of trade in agriculture in the World Trade Organization (WTO). To the extent that majority of poor families are dependent on traditional subsistence agriculture, success in raising agricultural productivity begets success in poverty alleviation.

The government recognizes that public policies based on privatization, liberalization, deregulation, and decentralization provide incentives for efficiency and growth. They expand the economic opportunities of people, enabling them to raise their standards of living.

The Ramos Administration is committed to pursue, and to accelerate where possible, these structural policy reforms, all of which have contributed to the sound economic performance from 1993 to 1995 and have provided a foundation for meeting any economic and social challenges in the future.

Long-term Objectives for Infrastructure Development

As the backbone of development of any economy, the provision of infrastructure is a prerequisite towards attaining economic growth and improving the country's productive capacity. The anticipated growth of the economy is expected to exert more pressure on infrastructure support facilities.

There are two major objectives for the infrastructure sector in the long-term: (1) to provide adequate, convenient, fast and safe facilities and competitively priced services to meet the primary needs of the population and; (2) to provide support facilities for the productive sectors and act as catalyst of development in desired areas.

Strategies for Infrastructure Development to Support National Objectives

The government has to design the proper policies and corresponding strategies for infrastructure development to ensure that the appropriate infrastructures will be provided in the right places at the right time. The following are the general policies and strategies to be pursued in the next three years in support of the sector's development under the Medium-Term Philippine Development Plan. (MTPDP):

1. Further encourage increased and broad-based private sector investments in the provision, operation and maintenance of infrastructure facilities through but not limited to the Build-Operate-Transfer (BOT) scheme;
2. Improve coordination among national government agencies, local government units (LGUs), the private sector and affected communities in the formulation and implementation of infrastructure plans and projects;
3. Ensure provision of adequate funds for required capital investment and operations and maintenance (O & M) with priority on the latter;
4. Strictly implement and upgrade maintenance and rehabilitation programs and standards;
5. Enhance integration of environmental and socio-cultural concerns in the planning and implementation of infrastructure projects;
6. Strengthen infrastructure support to socially depressed areas and to growth centres and areas with the highest growth potentials;
7. Promote, where feasible, labour-based technology in infrastructure activities;
8. Promote research, development and use of innovative construction materials and environment-friendly technology for energy-efficient structures and costefficient construction design;
9. Adjust fees and charges to approximate real costs incurred in the provision of infrastructure services;
10. Adopt the integrated area development approach in the

planning, programming and implementation of complementary support infrastructure for regional growth centres, tourism areas, and identified poverty areas;

11. Give priority to appropriate sanitation infrastructure facilities (e.g. toilets, water supply and sewerage) in Metro Manila and other urban centres, especially in depressed areas; and
12. Strengthen local technical and financial capacity for project implementation and service management through broad-based training programs and organizational and fiscal reforms.

Subsectoral Objectives, Policies Strategies and Priority Subsector Activities

Going down to the different subsector of infrastructure, the objectives and specific policies and strategies adopted for each and the corresponding priority activities are as follows:

Energy

The objectives of the energy subsector on ensuring the availability and security of market-based energy supply; promoting the judicious and efficient use of energy resources; and averting negative impacts of energy activities to health, safety and environmental quality in the design and operation of energy projects will be supported by the following policies and strategies.

To ensure energy availability and security:

1. Diversify sources and types of local and imported energy;
   i. utilization of natural gas for power generation or other competitive uses;
   ii. explore and develop oil and geothermal resource potential;
   iii. mine-mouth coal power plant operations for low-grade coal deposits;
   iv. large-scale utilization of new and renewable sources of energy including small-and mini-hydro resources, solar, wind and biomass-based resources;
   v. promote the use of decentralized energy systems for areas outside electricity grids; and

vi. rationalize expansion of petroleum distribution networks.

2. Expand coverage of electrification for the energy needs of countryside development;
3. Secure existing and future sites of power and energy resource development projects;
4. Enhance private sector participation in energy projects; and
5. Promote competition and long-term efficiency in the energy industry.

To promote judicious and efficient use of energy:

1. Pursue least-cost options;
2. Restructure electricity tariffs to reflect cost of provision;
3. Strictly implement comprehensive O & M and rehabilitation programs;
4. Enforce standards of efficiency and reliability in power generation and distribution utilities;
5. Promote energy conservation, energy efficient technologies, and energy R & D;
6. Move towards the deregulation of downstream oil industry to promote efficiency, e.g. petroleum product pricing and distribution.

To avert negative impacts of energy activities to health, safety and environmental *quality*:

1. Promote adoption of clean technologies for utilization of coal and other hydrocarbons;
2. Integrate environmental and socio cultural concerns in the planning and implementation of energy programs and projects, e.g., environmental management and community relations activities in energy project sites.

Priority Subsector Activities

1. Maintenance, rehabilitation and construction of power plants, transmission lines and substations in the Luzon, Visayas and Mindanao grids;

2. Exploration and development of indigenous energy resources including downstream activities;
3. Expansion of electrification coverage and improvement in the efficiency of distribution through the construction, rehabilitation, upgrading and maintenance of facilities; and
4. Implementation of research and development, institutional strengthening and energy conservation programs.

Transportation

As the economy expands toward the countryside and aims at global markets, the transport objective on strengthening interregional and urban-rural linkages to ensure people's mobility and continuous flow of goods; ensuring the safety and efficiency of transport services to meet the needs of an increasing population and dynamic market demands; and developing international gateways to optimum standards to enhance the country's global competitiveness; will be supported by the following policies and strategies:

1. Identify and provide basic transport infrastructure to ensure access and allow the integration of depressed communities;
2. Maintain existing transportation facilities properly to prolong their use;
3. Continuously upgrade transport facilities and service standards to make sure that their quality and quantity are responsive to traffic growth;
4. Promote multimodal transport to facilitate trade;
5. Develop the arterial road network consisting of a north-south backbone, east-west laterals, and other strategic roads;
6. Provide the transport facility requirements of agriculture, fishing, and agrarian reform areas, regional industrial centres, and tourism areas;
7. Proceed with the development of feeder ports under the Nationwide Feeder P. ts program in preparation for the devolution of their O & M to LGUs;

8. Establish specialized handling facilities for grains and bulk cargo in selected ports and construct additional fishing ports;
9. Implement urban transport management measures and develop alternative modes of transport in coordination with LGU's to alleviate traffic. Expand existing mass transit systems to provide affordable means of transport, and pursue new projects, including expressways and tollways;
10. Intensify transport safety programs to minimize accident risks and protect lives through the implementation of relevant recommendations of the Civil Aviation Master Plan, Maritime SafetyMaster Plan, and the Road Safety Program;
11. Strictly enforce environmental protection measures controlling vehicle emissions, water pollution, and noise pollution to safeguard the health of the population;
12. Strengthen institutional and inter-agency coordination of planning and project implementation to ensure effective and efficient intermodal linkage and reduce disruption of services;
13. Promote private sector participation in transport development, e.g., construction, maintenance, and operation of roads, expressways, mass transit systems, ports, railways, and terminals;
14. Enhance the capability of LGUs in administering, implementing and developing infrastructure facilities, i.e., local roads, municipal ports, as embodied in the Local Government Code;
15. Pursue efficiency-and competition-enhancing measures such as deregulation, decentralization, appropriate pricing mechanisms, and rationalization of user charges;
16. Adjust truck load limits along with road design standards to achieve a proper balance between trucking and infrastructure costs, and strictly enforce load limits;
17. Rehabilitate the PNR Mainline South, study the rehabilitation and possible extension of the northern line in Luzon and explore the feasibility of adopting rail as means of transportation in other areas of the country; and

18. Upgrade the NAIA and explore the use of the reverted baselands for its relocation or as a site for transport-related industrial complexes;

Priority Subsector Activities

1. Upgrading of national arterial and secondary roads to all-weather roads, and conversion of all bridges along these roads into permanent structures;
2. Construction and improvement of airport facilities including aircraft movement areas, terminal buildings, fire stations, etc.;
3. Upgrading and modernization of air navigation and communication facilities, and crash-fire-rescue vehicles;
4. Development and improvement of national ports and port facilities, feeder, fishing, and municipal ports, and river landings;
5. Acquisition and upgrading of aids to maritime navigation, search and rescue vehicles, hydrographic fire-fighting vessels, marine pollution control vessels, and other vessels;
6. Expansion and development of urban rail transit in Metro Manila, including the rehabilitation of LRT Line 1, the construction of new LRT lines, and the rehabilitation of PNR's Commuter Line South; and
7. Completion and the rehabilitation of PNR's Main Line South and study of viability of adopting rail transport in various areas of the country.

Communication

Increased globalization of production and finance requires that the Philippines keep pace with the latest advancements in the area of communications.

In this connection, the sector will strive to interconnect all local telephone exchanges into the main backbone; strengthen the regulatory and management capability of government to enable the private sector to meet the growing demand for telephone and other value-added services, and to achieve and maintain a high quality of telecommunications service; and expand postal service to far-flung/unserved areas and improve delivery efficiency in those areas covered. To attain these objectives; the following policies and strategies will be pursued:

1. Privatize all government telecommunications assets by 1998 as mandated by Republic Act 7925; allow more open entry of private firms to promote greater competition and efficiency in telecommunications services;
2. Phase out unnecessary taxes and fees that divert resources away from rapid growth of the sector, wean government away from the ownership, provision and direct operation of telecommunication services and privatize the postal service;
3. Adopt clear and simpler rules for interconnecting all public networks; encourage toll revenue sharing schemes that will ensure the financial viability of the local exchanges; and establish rules and regulations for a more rationalized delivery of broad band and personal communication services;
4. Reorient the regulatory system, initially towards forward arbitration of the issues arising from interconnection, revenue-sharing, rates restructuring based on cost radio spectrum usage, and complex technical options under a multi-operator business environment;
5. Increase telephone density and widen coverage consistent with the developmental stage of the various localities and the needs of the business, by private entities in concert with government investing their respective resources to anticipate and build capacities accordingly;
6. Upgrade the quality of postal communication service to internationally accepted standards; establish postal circuits in barangays not effectively covered by existing post offices and postal stations;
7. Introduce value-added services and initiate advanced users on the business and professional opportunities arising from the convergence of computers and communications; and
8. Modify the legal framework to permit and promote more electronic-based transactions, aside from phasing in deregulation measures as the sector achieves maturity.

Priority Subsector Activities

1. Installation of telephone main stations and public calling office (PCOs) throughout the country;
2. Construction of postal offices buildings and improvement of mail distribution service;
3. Improvement of the quality of telecommunications service; and
4. Establishment of telecommunication facilities to improve weather forecasting, enhance safety and improve information exchange.

Water Resources

In support to the objectives of increasing the provision of irrigation, safe and adequate water supply, sanitation services and appropriate flood control and drainage mechanisms are the following policies and strategies:

1. Pursue a decentralized, coordinated and efficient management of water resources; adopt an integrated planning and development strategy for an area-wide development schemes combining irrigation, power, flood control, and domestic and industrial water supply;
2. Determine investments in water resources and sanitation development would be based on demand and local initiative;
3. Encourage/facilitate participation of LGUs, NGOs, and private groups in sector development;
4. Integrate quality and quantity concerns in resource management and introduce appropriate environmental charges to protect public health and ensure environmental sustainability;
5. Implement cost-efficient water resources development projects for increased productivity and employment opportunities;
6. Integrate the provision of improved sewage and sanitation services in all water development programs and projects;
7. Determine the allocation of water among users where the primary bases shall be the socio-eocnomic consideration/ greater beneficial use.

Priority Subsector Activities

1. Construction, rehabilitation and maintenance of national and communal irrigation facilities nationwide;
2. Construction and upgrading of water supply and sewerage/sanitation facilities nationwide; and
3. Construction and implementation of flood control and drainage projects in the 12 major river systems in the country including Metro Manila.

Strategies for Supporting Regional Infrastructure Development

In support of programs for regional cooperation in infrastructure development, the following strategies shall be pursued in the sector:

1. Rapid expansion and integration of the network/facilities across urban and rural areas;
2. Active involvement of the private sector under the Local Government Code in local governance to ensure delivery of basic infrastructure facilities/services;
3. Integrate infrastructure planning with urban and regional planning, land use, environment, industry, agriculture, tourism and other sectors of the economy; and
4. In telecommunications, exploit the opportunities created by the overlaps of broadcasting and telecommunications through the production of cultural and entertainment programs geared for the Asia-Pacific market.

Scope and Priorities of Infrastructure Programs and Projects

Under the MTPDP, we have also identified specific programs and projects to implement such policies with corresponding key measurable targets. These targets will enable our government to monitor the implementation of programs and projects on infrastructure. They are the following:

Energy

1. More than 2,000 megawatts of new power-generating capacity to be put on stream up to the year 1998 to meet the projected 11.7 per cent yearly growth in power demand;

2. Integrate the three major island groups of the Philippines into a single grid in the next five years to strengthen system reliability and to allow the flexible shifting of power from areas with excess supply to deficient ones;
3. Dependence on imported energy to be reduced to 57 per cent of the total energy consumption of 258 million barrels of fuel oil equivalent by year 1998 from 67 per cent in 1995;
4. Expand rural electrification coverage to benefit an additional 1.1 million households under the government assisted electric cooperatives to 63 per cent by 1998 from 55 per cent in 1995;
5. Convert Clark Air Base into a freeport zone and investment haven just like Subic Bay Freeport Zone;
6. Rehabilitate and improve 100 per cent of national arterial roads and 95 per cent of national secondary roads into all-weather roads;
7. Improve major ports and airports and upgrade to international standards the Mactan, Davao and Zamboanga airports;
8. Construct new light rail transit lines in Metro Manila;
9. Install 4.2 million telephone lines to improve telephone density to 7.37 lines per 100 population from 2.01 in 1995;
10. Install public calling offices in all 1,565 municipalities;
11. Increase the proportion of the population served with potable water to 79 per cent from 72 per cent in 1995; and
12. Provide an additional 106,011 hectares with irrigation facilities.

Tourism Development

The overall objective for the development of the tourism sector hinges on the promotion of the Philippines as an attractive tourist destination not only for foreigners but also for Filipinos as well.

In support, the following policies and strategies will be aggressively pursued:

1. Promotion of destination clusters for major island groups, i.e., corresponding to the Luzon, Visayas and Mindanao

island groups, where each cluster will be supported by at least one major international gateway and tourism estates/ zones connected to a variety of satellite destinations;

2. Promotion of history, culture and arts;
3. Promotion of a mix of destinations and products for various tourist segments;
4. Conduct policy review in response to changing trends;
5. Establish and strengthen linkages and networking to ensure the provision of adequate infrastructure facilities and services in tourism areas, as well as the development, enhancement and promotion of existing and potential tourist attractions.

Priority Subsector Activities

1. Formulation of tourism master plans for all regions and detailed physical plans for priority tourism areas or 'must-see' destinations identified in the regional development framework;
2. Preparation of a Cluster Development Plan for Luzon, Visayas and Mindanao including the development of an integrated tourism infrastructure plan along the lines of conserving the socio-cultural heritage and preserving the environment;
3. Conduct of market research programs to identify target segment, product offerings, pricing, etc.;
4. Promotion of investments by both local and foreign developers in tourism priority areas;
5. Establishment of regional tourism training centres including the formulation of training modules at crafts/ skills level and mobile training units in the regions;
6. Establishment of cultural and heritage centres in areas identified in the TMP and regional master plans including the restoration of national parks, historical sites and shrines, e.g., Rizal Park, Intramuros, Vigan, Taal and Nayong Pilipino.
7. Conceptualization and packaging of "freedom trail tours" in line with the Philippine Freedom Centennial Celebration;

8. Pursuit of aggressive marketing campaigns focusing on the thematic campaign "Islands Philippines" during the Plan period culminating in the holding of a "Philippine Visit Year" Campaign in 1998.

Administrative Structure for Policy-making and for the Implementation of Infrastructure Programs and Projects

In explaining the administrative structure for the approval and implementation of infrastructure projects in the Philippines, discussions will be limited to BOT projects for brevity. The main actors in the BOT approval/implementation process are as follows:

Infrastructure Committee (INFRACOM) of the NEDA Board

The INFRACOM is a policy-level committee of the NEDA Board composed of the Secretaries of NEDA, DPWH, DOTC, DBM, DOF, DOE, and the Executive Secretary from the Office of the President. NEDA acts as the Secretariat to the Committee. In addition to its regular functions, it is tasked to coordinate the discussion/resolution/reformation of policies an issues pertinent to the implementation of the Build-Operate-Transfer Schemes. Investment Coordination Committee (ICC) of the NEDA Board The Investment Coordination Committee (ICC) is another cabinet committee of the NEDA Board composed of the Secretaries of DOF, NEDA, DBM, DTI, DA, BASP, DOE, CCPAP and the Executive Secretary from the Office of the President. Its basic mandate is to coordinate the utilization of fiscal resources for the public investment program, approve the implementation of major projects and monitor the same thereof.

With respect to BOT projects, ICC shall approve national projects costing up to 300 million and local projects costing more than 200 million pesos. ICC shall recommend the approval of national projects costing more than 300 million pesos to the National Economic Development Authority (NEDA) Board and all Build-Operate and Own projects to the President.

Implementing Agency

The implementing agencies for infrastructure development, such as the Department of Public Works and Highways, the Department of Transportation and Communications and the National Power Corporation, perform the following functions:

1. Identify and recommend particular projects for BOT;
2. Undertake at least the pre-feasibility studies for the projects;
3. Ensure that projects are part of its development program;
4. Secure ICC approval of the project before bidding;
5. Responsible for leading the project through bidding, negotiation and approval; and
6. In the absence of an appropriate regulatory body, issue a franchise to operate.

Local Government Unit (LGU)

The LGU identifies and recommends projects for BOT. It then secures project confirmation of the local development council or regional development council or the Metropolitan Manila Development Authority (for Metro Manila projects) prior to bidding. It is likewise responsible for leading the project though bidding, negotiation and approval. Finally, the LGU or appropriate regulatory body may issue a franchise to operate, as provided by existing laws.

Coordinating Council of the Philippine Assistance Program (CCPAP)

The Coordinating Council of the Philippine Assistance Program (CCPAP) has been tasked to handle the promotion of the BOT scheme and projects. It provides training/information to lead actors for BOT implementation, technical assistance for a prefeasibility study to assess if a project is suitable for BOT implementation, and support for tender document preparation, marketing and contract compliance.

Private Sponsors

The private sector agent is responsible for leading the project through packaging, negotiation and approval of the security package. It assembles the needed financial commitments for the project.

There are also other actors that have important roles to play in the BOT approval process. These are:

- *Local Development Council*

- Evaluates/approves/integrates the project into a larger development plan

o *Local Sanggunian or Council*

- Approves the project prior to call for bids

o *Board of Investments (BOI)*

- Decides if a project is eligible for investment incentives

o *Department of Environment and Natural Resources (DENR)*

- Reviews compliance with environmental laws
- Issues the Environmental Compliance Certificate

o *Regulatory Agencies*

- Ensures that tolls and fees are just

Market Preparations for Private Sector Investment

As in any country in the world, the Philippines' economic growth cannot be sustained and further improved without continuously adopting measures to enhance the infrastructure system. To realize this, a broad policy framework has been adopted by the government to encourage private sector to participate in economic development, e.g. financing, operation and construction of vital infrastructure facilities.

Current Laws Affecting Infrastructure Development

In the formulation of policies and programs for infrastructure development and in the course of implementation of such projects, we are bound by certain laws, foremost among which are the Build-Operate-Transfer (BOT) Law, the Public Service Law and other regulations.

BOT Law

Although provision of infrastructure facilities and services is mainly the responsibility of government because of its "public goods" aspect, severe fiscal constraints in the case of the Philippines, has resulted in the decline of public investment in infrastructure development. In consonance with the new era of low public sector deficits which the government aims to impose to contain inflation within manageable levels and ensure sustainable long-term growth, we are constrained to restrict our expenditure program. This means putting a limit to public investments in infrastructure projects. On the other hand this forces our government to seek other sources of financing such as Official Development Assistance (ODA) and private investments, either domestic or foreign. This kind of scenario opens a great number of opportunities for the BOT scheme.

Republic Act (RA) No. 6957 enacted on July 9, 1990 institutionalized the BOT/BT concept in the Philippines and this served as an avenue for the Philippine Government to address the following national concerns:

1. To encourage private sector participation in the financing, construction, operation and maintenance of infrastructure and power projects, the lack of which is considered one of the overriding barriers to economic growth in the Philippines;
2. To reduce the fiscal burden on the part of the Government of the Philippines (GOP) by making the private sector an effective partner and/or participant in infrastructure building; and
3. To effectively encourage the inflow of foreign capital financing, technology and expertise, especially in the operation of major and capital-intensive infrastructure projects.

Recognizing the need to put in place an environment conducive to private sector's entrepreneurial initiatives RA 6957 was enacted. RA 6957 initially sought to provide the necessary policy framework and clear-cut implementation of BOT/BT projects. In the course of its implementation, it became evident that further changes in some provisions were necessary in order to further stimulate private sector participation.

In line with the government's commitment to a liberal and facilitative socioeconomic environment, amendments to the Law were introduced through RA 7718 which was enacted on 05 May 1994. The amended BOT Law allows more types of infrastructure projects to be implemented by the private sector. In addition to traditional projects like power plants, highways, ports, airports and similar projects, new ones have been added. These are solid waste management, information technology networks and database infrastructure, education and health facilities, tourism projects, government buildings, and other projects that may be approved by the President of the Philippines. The scope of the amended BOT Law has also been liberalized and widened. Nine variations of contractual arrangements that go beyond building, owning, operating and transferring are now allowed. These new features include leasing, contracting, adding, rehabilitating, developing adjacent areas, etc.

Unsolicited project proposals may be accepted on a negotiated basis subject to certain conditions. Furthermore, direct negotiation shall be resorted to when there is only one complying bidder. This was not allowed before. The amended BOT Law likewise now allows government appropriation and/or access to ODA of up to 50 per cent of project cost for projects with difficulty in sourcing funds. The Implementing Rules and Regulations of the amended BOT Law also requires that the economic viability indicators of the project shall be evaluated against a hurdle rate of 15 per cent.

Rate setting will be deregulated for projects which are bid out. On the other hand, the appropriate regulatory agencies will approve the rates for negotiated contracts. In the case of negotiated contracts for public utility projects which are monopolies, the rate of return base will not exceed 12 per cent.

Investment incentives contained in the Omnibus Investment Code as well as direct cost-sharing and credit enhancements may be extended to projects as necessary. Considering the overwhelmingly favourable reactions to the new BOT law, we are very optimistic that more private investors will signify their interest to invest in infrastructure projects in our country.

Public Service Law of 1936

The Public Service Law defines "public utilities" as including:

1. Roads and thoroughfares
2. Railways and Urban Rail Mass Transit
3. Distribution (not production) of Electricity and Gas
4. Water Distribution and Sewerage Systems
5. Telephone Systems
6. Wireless Broadcast Stations
7. Any common carrier, either for freight or passenger.

Proposed amendments to the Public Service Law are now

pending in Congress which seek to remove the following activities from being classified as "public utilities":

1. Domestic messenger and parcel delivery services
2. Shipyards, marine railways, marine repair shops, wharves or docks
3. Ice plants and ice-refrigeration plants
4. Irrigation systems
5. Warehouses
6. Airships within the Philippines;
    - The Foreign Investments Act of 1991;
    - The Omnibus Investments Code of 1987 and
    - The Investment Priorities Plan.

The Foreign Investments Act identifies the areas where foreign investors can enter while the Omnibus investments Code identifies the kind of fiscal incentives that may be availed of by investors under certain conditions. The Investment Priorities Plan identifies the areas in which these incentives can be availed of. It is drawn up annually.

There are pending proposals in Congress to amend the Foreign Investments Act and the Omnibus Investments Code to further liberalize the entry of foreign investments into the country, including national treatment of equity investments put in by multilateral financing agencies.

The General Banking Code

Sections 111 and 112 of the General Banking Code establishes a single-borrower's limit of 15 per cent for Philippine banking institutions. This means that a Philippine bank cannot lend out more than 15 per cent of its capital base to any single entity.

This could have the effect of restricting domestic term loans to large BOT infrastructure projects. However, these projects would have to be very large, as the single borrower limit for the top five commercial banks is between five hundred million and one billion pesos per bank.

Executive Order No. 215

Executive Order No. 215 is the legal basis for tapping private sector power generation prior to the more expansive BOT Law. It is noteworthy for two reasons:

1. It allowed the private sector to participate in the generation of power.
2. It gave the National Power Corporation the authority to develop the implementing rules and regulations. In particular, NPC was given the leeway to determine (a) process of bidding and awarding of projects, thus allowing them to avoid-to some degree-the lengthy approval process for BOT projects, and (b) credit enhancements it could give in order to make the project more attractive to the private sector.

Local Government Code

The Local Government Code encourages the participation of the private sector in local governance, particularly in the delivery of basic services, to ensure the viability of local autonomy as an alternative strategy for sustainable development.

Government Commitment, Support and Riskmanagement

The critical challenge facing the government is to constantly monitor, improve, and refine policy measures and general guidelines when and where required. This is necessary to motivate and enable interested parties to take a more competitive form under a global climate of rapid change.

To encourage further private sector participation, the government has maintained its open-mindedness and receptiveness to suggestions on how to improve the process, e.g. possible amendment of the IRR of the amended BOT law to remove sources of irritants and bottlenecks and to resolve conflicts with other laws. In this regard, there is an inter-agency goverment committee that can be convened anytime there is a need to review or revise the IRR.

The country has come a long way since the path of liberalization was taken in developing the infrastructure crucial to the country's industrialization. Having put in place institutional measures to open up the sector to competition, coupled with a market demand projected to increase in size in the future, the government has succeeded in stimulating significant investment in the sector.

Since the adoption of policies geared towards a more liberal business environment, many foreign and local industry observers agree that the Philippine market is increasingly competitive, e.g. in telecommunications, power, transportation. These are on top of what the country now offers, e.g. political stability, an investor-friendly legal framework, free market for foreign exchange and guaranteed repatriation rights.

Bidding Procedures/Process For Government Infrastructure Projects

In line with its effort to achieve economy and efficiency in the implementation of public infrastructure projects, the government formulated in 1978 and in 1987 a standard set of rules and regulations for civil works and consultancy contracts, respectively, with the aim of: a) minimizing project cost through the adoption of sound practices in contract management; b) promote a healthy partnership between the government and the private sector in furthering national development; and c) enhance the growth of the local construction and consulting industries.

The government's bidding procedure generally advocates for an open competitive selection process. However, it also allows negotiated contracts under exceptional circumstances such as in times of emergencies or where there is lack of qualified bidders.

Foreign contractors/consultants may participate in the bidding of projects provided that they comply with the documentary requirements stipulated in the rules and regulations. In cases of consultancy contracts, foreign consultants are required to associate themselves with Filipino consultants in the interest of bringing about the transfer and introduction of new technologies into the country. The government's bidding process is similar to that of foreign lending institutions like the World Bank, ADB and OECF except for some extra features/provisions which are basically designed to address unique local conditions.

Following hereunder are the steps in the procurement of consulting services for government infrastructure projects. A flowchart of the process is presented in Annex 4.

1. Announcement of the project. The requirements for consulting services is announced for at least two (2) times within a period of not more than two (2) weeks in at least

two (2) newspapers of general circulation. Copies of the announcement are also posted in any conspicuous place in the agency concerned.

2. Issuance of qualification statements to interested consultants. Only those consultants who express their desire to offer their services for the work contemplated are included in the long list and requested to submit prequalification statements.
3. Preparation of the short-list of consultants. The pre-qualification statements are evaluated by the agency concerned to determine the short list of consultants. The following are considered in drawing-up the short list of consultants: applicable experience of the consultant, qualification of personnel to be assign to the project, and current work load relative to capacity.
4. Issuance of invitations to the short-listed consultants to submit proposals. The invitation generally includes the Terms of Reference, information required to be submitted by the consultants such as its experience and capability/ current work assignments, criteria and system of rating the consultants, etc.
5. Evaluation of technical proposals. As a general rule, the two envelope-two stage procedure is adopted whereby the short-listed consultants are requested to submit their technical and financial proposals in two (2) separate sealed envelopes. The first stage involves the evaluation and ranking of the consultants' technical proposals vis-à-vis certain predetermined criteria. Once the rankings of the consultants' technical proposals have been established and approved by the appropriate authority, the first-ranked firm is then invited for negotiation and their financial proposal opened in their presence (second stage). The first-ranked firm's financial proposal shall be the basis upon which negotiations shall be conducted to arrive at a fair and reasonable contract amount. Should negotiations with the first-ranked consultant fail, the financial proposal of the second-ranked consultant shall then be opened and negotiations conducted, and so on until an acceptable agreement with a consultant is reached.

6. Preparation of Agreement/Contract. The Agreement/ Contract is prepared after negotiations with the selected consultant had been finalized. The contract includes, among others, the scope and cost of services, method of payment, obligations of the consultant and agency concerned, and the list personnel to be involved in the project.
7. Approval of Agreement/Award of Contract. The Head of the agency shall approve the contract. In case of foreign-assisted projects, the agreement is submitted to the financial institution for concurrence.
8. Issuance of notice to proceed. After the contract had been approved, the agency concerned issue the notice to proceed to the selected consultant.

For civil works contracts, following hereunder are the procedures adopted by the government. A flowchart of the process is presented in Annex 5.

1. Announcement of the project. The project is advertised for at least three (3) times within a period of not less than two (2) weeks in at least two (2) newspapers of general circulation. Copies of the announcement are also posted at any conspicuous place in the agency concerned.
2. Issuance of qualification statements to prospective bidders. The agency concerned provides the prospective bidders with the notice to pre-qualification to guide them in evaluating their capabilities and decide whether or not to participate in the bidding.
3. Pre-qualification of contractors. In the evaluation of the qualification statements, both the technical capability and financial capacity of the contractor is considered. The technical capability of the contractor is gauged by the extent of his relevant experience, suitability of available construction equipment and adequacy of his proposed organization and personnel. The financial capacity of the contractor, on the other hand, is based on his ability to obtain a credit line statement from a reputable bank or financing institution licensed by the Central Bank of the Philippines.

4. Issuance of plans, specifications, proposal book forms and draft contract to pre-qualified bidders. The agency concerned issue the tender documents to the prospective bidders in accordance with the schedules stated in the rules and regulations. For projects costing less than P= 1.0 million, for example, the tender documents are issued to the bidders 15 days before the date of bidding. For projects costing more than P= 100.0 million, the tender documents are issued 90 days before the date of bidding.
5. Submission, opening and abstracting of bids. Bids are submitted in two (2) sealed envelopes. The first envelope contains, among others, the manpower schedule, construction schedule, equipment utilization schedule, and construction methods. The second envelope contains the bid prices, detailed estimates and cash flow by quarter.
6. Evaluation of bids. A bid which does not comply with the conditions of the bid documents is rejected by the agency. At the time of the opening of bids, there should be at least two (2) competing bidders. In case there is only one bidder, the agency can either consider the lone bid for award provided it does not exceed the approved agency estimate (AAE), or return the lone bid unopened and conduct a rebidding thru sealed canvass of at least five (5) qualified contractors.
7. Award/Approval of contract. No award of contract is made to a bidder whose bid price is higher than the allowable government estimate (AGE) or the AAE, whichever is higher, or lower than 70 per cent of the AGE. The AGE is equal to one half the sum of the AAE and the average of all responsive bids. Responsive bids pertain those bids not higher than 120 per cent of the AAE or lower than 60 per cent of the AAE. The head of the agency shall approve the contract.
8. Issuance of notice to proceed. Once the contract had been approved, the agency shall issue the notice to proceed to the successful bidder.

4

Competing by Collaborating in Hospitality

Tourism in Context

Tourism is a powerful driver of community prosperity. Tourism exports (ie; foreign revenue earned in Australia) are larger than coal exports, wool exports and most other categories. It makes both a direct (tourism industry jobs and income etc.) and an indirect (retail, hospitality, goods and services etc.) contribution to the Australian economy.

The tourism industry represents the quintessential expression of the small business ethic of Australia, with a large number of small and medium-sized operators, including many that are family run businesses. Tourism is a labour intensive activity overall, employing proportionally more people per dollar of GDP than most other industries.

Chief beneficiary industries are transport, accommodation, cafes and restaurants, manufacturing, retail and property and business services. After the airlines, large hotel chains, big tour companies and major man-made attractions, most tourism business is small, and reliant on local support for its viability. This is especially true in the CoPP.

An Australian snapshot: Tourism in Australia continues to trend upwards generally year on year at about 1%, despite periodic unforeseen spikes in the market occasioned by such factors as SARS or 9/11. Between 2000-2001, tourism contributed around $59 billion to Australia's GDP, which equates with 9% of GDP. Between 2004-05 tourism accounted for $18.3 billion in exports.

According to most recent available data, tourism in 2000-01 directly employed 549,000 people (6% of total employment). Indirect employment for the same 2000-01 period accounted for about 351,000 people, some 4.4% of the work force. When combined, in 2000-01 tourism accounted for the employment of around 900,000 people, or 10.4% of the Australian work force.

A Victorian Snapshot: According to the latest research, in 2003-2004, the combined direct and indirect contribution of tourism to Victoria's Gross State Product (GSP) is estimated to be 5.3% or $10.9 billion (a 49% increase from $7.3 billion in 1997-1998).

Overall, The tourism industry contributes more to the Victorian economy than many traditional industries including agriculture, forestry & fishing; mining; electricity, gas & water supply; Government administration and defence; and Cultural and recreational services.

Victorian Employment in the Tourism Industry

In 2003-2004 tourism accounted for 159,000 jobs or 6.6% of all people employed in Victoria (a 19% increase from 134,000 in 1997-1998).

Visitation to Victoria

Sixty-four percent of overnight visitors to Victoria were sourced from the intrastate market, followed by 28% from the interstate market and 7% from overseas. 37% of domestic visitor nights to Victoria were sourced from the intrastate market, followed by 36% from the international market and 26% from interstate.

Domestic Overnight Visitation

Victoria received 17.3 million domestic overnight visitors for the year ending June 2006 and 53.0 million domestic visitor nights. The average length of stay for the year ending June 2006 was 3.1 nights.

Domestic Daytrip Visitation

There were 31.8 million domestic daytrip visitors to Victoria for the year ending June 2006.

Domestic Visitor Expenditure

Domestic overnight expenditure in Victoria in 2005 is estimated to be $7.6 billion, with visitors spending on average $148 per night and $454 per visit. Domestic daytrip visitors spent $2.9 billion in Victoria in 2005, spending on average $92 per daytrip. Domestic overnight visitors to Victoria spent most of their money on food and drink (26% of total expenditure) and accommodation (20%).

Domestic Forecast

Over the period 2006 to 2015, domestic visitor nights to Victoria are expected to grow by an average annual rate of 0.5%, to reach 52.9 million nights in 2015. Holiday/Leisure travel to Victoria is forecast to grow at an annual average rate of 0.5% over the period 2006 to 2015 to reach 25.5 million nights.

A Melbourne Snapshot: In the year ended September 2005, Melbourne had almost 17.3 million visitors from all sources. Of those, nearly 5.9 million were domestic overnight visitors.

Total Travel to Melbourne in the YE Sep 2006

Looking at travel to Melbourne overall, there were nearly 40.7 million visitor nights. Of these, International overnight visitors to Melbourne numbered 1.3 million and they stayed 22.7 million nights or 55.9% of all visitor nights.

New Zealand is Melbourne's biggest international source market of visitors, with UK second, while China in third place, is the second biggest contributor of visitor nights in Melbourne. A significant proportion of the Chinese visitation is attributable to learning English.

A visit for 'Holiday/pleasure' continues to be the main purpose of visit for international overnight visitors to Melbourne, and 'Education' remained the biggest 'purpose of visit' contributor to international visitor nights in Melbourne. Because of people who come for education, and backpackers who use Melbourne as a work base, the average stay in Melbourne by international visitors is quite high at 18.1 nights (contributed mainly by education and backpackers). This makes sense of the notion that 'Rented house/apartment/unit/flat' remains the most popular accommodation type for international visitor nights in Melbourne.

Domestic visitors (from interstate and intrastate) made up 44.1% of Melbourne's visitation, while another 58% were on a domestic day trip.

Together, these visitors spent an estimated $7.1 billion in Melbourne, and almost certainly, a good proportion of that spending took place within the boundaries of the City of Port Phillip.

Domestic Overnight Travel

In the year ended September 06 Domestic visitors staying overnight in Melbourne numbered 6.6 million, and contributed 19.6 million nights, an increase on the previous year of 11.9%

The biggest source of interstate overnight travel to Melbourne is still NSW. The main purpose of a visit is 'Visiting friends or relatives', and the average stay in Melbourne by domestic overnight visitors is now 3.0 nights.

The most popular accommodation type remains a 'Friends or relatives property' and when here, eating out at restaurants' continues to be the most popular activity for domestic overnight visitors.

The Local Snapshot

CoPP is a significant beneficiary of visitation to Melbourne. Beyond anecdotal experience, understanding exactly what the share is, difficult to quantify other than to take a simple division of the Melbourne figures for visitation, and then apply those to CoPP.

It could be argued that on any given day or evening, many people dining in our restaurants and cafes, or gathering in our pubs and bars to listen to live music, laugh at a stand up comedian or meet friends are a mixture of local and inner Melbourne people. Added to this, the breadth of budget accommodation options within CoPP, means that additional visitors from elsewhere, including overseas might be numbered in the crowd, or staff behind the bar.

In addition, on weekends our local population swells considerably as leisure time pursuits are taken up within our city boundaries.

Measuring the impact of this visitation and the indirect economic impacts of tourism are difficult. Visitors do not recognise lines on a map, and in any given day, a single visitor from interstate, staying 2 nights and spending $500 may spend part of their time and money in several LGA's. Presently, best estimates suggest that most people staying more than one night in Melbourne will likely visit the City of Port Phillip as part of their itinerary.

Accounting Systems for Tourism in an International Context

Within the globalized economic and business environment, the assessment of accounting systems has become a crucial process for researchers. Accounting throughout history industry has undergone a drastic change. As a branch of economics, accounting provides information about a firm and its transactions to facilitate resource allocation decisions by users of that information. Via an extended literature review, researchers have attempted to approach theoretically accounting's catalytic contribution to the tourism business environment. However, a review of the hospitality literature revealed a paucity of academic research to assess the connection between accounting for tourism and its applications within the last five years. In this context the purpose of this paper is to provide the importance of accounting systems for tourism enterprises in an international context.

The next section presents the literature review. In this section, we analyse the concepts of "accounting", "tourism business" and "accounting systems for tourism". Then the research is specified in the applications of accounting systems in international hotel business. The results indicate that accounting is a catalytic element which offers additional value to the modern hotel business. Finally, the concluding remarks are discussed and some possible future research directions are highlighted.

Literature Review

General: This section presents the results of a literature review in order to illustrate the relevant theoretical models of accounting systems for tourism in an international context.

Conceptual Framework of "Accounting"

Accounting interest and approaches have expanded in recent years. Accounting history is worth studying since it puts contemporary accounting into perspective and may easily give us an account of all the information collected in the past which could provide solutions to the problems of the present. It is worth teaching as part of the overall cultural formation of future accountants, in particular to stress that "presently acceptable practices of accounting have not been immutable over the decades and centuries of environmental change".

Accounting historians have long been conscious that a full understanding of accounting's past needs to embrace international dimensions. The key role of accounting is to provide information for economic decision making (SAC 2, 1990) in support of the current political paradigm of economic growth and development.

Solomons (1991) describes accounting as being like a telephone – a neutral medium that promotes the exchange of information between the enterprise and the user; and while it is not an actor in the exchange, it is important that accounting measures be representationally faithful.

Miller and Napier (1993) argue that like any social phenomenon, accounting presents a "historically and geographically localised result", but that does not imply that accounting should be viewed in isolation at a particular point of space or time. Just as international accounting aims to situate local accounting practices of today within a comparative framework across space, so country-based histories of accounting attempt the same process across time.

In their prospectus for accounting history into the twenty-first century, Carnegie and Napier (1996) proposed the notion of "comparative international accounting history" (CIAH). This research field is not entirely unexplored. However, its expansion can assist in generating "a focus on examining and explaining cross-national differences in accounting development".

Accounting history literature witnessed a vast growth during the recent years. This growth has manifested itself not just in the number of publications but in the topics examined, research approaches adopted, and range of theoretical perspectives applied to the study of accounting through its history. Accounting concepts, techniques and institutions have been diffused through both space and time. Based on an admittedly limited population of English language papers appearing from 1996 to 1999 in the specialist accounting history journals, Carnegie and Potter (2000) concluded that their analysis indicates "the existence of a relatively insular international accounting history research community dominated by a small number of institutions and authors".

Carnegie and Potter contended that accounting history authors seldom engage in cross-border collaborative research and display a limited tendency to venture beyond core themes and the modern period. A subsequent study of the sex distribution of authors in the same journals revealed, unsurprisingly, that authorship and editorial board membership in accounting history is male-dominated. Furthermore, Edwards (2004) broader review of the accounting history literature identified concerns about areas of fading interest, publication media and the dissemination of research findings.

Fleischman and Radcliffe's (2005) celebration of the advance of accounting history during "the roaring nineties" is challenged by fears of its quiet demise in the United States. It takes accounting to be a translucent medium which presents factual data to the world about an enterprise's financial transactions and economic events. A good accounting is deemed to be one that represents the entity in a way that users recognize as commonsensical.

Theoretical Background of "Tourism Industry"

Tourism industry is of great importance for the world economy today. It is one of the largest single employers and in many countries it is the largest services exporting sector, making an outstanding contribution to the balance of payments.

Tourism industry has many of the characteristics of a competitive market:

* there are few barriers to enter;
* it is a truly global market with few unnatural barriers to trade;
* there is a large number of firms and
* prices are set on the basis of market expectations.

A lot of researchers have tried to define the concept of tourism. According to Monique Dacharry (1964), tourism owes to be delimited in its historical prospect. Years later, Kaspar (1976) defines tourism as the total of relations and events that arise from the travel and the eve of individuals, when the place of stay is neither the initial and permanent residence nor the usual place of work. In this context tourism, according to United Nations (1994) and Frechtling (1999) is the activities associated with travel away from a person's usual environment and most countries of the world are interested in the impact of tourism on their economies. Nowadays, tourism organizations are becoming truly international and the issues they face equally universal. In "the age of service competition" that is depicted by international hospitality and tourism, the customer reigns supreme.

Such is the power of customers that the term "service management" is increasingly used to emphasise management imperatives in this age of service competition and market forces. Therefore, to sustain competitiveness hospitality and tourism providers must continue to meet if not exceed customer expectations that are themselves dynamic. A properly planned, developed and controlled tourism industry will positively affect the society and the economy. Enrichment of the tourism industry with national characteristics is vital for a healthy development of tourism. Tourism has outperformed most other sectors and contributed significantly to the economic and employment growth. Generally speaking travel and tourism encompassing transport, accommodation, catering, recreation and developing economies worldwide.

Accounting Systems for Tourism

Consideration will also be made of the literature that reviews the impact of accounting systems for tourism, directly. It should be noted that there is little objective research on this specific impact. At first, Harris and Brown (1998) presented an overview of development in accounting management with particular emphasis on the contribution of applied work for the tourism industry. One year later, Graham and Harris (1999) presented a paper that illustrated the development and implementation management accounting techniques in the Europe, Middle East and Africa division of an international hotel chain.

In this context Mia and Patiarb (2001) stressed the use of management accounting system in hotels. More recently, Mongiello and Harris (2006) described the design of managerial accounting systems in multinational hotel companies. Moreover, Anderson and Guilding (2006) emphasized the potential of competitor-focused practice to hotel business. Finally Burgess (2007) emphasized the major importance of outsourcing accounting functions, particularly in the hotel sector.

Applications of Accounting Systems in International Hotel Business

There are many proponents who now define the industry as competing on global terms. Tse and West (1992) provide persuasive reasoning when they indicate that a firm competes on global terms when its competitive position in one country is significantly influenced by its position in other countries.

Internationalization has become a key research theme in the study of the hospitality industry and its constituents. Like its domestic counterpart, the international hotel industry competes via the placement of its units in significant and appropriate locations.

Recall that accounting entails several broad processes:

* *Measurement* is the process of identifying and quantifying economic activities. These measurements provide insights into the profitability of a firm's operations and the strength of its financial position.
* *Disclosure* is the process by which accounting measurements communicated to their intended users.
* *Auditing* is the process by which specialized accounting professionals attest to the reliability of the measurement and communication process.

The accounting procedure is considered to be the security belt of the business for avoiding either the involuntary or the intentional release of information as well as the avoidance of loss of income from misuse or from any errors in operation.

In this context, accounting plays a vital role in the verification of incomings and expenditure per field of operation in the hotel business. By the term 'fields of operation' of a hotel we mean those sections of the hotel in which the production procedure of the tourist goods and services occur with the purpose of achieving profit. The main fields of utilization within a modern hotel unit are:

* the bedrooms.
* the bar.
* the buffet.
* the restaurant.

A lot of researchers argue that all these fields of operation are the most essential centres of earnings and cost and accounting plays a vital role in them.

Furthermore, accounting includes those actions related to the funding of the hotel unit, that is, with the capital which is necessary for its smooth running. The risk of losing capitals and also credit risk appear to be the determining factors from its viability.

Within the framework of limiting the risk of correct constitution of financial affairs, the following actions are in effect:

* Controls of the procedures, whereby a check is held to ensure whether the investments are always in accordance with the approved investment policy.
* Controls of the evaluations, whereby the cost of the investments with the running values is mainly compared as well as a check of the "deposits" and the "loans".
* Controls of the availabilities, the bank deposits and loans, during which their frequent update and the confirmation of other ones is necessary.

Furthermore, accounting systems contribute to the provision of information for performance measurement. From the above mentioned, it is clear that accounting enables the hotel management to examine whether the right strategy of financial management is followed. Furthermore an appropriate accounting system is able to satisfy hotel managers' information needs aiming to support management decision-making. Simultaneously, accounting is essential in the correct valuation of mergers and acquisitions. Unfortunately, hotel companies do not fully utilize accounting information to assess the value of merger and acquisition, which is increasing to improve international competitiveness. This neglect of accounting information in merger and acquisitions leads to inappropriate evaluation of its value in markets.

The last few decades have been characterized by unparalleled change. Researchers have not paid much attention to accounting systems in tourism, despite its importance for the world economy. However, events may persuade many developing countries to reconsider their industralization policy: in this new world, tourism can provide a very important alternative for economic development and growth. The concept of tourism business was brought to the surface at the dawn of the 20th century. Simultaneously, accounting is established as an essential mean for the exact management of any business economic resources.

A possible limitation of the results is the short time interval covered. Furthermore with few exceptions such as Kreul (1993) and Burgess (1996) little work has been undertaken in an international context. There is also need for articles to which connect quality and environment with accounting systems for tourism.

Thus a suggestion for future research would be to examine the possible applications of accounting systems in tourism for a longer period. Another promising research initiative would be to further explore how an accounting system might be best operationalised to a tourism industry.

From the above it is clear that accounting adds up value, offering at the same time a systematic scientific approach on the improvement of the effectiveness of the tourism business. As the saying goes, "the future is bright, but the road ahead is tortuous". Realization of the major significance of accounting in tourism will set accounting as a priceless support in the hotel business management effort.

Geneva Seminar on International Sustainable Development Policy and Tourism

A Seminar on International Sustainable Development Policy and Tourism was held on Monday 25 November 2002, at the Palais des Nations in Geneva. It brought together much of the findings of UNRISD research in the area of tourism conducted in the late 1990s and early 2000s. The Seminar was organized by Institute jointly with the Geneva-based organization Europe-China Management Improvement Foundation (ECMI), presided by Professor Paolo Urio, former Dean of the Faculty of Economic and Social Sciences of the University of Geneva.

The 30 participants represented mostly the West-Central Qingshai province of China, with one representative from Hainan. They included senior representatives of the local government, heads of city and provincial tourism bureaus, university professors and academics, environmental specialists and lawyers as well as professional trainers.

The panel consisted of Krishna Ghimire, UNRISD Research Coordinator, who made a presentation on "Sustainable Development and Tourism: What Is New?"; Nicolas Bovay, UNRISD Information Officer, who presented a paper titled "Tourism, Ethics and Human Rights"; Behzod Mingboev, UNRISD Research Assistant, who spoke about "The Development of Tourism in Countries in Transition: The Case of the ex-Soviet-Union", and Li Zhaodong, correspondent in Geneva for the *Guangming Daily*, one of China's largest daily newspapers.

Krishna Ghimire, who moderated the seminar, made a presentation highlighting the linkages between sustainable development and tourism planning. He first presented a comparative analysis of tourism issues in Europe and developing countries which indicated many similarities in the evolution of lifestyles and rapid expansion in movements of people.

However, he said that many negative impacts of tourism were especially felt in the developing world. He then went on to discuss the context in which the 2002 World Summit on Sustainable Development in Johannesburg was organized and where, for the first time ever, tourism issues were included on the agenda in a major UN summit. Regrettably, however, the Summit merely called for increased investments in the tourism sector. In conclusion, Mr. Ghimire said that investment in small-scale community tourism projects should receive priority if tourism were to be used as a tool for poverty eradication. Tourism should be developed in an integrated manner with other sectors of livelihood provisioning so that local communities are not made helplessly dependent on tourism. In order to reduce vulnerability related to international tourism, developing countries should also explore the possibility of promoting national and regional tourism. He summed up by stating that the recent World Trade Organization's scheme to liberalize the service sector in tourism was especially unwelcome for developing countries as their tourism earnings are heavily derived from the service sector.

Nicolas Bovay pointed at the fact that tourism had an uneasy relationship with human rights and ecology. He recalled that human categories most at risk were children, indigenous peoples, women and local communities, and said that tourism, and particularly sex tourism, had led to violations of a number of existing international human rights standards and norms, including labour conventions and the concept of decent work.

He said that although present efforts to combat paedophilia in the context of tourism at the international and domestic levels were commendable, much more remained to be done in legal and policy terms. He also said that the development of tourism had led to ongoing violations of economic, social and cultural rights of the local communities in which it was taking place as well as the destruction of the local ecosystem and their peoples' ancestral ways of life. He went on to say that sustainable tourism would only succeed if it involves tourism workers that have a stake in it, and that means that they should be much more democratically involved at work. Workers needed livable salaries and better training in the environment if the industry was to have a beneficial impact on their local communities. He concluded by stating that if tourism wanted to survive as an industry it should not harm the local cultures and landmarks which are exactly what attract tourists in the very first place.

Behzod Mingboev stated that although all the countries of the former USSR were trying to develop their tourism industries, many factors limited their success. He recalled that many of the countries concerned lacked political stability and security and were economically and socially volatile. He also pointed at the fact that local touristic infrastructures, when they existed, were often well below international standards. In the case of Belarus there had even been a sharp decrease in the number of visitors due to the consequences of the 1986 Chernobyl disaster. Other forms of pollution, including the dumping of nuclear and industrial waste had taken a heavy toll on the environment. On a more positive tone, Mr. Mingboev said that the citizens of the newly independent states were now free to travel abroad and that the experiences and ideas that they gained abroad were proving useful to the nascence of a political culture in the post-Soviet geographical space.

Li Zhaodong made a presentation on the development of the tourism industry in Europe and particularly in Switzerland and its historical relevance to developing nations. In his presentation on the new phenomenon of outbound Chinese tourists he said that the new situation presented formidable opportunities for learning from past experiences of developed nations.

The presentations were followed by a lively debate. Professor Paolo Urio made the concluding remarks in which he stressed the importance for China of developing a tourism industry that would be sustainable and would be accessible to the emerging domestic touristic market. He concluded by saying that developing countries should privilege endogenous development and place more value on the development of their own local potentialities to diminish dependency on foreign interests.

Tourism And Environmental Issues

Environmental Implications of the Tourism Industry

Energy Consumption: Preliminary figures from a draft Sustainable Tourism Roundtable Report indicate that the tourism industry uses 72.1 Gwhours of energy per year. This amount is only a very small percentage of total U.S. energy consumption approximately 0.3% in 1997.

Water Consumption

The preliminary figures from the above-mentioned report indicate that the tourism industry in the aggregate uses 93.9 billion gallons of water per year. This amount is 4.0% of total U.S. commercial consumption (including the chemical, pulp and paper, primary metals, and the textiles industries). Tourism-related water use in the lodging industry accounts for approximately 46.2 billion gallons of water per year. In 1995, total freshwater withdrawals in the United States for offstream uses (e.g., withdrawal of surface and ground-water for public supply; domestic use; agriculture, including irrigation and livestock watering; industry, including mining; and thermoelectric power uses) was 340 billion gallons per day. By contrast, tourism related hotel water use accounted for under.04% of the total.

Pollution and Waste Outputs

Water Quality: The tourism industry impacts water quality through construction and maintenance of tourist infrastructure, recreational boating, and certain activities of the cruise industry. Tourist infrastructure increases the pressure on existing sewage treatment plants and can lead to overflows during peak tourist times. A more gradual impact is the leaching of nutrients from septic systems of tourists' waterfront homes, accelerating eutrophication of adjacent water bodies, and depleting dissolved oxygen supplies. The construction of tourist facilities and infrastructure also increases the amount of impervious surfaces, which in turn increases the amount of polluted runoff reaching water bodies.

The most significant problem from the standpoint of human health associated with recreational boating and water quality is the discharge of sewage into water bodies with limited flushing, where the discharge occurs near the location of shellfish beds. Diseases that can be potentially transmitted through human contact with fecal discharge and/or ingestion of contaminated shellfish include typhoid fever, dysentery, infectious hepatitis, and nonspecific gastroenteritis.

Spills and discharges of oil and toxic chemicals are other impacts that recreational boats and the cruise industry can have, although such impacts are not necessarily significant. In 1997, recreational vessels were responsible for 535 reported oil spills, comprising 6.2% of the total spill incidents in U.S. waters. The cruise industry was responsible for an even smaller percentage, at 1.6% of total spills in U.S. waters.

Air Quality

Most tourism-related air pollution comes from automobiles. Automobiles emit by far the most carbon monoxide of all transportation modes. In 1997, they emitted 26 million short tons of carbon monoxide, compared with 1.7 million short tons from recreational marine vehicles, and 1 million from aircraft. Specific information on tour bus emissions was not available, but all heavy-duty diesel vehicles (most tour buses fall into this category) emitted 1.4 million short tons in 1997.

Habitat/Ecosystem Alteration and Fragmentation

Ecosystems and natural habitat can be damaged by tourist infrastructure, tourist activities, recreational boating, and the cruise industry. Recreational boats and cruise vessels can damage aquatic vegetation by cutting it with their propellers or otherwise damaging it when running aground. Wetlands have been destroyed in order to build tourist-related infrastructure, such as airports, roads, and marinas. For example, in Jamaica over 700 acres of wetlands have been destroyed since the 1960s for tourism development.

When snorkelling and hiking, tourists can damage ecosystems by littering, and trampling coral and vegetation. This type of damage is cumulative in nature. One or two tourists may not cause visible harm, but hundreds over time can do substantial damage.

Impacts on Wildlife

Wildlife can be adversely affected by the construction and maintenance of tourist infrastructure, and by tourist activities. Impacts from tourist infrastructure can be direct, such as when development in lower elevations of mountain resorts restricts the migratory range of certain wildlife, or indirect, such as when marine turtles are disoriented by automobile headlights and resort illumination. The two primary ways in which tourist activities disturb wildlife are by altering their eating habits and feeding patterns, and by altering their habitat. Feeding patterns are altered directly by tourists feeding animals, and indirectly by littering, which encourages wildlife to scrounge for food. Wildlife habitat is altered by tourists' trampling and by the use of off-road vehicles (ORVs).

Aesthetic and Cultural Impacts

Tourism can diminish the aesthetic appeal of a destination through the construction of buildings that clash with the surrounding environment, creating "architectural" or "visual" pollution. The high-rise hotels along the coastal zone of Atlantic City and Miami are examples, as are several high-rise hotels in Jerusalem, whose construction arguably damaged the city's architectural beauty.

Impact on Gateway Communities Outside National Parks and Other Host Communities

Tourism affects the natural landscape and character of "gateway communities," which are adjacent to national parks, and other significant tourist destinations. Development related to tourist activity can be detrimental to cultural and aesthetic aspects of these communities if undertaken in an indiscriminate and/or scattered manner. For example, Tusayan, the town near the south rim of the Grand Canyon is "dominated by a gaggle of fast-food restaurants, motels, and trinket shops along the highway, has been likened to a strip mall on the way to the Vatican".

Positive Impacts

Despite its many adverse impacts, tourism can have positive impacts on both natural and artificially constructed environments, as well as on destination communities. In fact, tourism has motivated the preservation of such sensitive ecosystems as the Everglades National Park in Florida. Furthermore, tourism that focuses on cultural and historic sites (sometimes referred to as "heritage" tourism) can be the impetus for the preservation and rehabilitation of existing historic sites, buildings, and monuments. For example, historic lighthouses and piers in Cape Cod, Massachusetts and historic buildings in Williamsburg, Virginia have been transformed and preserved for the purpose of tourism. In addition, the economic benefits of tourism partially balance its negative environmental impacts. For example, gateway communities adjacent to national parks exist primarily because of the economic benefits of tourism. The parks attract more visitors to these communities, resulting in increased employment opportunities and an improved standard of living.

Upstream and Downstream Impacts

In addition to direct environmental impacts, impacts from tourism occur at every point along the supply chain. The "supply chain" with respect to service industries refers to all the actors involved in the provision of a service, including the consumer. The supply chain in the tourism industry consists of those industries that provide accommodations, provide transportation, make arrangements for travellers, and supply equipment. It also includes the tourists themselves. The degree of environmental impact of tourism can be influenced by actors along the supply chain.

For example, a hotel can exert "upstream" influence on its suppliers to provide products that minimize environmental impacts, such as recyclable toiletries. There are several existing initiatives within the private and non-profit sectors to work with the lodging industry to reduce environmental impacts through supplier relations. The extent to which a hotel can leverage its suppliers depends upon several factors, including type of hotel and type of supplies.

Similarly, travel service providers can have "downstream" impacts by influencing tourists through education and provision of options to reduce resource use. For example, hotels can give guests the option not to have their linens washed daily, and cruise lines can limit the number of tourists that go ashore at sensitive destinations. Downstream influence through tourist education is seen most clearly with ecotourism, defined as travel and tourism that attempts to minimize impacts on the environment. Tour operators specializing in ecotourism influence their customers through provision of environmental guidelines before and during trips.

Impact of Technology on Travel Services

The growth of the Internet has begun to influence the interactions among travel agents, suppliers, and consumers. The sophistication of information technology has already begun to allow tourists to bypass traditional methods of making travel arrangements. For example, Southwest Airlines now sells most of its tickets without the use of travel agents, using the Internet instead. The full impact of this technological change has yet to be realized. However, it has the potential to effect significant changes. The interactive nature of the Internet allows for the values of tourists to register directly with providers of tourist services. If there is a strong demand for environmentally sensitive services, it is likely that the demand will be met.

Regulation of Industry Activities

Regulation of the tourism industry reflects its fragmented nature. Different aspects of the industry are regulated by different (primarily federal) agencies, with some overlap. The Environmental Protection Agency (EPA) and the U.S. Coast Guard regulate oil and sewage discharges from recreational marine vessels. The EPA under the Clean Air Act (CAA) amendments now regulates air emissions from selected marine engines. Emissions from land vehicles are regulated under the Clean Air Act.

The EPA also regulates smoke, hydrocarbons, nitrogen oxide, and carbon monoxide from aircraft engines. The Federal Aviation Administration (FAA) in the Department of Transportation (DOT) is responsible for enforcing those emission standards. The FAA is also responsible for regulating noise pollution from aircraft under the 1990 Airport Noise and Capacity Act. The cruise industry is regulated by both international and federal regulations. The primary international regulatory framework for the cruise industry is the International Convention for the Prevention of Pollution from Ships, commonly referred to as MARPOL 73/78. Three relevant annexes regulate the discharge of sewage, oil, and solid wastes.

The U.S. Coast Guard is responsible for enforcing these regulations in the United States. The International Maritime Organization (IMO) has requirements for solid waste generation and incineration on board cruise vessels, NOx emission limits, and guidelines to minimize transfer of non-native species. Regulation of the development of tourist infrastructure occurs at the state or local level, through planning and zoning laws. The efficacy of these regulations varies depending on location.

Policy Implications

As indicated by the regulatory framework highlighted above, the fragmented nature of the tourism industry is not conducive to integrated, holistic regulation that encompasses all aspects of the industry. The dispersed nature of the tourism industry produces diffuse impacts that fall under the jurisdictions of different federal, state, and local agencies. Moreover, enforcement and compliance problems make it particularly difficult to regulate tourist activities. For these reasons educational efforts seem more promising than regulation to minimize many of the environmental impacts of tourism that are not now regulated. Education can be used to support existing regulations, and to encourage environmentally responsible behaviour where no regulations exist.

Educational efforts to promote environmentally responsible tourism should be framed in accordance with the targeted audience. Tourists may be more receptive to educational efforts that focus on the environmental benefits of altering their behaviour than to regulatory prohibitions per se. For example, a sign that prohibits anchoring in a sensitive marine ecosystem could be more effective if accompanied by an explanation of the potential damage a boat can do to the ecosystem.

However, educational efforts geared towards industry sectors seem most effective when cost savings and the marketing benefits of "being green" are emphasized. A study of 13 corporate executives of hotel chains found that the two most important factors that contributed to their decision to implement a solid waste program were waste disposal fees and the betterment of public image. Some hotels have found that their environmental initiatives have resulted in an increase in business. Although environmental awareness has had an important impact on the tourism industry, economic motives are still primary. Therefore, educational programs aimed at tourism service providers should emphasize the potential economic and marketing benefits of environmental stewardship.

Environmental Implications of the Tourism Industry

Environmental management in the United States over the past several decades has focused on regulating production industries, such as manufacturing and mining. However, there has been increasing interest in the environmental effects of the service industry. Generally speaking, a service is as an activity done for others. A perhaps even broader definition of a service is "anything sold in trade that cannot be dropped on your foot". The service industry therefore comprises a variety of activities, from restaurants to hospitals to financial institutions. It accounts for 75% of the U.S. gross domestic product ($3.8 trillion in 1997) (U.S. Census Bureau, 1998) and 80% of U.S. employment.

The service industry merits attention because of its large size and consequently its potential for environmental impacts (both negative and positive). There is a small but growing body of literature discussing the influence of the service sector on environmental quality. Three categories of influence have evolved from these discussions:

1) direct impacts of the service itself,
2) upstream impacts, arising from the service provider's ability to influence its suppliers, and
3) downstream impacts, where the service provider can influence its customers' behavioral or consumption patterns.

It is necessary to look at all three categories to develop a complete picture of the influence of the service sector on environmental quality. The tourism industry is one of the largest components of the service sector, and has considerable ability to influence environmental quality. Travel and tourism contributed $91 billion in revenue into the U.S. economy in 1998, supporting 16.2 million jobs directly and indirectly. Over forty-three million tourists visited the United States in 1998. Furthermore, the tourism industry is projected to be the largest U.S. private employer by 2000, and now represents 10% of the national private gross domestic product.

Tourist destinations tend to be places of the highest amenities, whether the amenities are social, cultural, or natural. These destinations, due in part to their high quality, are often in short supply relative to demand. This scarcity leads to the potential for degradation of tourist areas, as they reach and in some cases exceed their carrying capacity.

The tourism industry is complex; being fragmented into several industries that, taken together, constitute what is commonly referred to as the travel and tourism industry. It comprises components of other industries that do not cater exclusively to tourists; therefore a discussion of the environmental impacts of tourism needs to consider what percentage of use is related to tourism in each industry.

Sectors of the tourism industry include transportation (e.g., airlines, buses, automobiles), lodging, restaurants, the cruise industry, amusement parks and resorts, and general retail and merchandise stores. Included in the definition of the tourism industry is the associated development (e.g., tourist infrastructure) of tourist destinations, and tourist activities. We have identified impacts from tourist-related transportation, tourist-related development, tourist activities including some recreational activities such as boating, and direct impacts of the lodging and cruise industries.

Quantitative data help to illustrate impacts where available; otherwise qualitative data supported by relevant examples are used. Although this discussion focuses on environmental impacts in the United States, some international examples are drawn upon when applicable. After presenting these impacts, we analyse the influence that providers of tourism services can have on their suppliers as well as the tourist. While there are many more industries that provide services to tourists, this discussion focuses on the upstream and downstream leveraging potential of four service providers: the lodging industry, the cruise industry, travel agents, and tour operators.

Section 1 presents both beneficial and adverse environmental impacts of tourism, including tourist activities, development, transportation, and direct impacts of the lodging and cruise industries.

Section 2 explores the relationships among travel agents, tour operators, and service providers, and tourists. The structure of selected components of the tourism industry is presented, and opportunities for upstream leverage on suppliers and downstream leverage on tourists are discussed. Finally, this section briefly analyses the impact of technology on travel services. Section 3 discusses steps within the tourism industry as well as government to lessen the adverse environmental impacts of tourism. This section concludes with a brief presentation of the benefits of educational efforts to minimize impacts.

Environmental Impacts of Tourism

Definition of Tourism: Tourism is "the temporary movement of people to destinations outside their normal places of work and residence, the activities undertaken during their stay in those destinations, and the facilities created to cater to their needs". It is often difficult to distinguish between tourism and recreation, as they are interrelated. Tourism involves travelling a distance from home, while recreation is defined as the activities undertaken during leisure time. Outdoor recreation is even more closely related to tourism.

The extent of the overlap depends in part on the length of time of the activity and its location. For example, a boater who uses his or her boat for one day and who stays near his or her home may be considered a recreational boater; while a boater who travels on his or her boat overnight to a destination may be considered a tourist. Therefore while this discussion paper focuses primarily on tourism, selected recreational activities and their impacts are considered as well. The degree of environmental impact varies, depending on the type of tourist and the intensity of site use. There are day tourists, who visit a destination for a day and then leave; summer residents who are in effect tourists for a season; and tourists on bus tours and other trips that may visit a location for a few minutes or a number of days. Day tourists have an impact on the environment through their transportation to their destination as well as their activities once there. This is true for summer residents, but these tourists also have a cumulative impact, as they are in one place for a longer period of time. For example, nutrients leaching from the septic systems of tourists' waterfront homes can accelerate eutrophication and contribute to depletion of dissolved oxygen supply of the adjacent water body.

On the other hand, summer residents often are an important force in preserving the natural beauty of an area (e.g., the Adirondacks). Tourists who visit an area for longer than a day and choose to stay in hotels contribute to the impacts that the lodging industry has on the environment. In addition to the length of stay, tourist impacts depend on the type of activity undertaken. Passive activities such as birdwatching have different impacts than more active pursuits, such as snowmobiling or boating. There are environmental impacts from the travel to a destination, the tourist activities in and of themselves at that destination, such as hiking or boating, and from the creation, operation, and maintenance of facilities that cater to the tourist, such as hotels. This discussion addresses impacts from tourism-related transportation, development, the lodging and cruise industries, and tourist activities including selected forms of recreation.

Transportation

Airlines: In 1995, twenty percent of U.S. commercial air travel was attributed to leisure, including rest and relaxation, sightseeing, and outdoor recreation. The total and tourism-related contribution of air pollutants from the air transportation industry. Aircraft emit the most carbon monoxide of any of the five listed air pollutants, but it is a small amount relative to other modes of transportation. In total, aircraft are responsible for approximately one percent of the total ground-level emissions from mobile sources; therefore tourism-related air travel is responsible for only.2% of total ground-level emissions. Furthermore, tourism-related air travel contributes less than 1% of total U.S. emissions of each of the listed criteria pollutants.

Although aircraft contribute only a small amount to total air pollution, emissions from this source is increasing. Between 1970 and 1995, hydrocarbon and NOx emissions from aircraft sources have grown 53%. Projections to 2010 indicate that aircraft emissions will continue to increase. Aircraft emissions in nonattainment areas with large airport facilities in particular are projected to represent a growing percentage of regional sources of air pollutants.

The projections indicate an increase in the aircraft component of total regional emissions between 1990 and 2010 in ten metropolitan regions (nine of which are currently not in attainment of the National Ambient Air Quality Standards (NAAQS) for ozone; the tenth city has attained the ozone standard, but is considered an ozone "maintenance" area).

The 2010 percentages are still relatively low, ranging from 0.2% volatile organic compounds (VOC) in Philadelphia to 5.1% VOC in Charlotte; and 1.8% NOx in Philadelphia to 7.6% in Charlotte. The percentages are higher in Charlotte in part because other sources contribute less. The EPA has had regulations for smoke and hydrocarbon emissions from aircraft engines in place since 1984. In 1997, the agency promulgated new emission standards for nitrogen oxides and carbon monoxide. This rule was adopted to codify the existing voluntary emission standards of the United Nations International Civil Aviation Organization (ICAO). The DOT's Federal Aviation Administration (FAA) is responsible for enforcing these aircraft emissions standards.

With increased awareness of the fragile nature of our planet and its beauty, it is not surprising that there has also been an increased demand for travel to unique and remarkable environments around the world, known as environmental tourism. Environmental tourism is the phenomenon of increasing travel to places of environmental interest. It is travel that focuses on the ecological surroundings of the destination, which is generally a place overflowing with natural beauty and wonder.

Environmental tourism can include travel to unique and endangered areas, such as the Galapagos Islands. In addition to visiting places for its uniqueness, many people engage in environmental tourism as a "voluntourism" mission – this is a form of tourism in which people travel to a destination for a short period of time to volunteer in some capacity. In the case of environmental tourism, volutourism means travelling to an ecologically fragile part of the world to offer assistance in repairing it – such as cleaning an oil spill. The concept of environmental tourism is that people will become more engaged with the ecological and sociocultural concerns of the world through firsthand experience, and thus be more active in conservation and making change. The idea evolved in the late 1980s along with growing consumer awareness of issues surrounding conservation and consumption. Not only is environmental tourism an adventure into the wilderness aimed at helping save the planet, but it also expands the profitable travel industry to developing countries where jobs are scarce and economies are struggling. Although the objectives of environmental tourism are well meaning, there are consequences that arise from the practice.

When people travel to places that have historically been disparately inhabited, the presence of increased and new populations inevitably impacts the environment and the culture of the location. The first impact on the environment comes from getting to the destination. Travel to remote locations where wildlife thrives can be costly to the environment using more fuel than that of an ordinary vacation, at times. Lodging and living are further strains the local environment.

Constructing new lodging often means destroying a natural ecosystem and bringing a Western lifestyle to a developing country often means improper disposal of the increased amounts of waste. In a sociocultural sense, environmental tourism can present a problem with the displacement of people and their resources as well as impede and endanger their daily customs by introducing new difficulties and cultures.

Tourism's Three Main Impact Areas

Negative impacts from tourism occur when the level of visitor use is greater than the environment's ability to cope with this use within the acceptable limits of change. Uncontrolled conventional tourism poses potential threats to many natural areas around the world. It can put enormous pressure on an area and lead to impacts such as soil erosion, increased pollution, discharges into the sea, natural habitat loss, increased pressure on endangered species and heightened vulnerability to forest fires. It often puts a strain on water resources, and it can force local populations to compete for the use of critical resources.

Depletion of Natural Resources

Tourism development can put pressure on natural resources when it increases consumption in areas where resources are already scarce.

Water resources: Water, and especially fresh water, is one of the most critical natural resources. The tourism industry generally overuses water resources for hotels, swimming pools, golf courses and personal use of water by tourists. This can result in water shortages and degradation of water supplies, as well as generating a greater volume of waste water..

In dryer regions like the Mediterranean, the issue of water scarcity is of particular concern. Because of the hot climate and the tendency of tourists to consume more water when on holiday than they do at home, the amount used can run up to 440 litres a day. This is almost double what the inhabitants of an average Spanish city use.

Golf course maintenance can also deplete fresh water resources. In recent years golf tourism has increased in popularity and the number of golf courses has grown rapidly. Golf courses require an enormous amount of water every day and, as with other causes of excessive extraction of water, this can result in water scarcity. If the water comes from wells, over pumping can cause saline intrusion into ground-water. Golf resorts are more and more often situated in or near protected areas or areas where resources are limited, exacerbating their impacts.

Local resources: Tourism can create great pressure on local resources like energy, food, and other raw materials that may already be in short supply. Greater extraction and transport of these resources exacerbates the physical impacts associated with their exploitation. Because of the seasonal character of the industry, many destinations have ten times more inhabitants in the high season as in the low season. A high demand is placed upon these resources to meet the high expectations tourists often have (proper heating, hot water, etc.).

Land degradation: Important land resources include minerals, fossil fuels, fertile soil, forests, wetland and wildlife. Increased construction of tourism and recreational facilities has increased the pressure on these resources and on scenic landscapes. Direct impact on natural resources, both renewable and nonrenewable, in the provision of tourist facilities can be caused by the use of land for accommodation and other infrastructure provision, and the use of building materials. Forests often suffer negative impacts of tourism in the form of deforestation caused by fuel wood collection and land clearing. For example, one trekking tourist in Nepal-and area already suffering the effects of deforestation-can use four to five kilograms of wood a day.

Pollution

Tourism can cause the same forms of pollution as any other industry: air emissions, noise, solid waste and littering, releases of sewage, oil and chemicals, even architectural/visual pollution.

Air pollution and noise: Transport by air, road, and rail is continuously increasing in response to the rising number reported that the number of international air passengers worldwide rose from 88 million in 1972 to 344 million in 1994. One consequence of this increase in air transport is that tourism now accounts for more than 60% of air travel and is therefore responsible for an important share of air emissions. One study estimated that a single transatlantic return flight emits almost half the CO2 emissions produced by all other sources consumed by an average person yearly. (Mayer Hillman, Town & Country Planning magazine, September 1996. Source: MFOE).

Transport emissions and emissions from energy production and use are linked to acid rain, global warming and photochemical pollution. Air pollution from tourist transportation has impacts on the global level, especially from carbon dioxide (CO2) emissions related to transportation energy use. And it can contribute to severe local air pollution. Some of these impacts are quite specific to tourist activities. For example, especially in very hot or cold countries, tour buses often leave their motors running for hours while the tourists go out for an excursion because they want to return to a comfortably air-conditioned bus.

Noise pollution from airplanes, cars, and buses, as well as recreational vehicles such as snowmobiles and jet skis, is an ever-growing problem of modern life. In addition to causing annoyance, stress, and even hearing loss for it humans, it causes distress to wildlife, especially in sensitive areas. For instance, noise generated by snowmobiles can cause animals to alter their natural activity patterns.

Solid waste and littering: In areas with high concentrations of tourist activities and appealing natural attractions, waste disposal is a serious problem and improper disposal can be a major despoiler of the natural environment-rivers, scenic areas, and roadsides. For example, cruise ships in the Caribbean are estimated to produce more than 70,000 tons of waste each year. Today some cruise lines are actively working to reduce waste-related impacts. Solid waste and littering can degrade the physical appearance of the water and shoreline and cause the death of marine animals.

In mountain areas, trekking tourists generate a great deal of waste. Tourists on expedition leave behind their garbage, oxygen cylinders and even camping equipment. Such practices degrade the environment with all the detritus typical of the developed world, in remote areas that have few garbage collection or disposal facilities. Some trails in the Peruvian Andes and in Nepal frequently visited by tourists have been nicknamed "Coca-Cola trail" and "Toilet paper trail".

Sewage: Construction of hotels, recreation and other facilities often leads to increased sewage pollution. Wastewater has polluted seas and lakes surrounding tourist attractions, damaging the flora and fauna. Sewage runoff causes serious damage to coral reefs because it stimulates the growth of algae, which cover the filter-feeding corals, hindering their ability to survive. Changes in salinity and salutation can have wide-ranging impacts on coastal environments. And sewage pollution can threaten the health of humans and animals.

Aesthetic Pollution: Often tourism fails to integrate its structures with the natural features and indigenous architectural of the destination. Large, dominating resorts of disparate design can look out of place in any natural environment and may clash with the indigenous structural design.

A lack of land-use planning and building regulations in many destinations has facilitated sprawling developments along coastlines, valleys and scenic routes. The sprawl includes tourism facilities themselves and supporting infrastructure such as roads, employee housing, parking, service areas, and waste disposal.

Physical Impacts

Attractive landscape sites, such as sandy beaches, lakes, riversides, and mountain tops and slopes, are often transitional zones, characterized by species-rich ecosystems. Typical physical impacts include the degradation of such ecosystems.

An ecosystem is a geographic area including all the living organisms (people, plants, animals, and microorganisms), their physical surroundings (such as soil, water, and air), and the natural cycles that sustain them. The ecosystems most threatened with degradation are ecologically fragile areas such as alpine regions, rain forests, wetlands, mangroves, coral reefs and sea grass beds. The threats to and pressures on these ecosystems are often severe because such places are very attractive to both tourists and developers. Physical impacts are caused not only by tourism-related land clearing and construction, but by continuing tourist activities and long-term changes in local economies and ecologies.

Physical Impacts of Tourism Development

- Construction activities and infrastructure development: The development of tourism facilities such as accommodation, water supplies, restaurants and recreation facilities can involve sand mining, beach and sand dune erosion, soil erosion and extensive paving. In addition, road and airport construction can lead to land degradation and loss of wildlife habitats and deterioration of scenery.

  In Yosemite National Park (US), for instance, the number of roads and facilities have been increased to keep pace with the growing visitor numbers and to supply amenities, infrastructure and parking lots for all these tourists. These actions have caused habitat loss in the park and are accompanied by various forms of pollution including air pollution from automobile emissions; the Sierra Club has reported "smog so thick that Yosemite Valley could not be seen from airplanes". This occasional smog is harmful to all species and vegetation inside the Park.
- Deforestation and intensified or unsustainable use of land: Construction of ski resort accommodation and facilities frequently requires clearing forested land. Coastal wetlands are often drained and filled due to lack of more

suitable sites for construction of tourism facilities and infrastructure. These activities can cause severe disturbance and erosion of the local ecosystem, even destruction in the long term.

- Marina development of marinas and breakwaters can cause changes in currents and coastlines. Furthermore, extraction of building materials such as sand affects coral reefs, mangroves, and hinterland forests, leading to erosion and destruction of habitats. In the Philippines and the Maldives, dynamiting and mining of coral for resort building materials has damaged fragile coral reefs and depleted the fisheries that sustain local people and attract tourists.

Overbuilding and extensive paving of shorelines can result in destruction of habitats and disruption of land-sea connections (such as sea-turtle nesting spots). Coral reefs are especially fragile marine ecosystems and are suffering worldwide from reef-based tourism developments.

Evidence suggests a variety of impacts to coral result from shoreline development, increased sediments in the water, trampling by tourists and divers, ship groundings, pollution from sewage, overfishing, and fishing with poisons and explosives that destroy coral habitat.

Physical Impacts from Tourist Activities

- Trampling Tourists using the same trail over and over again trample the vegetation and soil, eventually causing damage that can lead to loss of biodiversity and other impacts. Such damage can be even more extensive when visitors frequently stray off established trails.

Trampling impacts on vegetation	Trampling impacts on soil
Breakage and bruising of stems	Loss of organic matter
Reduced plant vigour	Reduction in soil macro porosity
Reduced regeneration	Decrease in air and water permeability
Loss of ground cover	Increase in run off
Change in species composition	Accelerated erosion

Source: University of Idaho

- Anchoring and other marine activities In marine areas (around coastal waters, reefs, beach and shoreline, offshore waters, uplands and lagoons) many tourist activities occur in or around fragile ecosystems. Anchoring, snorkelling, sport fishing and scuba diving, yachting, and cruising are some of the activities that can cause direct degradation of marine ecosystems such as coral reefs, and subsequent impacts on coastal protection and fisheries.
- Alteration of ecosystems by tourist activities Habitat can be degraded by tourism leisure activities. For example, wildlife viewing can bring about stress for the animals and alter their natural behaviour when tourists come too close. Safaris and wildlife watching activities have a degrading effect on habitat as they often are accompanied by the noise and commotion created by tourists as they chase wild animals in their trucks and aircraft. This puts high pressure on animal habits and behaviours and tends to bring about behavioural changes. In some cases, as in Kenya, it has led to animals becoming so disturbed that at times they neglect their young or fail to mate.

Loss of Biological Diversity

The effects of loss of biodiversity:

- It threatens our food supplies, opportunities for recreation and tourism, and sources of wood, medicines and energy.
- It interferes with essential ecological functions such as species balance, soil formation, and greenhouse gas absorption.
- It reduces the productivity of ecosystems, thereby shrinking nature's basket of goods and services, from which we constantly draw.
- It destabilizes ecosystems and weakens their ability to deal with natural disasters such as floods, droughts, and hurricanes, and with human-caused stresses, such as pollution and climate change.

Tourism, especially nature tourism, is closely linked to biodiversity and the attractions created by a rich and varied environment. It can also cause loss of biodiversity when land and resources are strained by excessive use, and when impacts on vegetation, wildlife, mountain, marine and coastal environments and water resources exceed the carrying capacity. This loss of biodiversity in fact means loss of tourism potential.

Introduction of exotic species: Tourists and suppliers-often unwittingly-can bring in species (insects, wild and cultivated plants and diseases) that are not native to the local environment and that can cause enormous disruption and even destruction of ecosystems.

Depletion of The Ozone Layer

The ozone layer, which is situated in the upper atmosphere (or stratosphere) at an altitude of 12-50 kilometres, protects life on earth by absorbing the harmful wavelengths of the sun's ultraviolet (UV) radiation, which in high doses is dangerous to humans and animals. For instance, one of the reasons scientists have put forward for the global decrease of amphibian populations is increased exposure to UV radiation.

Ozone depleting substances (ODSs) such as CFCs (chlorofluorocarbon) and halons have contributed to the destruction of this layer. The tourism industry may be part of the problem; direct impacts start with the construction of new developments and continue during daily management and operations. Refrigerators, air conditioners and propellants in aerosol spray cans, amongst others, contain ODSs and are widely used in the hotel and tourism industry. Emissions from jet aircraft are also a significant source of ODSs. According to Tourism Concern, scientists predict that by 2015 half of the annual destruction of the ozone layer will be caused by air travel.

UNEP's OzonAction Programme works with governments and industries, including the tourism industry, to phase out ODSs and find safer alternatives. UNEP has developed extensive information and guidance on how many types of businesses can eliminate ODSs and contribute to preservation of the ozone layer. For further reading see the publication How the Hotel and Tourism Industry can Protect the Ozone Layer.

Climate Change

Climate scientists now generally agree that the Earth's surface temperatures have risen steadily in recent years because of an increase in the so-called greenhouse gases in the atmosphere, which trap heat from the sun. One of the most significant of these gases is carbon dioxide (CO_2), which is generated when fossil fuels, such as coal, oil and natural gas are burned and when there are changes in land use, such as deforestation. In the long run, the accumulation of CO_2 and other greenhouse gases in the atmosphere can cause global climate change-a process that may already be occurring.

Global tourism is closely linked to climate change. Tourism involves the movement of people from their homes to other destinations and accounts for about 50% of traffic movements; rapidly expanding air traffic contributes about 2.5% of the production of CO2. Tourism is thus a significant contributor to the increasing concentrations of greenhouse gases in the atmosphere. Air travel itself is a major contributor to the greenhouse effect. Passenger jets are the fastest growing source of greenhouse gas emissions. The number of international travellers is expected to increase from 594 million in 1996 to 1.6 billion by 2020, adding greatly to the problem unless steps are taken to reduce emissions.

For more information on the relationship between energy and the environment, see UNEP's Energy Programme, which provides information and publications on energy efficiency and alternative energy sources to reduce the environmental impacts of energy use and of transportation.

How Global Environmental Impacts Affect Tourism

Natural disasters: Catastrophes like floods, earthquakes, wildfires, volcanoes, avalanches, drought and diseases can have a serious effect on inbound and domestic tourism and thus on local tourism industries. The outbreak of the foot and mouth disease epidemic in England earlier this year (2001), for instance, has severely affected Great Britain's inbound tourism market. A BHA/Barclays Hospitality Business Trends Survey found that 75% of hotels in England, 81% in Scotland and 85% in Wales continued to be affected by the foot and mouth outbreak, and over 60% forecast a decline in business in the June-September 2001 period.

Climate change: Tourism not only contributes to climate change, but is affected by it as well. Climate change is likely to increase the severity and frequency of storms and severe weather events, which can have disastrous effects on tourism in the affected regions. Some of the other impacts that the world risks as a result of global warming are drought, diseases and heat waves.

These negative impacts can keep tourists away from the holiday destinations. Global warming may cause:

- Less snowfall at ski resorts, meaning a shorter skiing seasons in the Alpine region. In already hot areas like Asia and the Mediterranean, tourists will stay away because of immense heat, and out of fear of diseases and water shortages.
- Harm to vulnerable ecosystems such as rainforests and coral reefs because of rising temperatures and less rainfall. A major risk to coral reefs is bleaching, which occurs when coral is stressed by temperature increases, high or low levels of salinity, lower water quality, and an increase in suspended sediments. These conditions cause the zooxanthallae (the single-celled algae which forms the colours within the coral) to leave the coral. Without the algae, the coral appears white, or "bleached"-and rapidly dies. The Great Barrier Reef, which supports a US$ 640 million tourism industry, has been experiencing coral bleaching events for the last 20 years.
- Rising sea levels, the result of melting glaciers and polar ice. Higher sea levels will threaten coastal and marine areas with widespread floods in low-lying countries and island states, increasing the loss of coastal land. Beaches and islands that are major tourism attractions may be the first areas to be affected.
- Increased events of extreme weather, such as tornadoes, hurricanes and typhoons. These are already becoming more prevalent in tourist areas in the Caribbean and South East Asia. Hurricane Mitch in 1998, for instance, heavily affected tourism in the Caribbean. Wind damage, storm waves, heavy rains and flooding caused major losses in the local tourism sector.

Effects of Other Industries on Tourism

Impacts from other industries often have a more dramatic effect on the environment and can seriously affect tourism.

- Oil spills, like the oil tanker disaster that occurred off the Galapagos Islands (Ecuador) in January 2001, can cause severe short-term damage to tourist attractions. In that case, a freight ship loaded with 160,000 gallons of diesel fuel and 80,000 gallons of other petroleum products ran aground on the coast of San Cristóbal and spilled nearly all of its load. Unique local marine and land species and the tourism potential of the area were badly affected.
- Agricultural runoff or industrial discharges can cause water pollution and may cause algae blooms like those that occurred in the Adriatic Sea in the early 1990s. In spite of improved control of sewage from tourism developments, the Mediterranean sea floor is increasingly carpeted with these quick-growing invaders, many rising 30 inches or more above anchoring runners. They appear equally adept at colonizing rock, mud, and sand in a virtually continuous swath that can extend from the beach out to a depth of about 150 feet, smothering coral reefs, fish and other sea flora and fauna in the process.
- Destructive practices such as blast fishing, with poisonous chemicals like cyanide, and muro-ami netting (pounding reefs with weighted bags to scare fish out of crevices) directly destroy corals. They can also destroy a major draw for tourists.

How Tourism Can Contribute to Environmental Conservation

Financial contributions:

- Direct financial contributions: Tourism can contribute directly to the conservation of sensitive areas and habitat. Revenue from park-entrance fees and similar sources can be allocated specifically to pay for the protection and management of environmentally sensitive areas. Special fees for park operations or conservation activities can be collected from tourists or tour operators.
- Contributions to government revenues: Some governments collect money in more far-reaching and indirect ways that are not linked to specific parks or conservation areas. User fees, income taxes, on sales or rental of recreation equipment, and license fees for activities such as hunting

and fishing can provide governments with the funds needed to manage natural resources. Such funds can be used for overall conservation programs and activities, such as park ranger salaries and park maintenance.

For Costa Rica, for example, tourism represents 72% of national monetary reserves, generates 140,000 jobs and produces 8.4% of the gross domestic product. The country has 25% of its territory classified under some category of conservation management. In 1999, protected areas welcomed 866,083 national and foreign tourists, who generated about US$ 2.5 million in admission fees and payment of services.

Improved Environmental Management and Planning

Sound environmental management of tourism facilities and especially hotels can increase the benefits to natural areas. But this requires careful planning for controlled development, based on analysis of the environmental resources of the area. Planning helps to make choices between conflicting uses, or to find ways to make them compatible. By planning early for tourism development, damaging and expensive mistakes can be prevented, avoiding the gradual deterioration of environmental assets significant to tourism.

Cleaner production techniques can be important tools for planning and operating tourism facilities in a way that minimizes their environmental impacts. For example, green building (using energy-efficient and non-polluting construction materials, sewage systems and energy sources) is an increasingly important way for the tourism industry to decrease its impact on the environment. And because waste treatment and disposal are often major, long-term environmental problems in the tourism industry, pollution prevention and waste minimization techniques are especially important for the tourism industry. A guide to sources of information on cleaner production (free) is available here.

Environmental Awareness Raising

Tourism has the potential to increase public appreciation of the environment and to spread awareness of environmental problems when it brings people into closer contact with nature and the environment. This confrontation may heighten awareness of the value of nature and lead to environmentally conscious behaviour and activities to preserve the environment. For instance, Honduran schoolchildren from the capital city of Tegucigalpa are routinely taken to visit La Tigra cloud forest visitor centre, funded in part by eco-tourist dollars, to learn about the intricacies of the rainforest.

If it is to be sustainable in the long run, tourism must incorporate the principles and practices of sustainable consumption. Sustainable consumption includes building consumer demand for products that have been made using cleaner production techniques, and for services-including tourism services-that are provided in a way that minimizes environmental impacts.

The tourism industry can play a key role in providing environmental information and raising awareness among tourists of the environmental consequences of their actions. Tourists and tourism-related businesses consume an enormous quantity of goods and services; moving them toward using those that are produced and provided in an environmentally sustainable way, from cradle to grave, could have an enormous positive impact on the planet's environment.

Protection and Preservation

Tourism can significantly contribute to environmental protection, conservation and restoration of biological diversity and sustainable use of natural resources. Because of their attractiveness, pristine sites and natural areas are identified as valuable and the need to keep the attraction alive can lead to creation of national parks and wildlife parks.

In Hawaii, new laws and regulations have been enacted to preserve the Hawaiian rainforest and to protect native species. The coral reefs around the islands and the marine life that depend on them for survival are also protected. Hawaii now has become an international centre for research on ecological systems-and the promotion and preservation of the islands' tourism industry was the main motivation for these actions.

Grupo Punta Cana, a resort in the Dominican Republic, offers an example of how luxury tourism development and conservation can be combined. The high-end resort was established with the goal of catering to luxury-class tourists while respecting the natural habitat of Punta Cana. The developers have set aside 10,000 hectares

(24,700 acres) of land as a nature reserve and native fruit tree garden. The Punta Cana Nature Reserve includes 11 fresh water springs surrounded by a subtropical forest where many species of unusual Caribbean flora and fauna live in their natural state.

Guests can explore a "nature path" leading from the beach through mangroves, lagoons of fresh water springs and dozens of species of Caribbean bird and plant life. The Punta Cana Ecological Foundation has begun reforesting some parts of the reserve that had been stripped of their native mahogany and other trees in the past. Other environmentally protective policies have been put into effect at the resort, such as programs to protect the offshore barrier reefs and the recycling of wastewater for use in irrigating the grounds.

The fairways of the resort's new golf course were planted with a hybrid grass that can be irrigated with sea water The grass also requires less than half the usual amounts of fertilizer and pesticides. The resort has also established a biodiversity laboratory run by Cornell University.

Tourism has had a positive effect on wildlife preservation and protection efforts, notably in Africa but also in South America, Asia, Australia, and the South Pacific. Numerous animal and plant species have already become extinct or may become extinct soon. Many countries have therefore established wildlife reserves and enacted strict laws protecting the animals that draw nature-loving tourists. As a result of these measures, several endangered species have begun to thrive again.

Alternative Employment

Tourism can provide an alternative to development scenarios that may have greater environmental impacts. The Eco-escuela de Espanol, a Spanish language school created in 1996 as part of a Conservation International project in the Guatemalan village of San Andres, is an example.

The community-owned school, located in the Maya Biosphere Reserve, combines individual language courses with home stay opportunities and community-led ecotours. It receives around 1,800 tourists yearly, mostly from the US and Europe, and employs almost 100 residents, of whom around 60% were previously engaged in mostly illegal timber extraction, hunting and *milpas*, or slash-and-burn agriculture. Careful monitoring in 2000 has shown that, among the families benefiting from the business, the majority has significantly reduced hunting practices, and the number and extension of "slash-and-burn" agricultural plots. Furthermore, as most families in the village benefit directly or indirectly from the school, community-managed private reserves have been established, and social pressure against hunting has increased.

Regulatory Measures

Regulatory measures help offset negative impacts; for instance, controls on the number of tourist activities and movement of visitors within protected areas can limit impacts on the ecosystem and help maintain the integrity and vitality of the site. Such limits can also reduce the negative impacts on resources.

Limits should be established after an in-depth analysis of the maximum sustainable visitor capacity. This strategy is being used in the Galapagos Islands, where the number of ships allowed to cruise this remote archipelago is limited, and only designated islands can be visited, ensuring visitors have little impact on the sensitive environment and animal habitats.

Tourism and the Environment

Tourism plays an important role in the economies of both Goa and the Maldives. For the Maldives, it provides 17 percent of the gross domestic product, over 25 percent of government revenue and around 60 percent of the foreign exchange earnings; and for Goa, it generates 13.7 percent of the state's net domestic product, 7 percent of employment, and 7 percent of state tax revenues.

Although both states capitalize on their comparative environmental advantages, that is beach and sunshine, Goa also capitalizes on its unique historical and cultural heritage while the Maldives on its unique archipelagic and coral reef marine environment. Their products and approaches to tourism development are very different: Goa promotes heterogeneous tourism development with upscale and inexpensive charter tourism to international and domestic audiences while the Maldives concentrates on upscale, international tourism. The experiences in tourism of Goa and the Maldives vary in terms of their environmental impacts, social issues and conflicts and institutional responses. There is much that Goa and the Maldives can learn from each other. Other states could also learn from the experiences of these two tourist spots in South Asia.

Tourism and the Environment

The two papers included in this set, presented at an EDI/ SAARC Regional Seminar on. Economic Globalization and Environmental Sustainability in Goa in June 1997, review the impacts of tourism on the environment in the State of Goa, India and in the Republic of the Maldives. Compared with their giant neighbouring states, Goa (population 1.2 million) and the Maldives (population 244,000) are small, but blessed among others with local attractions, good beaches and sunshine that draw tourists from near and far.

Tourism plays an important role in the economies of both Goa and the Maldives. For the Maldives, it provides 17 percent of the gross domestic product, over 25 percent of government revenue and around 60 percent of the foreign exchange earnings. For Goa, tourism generates 13.7 percent of the state's net domestic product, 7 percent of employment and 7 percent of tax revenues. Both states capitalize on their comparative environmental advantages: beach and sunshine. Goa also capitalizes on its unique historical and cultural heritage while the Maldives on its unique archipelagic and coral reef marine environment. Their products and approaches to tourism development are very different: Goa promotes heterogeneous tourism development with upscale and inexpensive charter tourism to international and domestic audiences. The Maldives concentrates on upscale, international tourism. The experiences in tourism of Goa and the Maldives vary in terms of their environmental impacts, social conflicts and institutional responses. After reviewing both experiences, there is much that Goa and the Maldives can learn from each other. Other states could also learn from the experiences of these two tourist spots in South Asia.

The preservation of the natural environment, the prudent use of natural resources, disposal of solid waste and sewage, and the depletion and deterioration of ground-water attributable to tourist inflows are, among others, issues which both governments face. In Goa, the growth of coastal tourism has been rapid and uncontrolled, notes the paper by Sawkar *et al*. Tourism development has resulted in, the loss of biodiversity, erosion of sand dunes, declining fish catches, accretion and salutation and depletion of ground-water.

Although the environmental diversity and sensitivity of Goa has been widely known, a complex mixture of customary rights, land ownership, a variety of stakeholders with very differing interests, and ineffective institutional and political structures seem to have made it difficult for Goa to define a tourism strategy and to enforce its implementation. In the Maldives, the rapid increase, *albeit* government controlled, in the number of resorts over the last two decades has also taken its toll on the environment. The paper on the Maldives by Saeed, acknowledges environmental damage from beach erosion, an alteration of ocean currents, loss of biodiversity, water, soil and nutrient pollution and damage to its coral reefs most notably from mining for construction, anchoring of boats and diving. The Government has played a key role in promoting tourism on unoccupied islands (or abandoned islands where customary usufruct rights were compensated) through certain traditionally powerful families and with certain funding arrangements to encourage foreign investments; the government has been closely monitored the development of tourism.

Tourism development has many social impacts. The Maldives has avoided much social conflict due to its relatively isolated geographical location and small, somewhat homogenous population and culture. The Maldives strategy of separating foreign tourists from the local residents by developing tourist resorts on uninhabited islands is critical to minimizing social impacts.

This strategy has managed thus far to avoid social conflicts, but with the leakage of information from tourist areas, and the separation of resort employees from their families, the sustainability of this strategy under existing institutional and political structures remains to be seen. In contrast, as Goa does not have land which is untitled or unowned or which is not of some historical significance, the needs of tourists and the local population in Goa come into frequent conflict over the use of local resources. The Goan social scene is further complicated by the states porous borders with the rest of India. While Goas geographical location improves domestic demand for tourism, it has also lead to a large influx of labour from adjoining states, further exasperating social impacts.

Conflicts over resource use and institutional responses to them is another area in which the experiences of Goa and the Maldives differ. The situation in Goa is rather complex due largely to the number of stakeholders involved in tourism: luxury hotels, family-run guest houses, the needs of tourists, local residents, and other sectors of the economy. Mechanism for resolving conflicts among the various resource users do exist, such as the panchayats (.communidades.) and the courts, but the long backlog of cases has delayed justice.

The high number of conflicts among users suggests that an improved institutional response is necessary. Comparatively, the situation seems less complex in the Maldives. At this point, legislating and enforcing environmental quality controls for tourism appears to create fewer conflicts among residents because of the geographical separation of resorts, the small number of facilities and the limited number of stakeholders involved in tourism. As tourism expands in the Maldives, additional review of potential conflicts over resource use must be considered. Environmental legislation and regulatory mechanisms are in place in both states. The Maldives has developed its institutional capacity to address these problems and to facilitate unique solutions. Having carried out a proper evaluation of tourism in 1983 and a survey in 1995 to identify the major existing environmental problems facing the resorts, the Maldives seems further down the road in its development of tourism. But, while the Maldives has increased its regulation of tourism, it tends to focus on future environmental damage, viewing current damage as more aesthetic rather than a serious threat.

The sustainability of such policy is questionable. In Goa, while a Master Tourism Plan is in place, the implementation of the laws and regulations appears to be somewhat tardy. Although the paper alludes to several government department charged with varies aspects of tourism planning in Goa, institutional strengthening is a clear issue. Similarly, a systematic study of the environmental impacts of tourism and the implementation of a monitoring and management system would also aid Goa. Fortunately, some of these issues will be covered by the. India Environmental

Management Capacity Building Technical Assistance Project, supported by the World Bank, in which Goa is included.

In sum, these two cases provide a brief introduction to the complexity of pursing tourism as an avenue to development. Much can be highlighted from the two. The Maldives has excelled in moving forward with strengthening its environmental regulatory and enforcement framework. Not only has it increasingly developed its institutional capacity to address environmental problems related to tourism, but it has also concentrated its efforts on the polluter pays principle. In Goa, although institutional responses and the development of a tourism strategy which integrates the needs of all stakeholders has lagged, the active lobby of its citizenry at all levels, which has intensively documented its environmental impacts and brought environmental concerns to the public agenda, should be highlighted. The active participation of all stakeholders in the planning process lends itself to greater sustainability of tourism in the long-run.

Clearly the complexity of both cases requires that Goa and the Maldives carefully review the sustainability of their approaches and how to strike a balance between tourism development and protecting the natural and social environments. As in any other sector of an economy, tourism requires a sound, well-defined and executed approach in which the government, the various stakeholders and the public cooperate. We wish to acknowledge the contributions of the two papers and the comments of Mr. Gert van Santen.

Issues of Concern in the Coastal Zone of Goa

When Goa joined the Indian Union in December 1961, its only large industry was the export of its rich ores of iron and manganese. Goans depended on indigenous fish and coconuts for their vital nutritional requirements. The popularity of milk and vegetables amongst local inhabitants was low, and most of their dietary and other consumer items were imported. Before 1961, Goa had very little development in the modern sense of the term. With rich coastal biodiversity and abundant natural resources, the quality of life and the social fabric was good.

Its main assets were its genial and peace loving people, a tranquil and unspoiled environment, and an absence of population pressure. Tourism was adopted as a key sector for Goa development, not only for the well-established reasons of increasing income and employment but also for its potential to generate non-manual employment in a state with an increasingly educated work force and limited industrial growth. Fearing industrial pollution, the planners and decision-makers opted for tourism as an avenue to earn the states income over increased industrial development in addition to mining.

Except at academic levels, very little awareness and understanding existed back then among planners about the processes of the life support systems of the coastal environment and the interactive roles played by each component. This paper highlights the issues and the implications of tourism on the coastal marine and the socioeconomic environment of Goa.

Nature and Growth of Tourism in Goa

Most of the tourism in Goa is concentrated in the coastal stretches of Bardez, Salcete, Tiswadi and Marmagao. Over 90 percent of domestic tourists and over 99 percent of the international tourists frequent these areas. Consequently, beach tourism is the only type that is avidly encouraged by policy makers and other concerned parties alike.

Goa is visited by two types of tourists with distinct needs which this state satisfies. The first is the domestic tourists, who comprise 80 percent of all tourists. These people come in search of the culture that is different from the rest of India, as the Goan image holds a degree of mysticism, a sense of freedom and unconventional dress style. The second is the international tourists who visit Goa purely for the natural environment sun and beaches. Within the category of international tourists are there are two sub-categories: backpackers and charter tourists. Although both visit Goa for the beaches, they stay away from each other. The backpackers are not found in areas of charter tourists; they prefer to mingle and live with the local communities. Whereas, the charter tourists tend to stay in the luxury starred hotels. Domestic and international tourists also differ in terms of the areas they frequent. For the domestic tourist, the beaches hold limited appeal, so domestic tourists remain away from the places frequented by the international tourists.

The timings of visits are clearly different for the domestic and the international tourists. In previous decades, a clear off season for all tourists could be identified, today this is not so for domestic tourists, who come throughout the year albeit in larger numbers in the non-monsoon months. Conversely, international tourists avoid the monsoon months, as for them the use of the beach is the prime attraction to come to Goa.

In the earlier years, the international tourist was one in search of alternative lifestyles and mingling with local communities; however, in more recent years, a considerable homogenization of the traveller has occurred in terms of package tourism. In the 1980s, the domestic tourist came from the middle class and from the adjoining states; however, now domestic tourists that come to Goa are diversifying, as the place attracting a number of the rich young elites from more distant states. In response to these changes, the tourism industry in Goa has evolved into a curious mix of low-budget tourism and up-market hotel development, a mix that is marked with tensions and potential conflicts over the appropriation of resources.

Impacts of Tourism in Goa

Tourism development among policy-makers tends to be discussed in terms of the factors that are of concern to the national and the state governments. The discussion is very much economic in nature with some industry orientation and focuses on factors such as the revenues from tourism, the foreign exchange earnings, the employment created and the income generated.

The focus has always been on the implications of tourism development on the economy of Goa and on the relations among the various components of its tourism industry. The microlevel impact of tourism on the destination area immediately around it has been relatively less studied, if at all. The impacts of such a large-scale, diversely interactive activity as tourism should be more inclusive of all components. Tourists travel to and from their destinations, are accommodated, fed and entertained. All these activities require extensive infrastructural networks and support services that may not remain limited to the geographical positions of a tourists movements. Moreover, the effects result very much from the interactions among the tourists and the agents in the destination area.

Economic Aspects

The foreign exchange earning potential of the tourism industry is one of the main attractions for its support by national governments, while state governments are more concerned with its contribution to local income, taxes and employment. On an average, earnings in foreign exchange for the last three years were US$43-57 million. It is estimated that tourism contributes to around 13.7 percent of Net State Domestic Product; 7 percent of employment and 7 percent to state tax revenues. The money spent by domestic and international tourists is received by different segments of the industry which provide the supporting goods and services.

Tourist receipts can be classified into five categories: accommodation and food, shopping, internal travel, entertainment and miscellaneous items. An overview of the distribution of expenditures among the five categories for international and domestic tourists. Moreover, in 1992, about 90 percent of the domestic tourists who came to Goa spent less than US$35 per capita per day. Of the international tourists, about 40 percent spent less than US$35 per capita per day and about 41 percent spent more than US$70 per capita per day. As mentioned earlier, however, this trend is changing today. In the last few years indications are that the domestic tourist coming to Goa is increasingly from the more affluent segments of society, and the international tourist have increasingly been more of the inexpensive charter packages.

As previously mentioned, most of the tourism development in Goa is concentrated in the four coastal stretches of Bardez, Salcete, Tiswadi and Marmagao. These areas are, similarly, the most developed regions of Goa, accounting for approximately 66 percent of Goa's Gross State Domestic Product (GSDP). They have dense settlements and are more developed in terms of infrastructural support services.

About 70 percent of small-scale units, 78.5 percent of the capital investment in small industry and over 68 percent of the employment in this sector are found here. Historically, the region developed relatively faster than the rest of the state due to its coastal location, which provided easy access for sea trade and was attractive for settlement. There are a number of interesting locations with tourism potential exist in the hinterland; however, very little has been done to develop them. Hence, there is a considerable imbalance between the coastal and the hinterland regions in infrastructural and other indicators of economic development. Investment in the Tourist Industry Since tourisms acceptance as the primary avenue through which to develop, it has grown in scope to be comparable with mining, the only other industry in Goa. State expenditures on the tourism industry has doubled over a period of 10 years. Expenditures amounted to approximately Rs.15 million in 1986-87, and they grew to approximately Rs.30 million by 1996-97.

Private investment also increased. If the investment per room by hotel category, which was estimated by Kirloskar Consultants 1994, investment in the hotel industry has risen from Rs.2.08 billion to Rs.3.25 billion in 1996, an increase of Rs.1.19 billion in just 2 years. If the type of hotels that have been built over the last two years is analysed, investment in starred hotels increased by 39.5 percent during this period while that in other hotels has gone up by 47.5 percent. Tourism studies suggest that the financial performance of the hotel industry is poor compared to several other industries in the state although no evidence has been presented to back this claim.

From the statistics available and through observation, local participation in the tourism industry is high in terms of the number of small hotels and paying guest accommodations, yet the bulk of economic investment is concentrated in just a few hotels. Thus, using just the accommodation sector as a proxy for the tourism industry as a whole in 1996, almost half of all investment in the sector was in the hands of just four large hotels; the largest hotels together controlled 69 percent of all investment, and the balance was made up by smaller hotels. Seasonality of Income and Employment The industry peaks and troughs: October-February being the good months and June-August being the lean months due to the monsoon. This seasonality requires the tourism industry to respond by adjusting the output in terms of the services it provides which affects hotels, restaurants and their employees. Because of the search and initial training costs that the employer faces, and because of the need to cater to sudden spurts of demand, a hiring and firing policy is not cost-effective to an employer. The first reaction of employers is to keep labour, but reduce the work hours, a situation akin to holding inventories of labour in excess of demand. This strategy is supported by employing unskilled labour during the peak season, who are then laid off during the off season as the costs of hiring and firing unskilled labour are not high. A sample survey indicates that the highest seasonality of income (in terms of lower off season earnings) and the highest seasonality of employment (in terms of hours worked per week) are experienced by the smaller hotels. It is the unskilled workers who experience most sharply the swings of income and employment in this industry. This is a social cost of the industry to which hitherto scant attention has been paid.

Shifts in Population and Traditional Occupations

In the tourist belts of Calangute-Candolim in Bardez, a shift in the composition of the resident population has occurred to include a large number of migrants from the states of Karnataka, Rajasthan and Kashmir due to potential employment in the tourism industry. Most of these people are engaged in selling artisanal pieces, handicrafts and garments. It cannot be denied that tourism has also given a boost to local art and handicrafts; however, the commercialisation of such arts and crafts has resulted in a certain deterioration in their quality as they are being manufactured for bulk sale. At another level, Goan cultural practices are being used as tourist attractions, such as Carnival and Shigmo, which have been given a certain orientation to suit the demand of tourists. Much of the spontaneity of these practices has been lost.

Moreover, some of the villages along the coasts have become very tourist-oriented and thus, shifted away from their traditional occupations. A couple of decades ago, these villages were predominantly fishing-or agricultural-oriented. Tourism has increased land prices and encouraged locals to sell their land, thereby sharply increasing the competition for land in the tourist belt. It can be argued that tourism has accelerated the decline of agriculture in Goa, by providing a viable alternative for the lateral transfer of investment capital, land, and labour by the locals. In the tourist belt, land conversion from agriculture to non-agriculture uses has occurred. In the fishery sector, while fishermen do not always compete with tourists for shore space, there are instances on the Goan coasts where traditional fishing operations have been constrained by lack of shore space. In some areas, fishing ports and the houses of fishermen have been displaced by resort development. Economic forces are driving social forces here. On the one hand, expectations of higher returns, from the sale of land to builders and/or from hiring out houses to tourists rather than from actively engaging in agriculture or fishing are creating incentives for shifting occupations.

On the other hand, social forces are at work in the sense that tourism provides locals with an opportunity to keep their women at home rather than have them till the soil or sell fish in the market. This is perceived as a movement upwards for the locals, and a factor that cannot be ignored in the dynamics of the intersectoral movement of land and labour. Often large tourism development projects require the displacement of some of the original inhabitants of the area. Some of those displaced by present projects, chose to invest their compensations in capital assets, e.g., taxis, and have become to a degree upwardly mobile in an economic sense. However, there are others who due to their initial circumstances are unable to move along the same path, and instead become marginalized, having to replace self-employment for menial jobs in the very resorts that have displaced them. The issue of income distribution needs to be examined.

Impacts on the Goans. Sense of Community

One of the impacts of tourism on the Goan community is the creeping expropriation felt by the locals. This feeling of being pushed out arises from the fact that starred hotels have effectively gained control over beach resources, which locals have used for generations, and are selling access to them at a price. The area that is available to them as commons is increasingly reduced and overpopulated, causing the locals to avoid the beaches as a whole. Consequently, the growth of tourism in Goa has been accompanied by strong anti-tourism activism. Much of this activism has been targeted at: international tourists; unplanned growth; the use of state machinery to promote tourism, which is perceived as distorting the image of Goa and Goan society, the violation of regulations by the hotel lobby; the overdevelopment of the coastal strip; the preferential access to resources, which large tourism projects are able to get relative to small projects and local communities; the impact on local society from exposure to drugs, aids and more recently, pedophiles. The bottom-line is that there has been little involvement of the public in the policy decision-making process resulting in a strong sense of alienation about decisions that are affecting the lives of the local community.

Environmental Aspects

Coastal zone environment is particularly fragile and can be divided into two areas: the marine part and the land part. For the purpose of this discussion, coastal waters, bays, backwaters, creeks, tidal inlets, and estuaries are considered as components of the marine part of the coastal zone. The sandy beaches along with two dunes (one which runs along the seashore, and another that runs parallel but about 100 to 500 meters away from the seashore) and their vegetation are considered components of the land part. In between these dunes there lies a sandy plain, which acts as a buffer zone between the main land and the sea.

Impacts to the Marine Part of the Coastal Zone

The marine part of the coastal zone provides many functions and in the present context are:

- To support marine flora including subtidal varieties, such as mangroves. The mangrove ecosystem itself serves as a habitat for diverse types of species of birds and marine biota, in addition as the protection of the coastline from erosion, tides and storms.
- To support a wide variety of marine organisms including mammals. The marine organisms among themselves form a very intricate, well-established food chain starting with the chemical constituents of sea water called nutrients.
- To function as a natural thermostat which balances the climate on the subregional, regional and global scales.
- To disperse riverine load effectively in near-shore regions.

Most of the above functions are interactive in nature. In the coastal current movement, the most important force is the tidal cycle, which drives the sea water along the shoreline, bays, creeks and upstream through the mouths of rivers and estuaries. Other important forces are the near shore and riverine, or estuarine currents. All these currents carry natural sediment load and any other marine discharge, resulting from man-made activities, and deposits them at a site defined by an equation containing parameters, such as current velocity, counter currents, topography of the seabed or riverbed and other oceanographic factors. The transportation capacity of the currents has to be understood in terms of its effect on marine biota. For example, a rise of a few degrees in temperature of a sea water body would adversely effect species occurrence and predominance among biota, which in turn could influence other life forms. Also, a sudden appearance or disappearance of a species due to anthropogenic factors may cause stress in other species. Given the interactiveness and complexities of the coastal environment, any developmental activity should to be preceded by the Environmental Impact Assessment studies to forestall environmental degradation.

The following impacts on the marine part of the coastal zone have been observed while surveying the ecosensitive coastal areas of Goa. They have been represented in a flowchart in the Annex. The work was carried out by National Institute of Oceanography on request from the Ministry of Environment and Forests, Government of India, in August/September, 1996.

- Loss of mangroves: Thick mangroves on the outskirts of Panaji, at Sao Pedro near Old Goa, around Talpona backwaters and at innumerable other locations are being reclaimed. In addition to the biological impacts of the loss of mangroves, the tidal waters could flood the surrounding coastal areas causing erosion and thus opening the estuarine banks to storm surges.
- Reduced fish catch and species: A steady decrease in the total annual fish catch has been observed in Goa. The catch has declined from 105.44 thousand tones in 1993-94 to 101.90 in 1994-95 and in 1995-96, to 87.82 thousand tones. More specifically, at Sancoale-Chicalim Bay, the decrease in production of certain varieties of shellfish and crabs, both local delicacies, is believed to be due to the land reclamation of mangrove swamps and to the construction of roads to the Sao Jacinto Island and at Talpona. More generally, one or more of the following factors may be responsible for the reduction in fish catch:

  a) Unscientific fishing practices: These can include the use of nets with a mesh size smaller than permissible during spawning periods and the fishing beyond sustainable yields. These practices are pursued due to high demand for fresh seafood in the market.

b) Loss of spawning grounds: Reasons for this could be mangrove deforestation, land reclamations and salutation. Short-term economic gains from the development of these areas is obviously preferred over the long-term benefits of the conservation of ecology.

c) Introduction of anthropogenic material: Any disturbance at any step in the marine food web may inadvertently affect other species. The introduction of untreated sewage and waste to the environment would give rise to toxic algal blooms wiping out many species. Increased turbidity and sedimentation can also affect the benthic communities.

- Erosion: Dispersion of sediment load at any given point depends upon a number of parameters related to marine currents. Any activity which causes disturbances in these parameters, could alter the sites of deposition and result in erosion, accretion or salutation and changes in the ecology of that area, such as land reclamations, the extraction of sand or the construction of jetties. Consequently, there are a large number of cases where coastal stretches have been subjected to the forces of erosion. Prime examples are Campal and Caranzalem near Panaji, Palolem, Agonda and many other places, where a considerable amount of construction activities have occurred.
- Accretion/salutation: Accretion and salutation is occurring. An island is in the process of formation upstream of the mouth of River Talpona. Due to sand bar formation at the mouth itself, which has been more pronounced in the last few years, the river is navigable only during high tides. In addition, local fishermen have noted salutation in the river bed. All these observations suggest disturbances in the natural sediment load dispersion patterns in the River Talpona. Impacts to the Land Part of the Coastal Zone

The land part of the coastal zone mainly comprises sandy areas along with the dunes and its vegetation cover. This part provides the following functions:

- To protect the coast from the forces of the oceans,
- To replenish the sand on the beach that is carried away by the sea,
- To gather the sand that is blown landward by the wind with the help of dunes and its vegetation, and
- To serve as habitats for numerous organisms, including turtles. Sandy areas are also used for tourism development:
- To mix the sand with cement for construction purposes, and
- To develop the land.

All along the coastline of Goa, for example, between Chapora and Sinquerim in Bardez, Caranzalem and Miramar in Panaji, Salcete Coast in Central Goa and in Galgibaga, Talpona, Palolem in South Goa, there has been a boom in construction activities, most of which are for tourism or for associated purposes. To make space for and to use them as a component of cement for construction, sand is being extracted in substantial amounts.

When the environmental functions are weighed against the economic services that sand performs, the fact that the former are not priced, tilts the demand in favour of the economic user-groups. There is need to quantify and monitor such sand losses and their ecological impacts. The following impacts have been observed on the coastal stretches of Goa due to development activities:

- Loss of sand dunes: Sand dunes have borne the brunt of construction activities along the coastal stretches of Goa. Anjuna and Baga-Calangute-Candolim stretches in North Goa, and Salcete beaches comprising Betalbatim, Colva, Varca, Cavelossim and Mobor in central Goa, were the first beaches to lose their dunes. Our survey showed South Goa to be the next in line as in Galgibaga, two dunes, 10 meters high, have already been flattened into plateaus at half the heights to make way for construction.
- Endangered species: Four species of turtles have been reported to frequent the beaches at Morjim, Miramar,

Bogmalo and Palolem, covering almost the entire stretch of the Goan Coast. The Save The Turtles. campaign of the Goa Foundation, a local Non-Governmental Organization, carried jointly with the Forest Department of the Government of Goa, reported that the number of seaturtles visiting their nesting sites on different beaches in Goa particularly in Morjim, is steadily decreasing.

- Tidal ingress: The ceaseless mining of sand and sand-dunes have effectively razed gentle slopes of sand which stop the tides from rushing further on the shore. The consequent tidal ingress has reduced the area of beach at different places, such as Miramar in Panaji, Baga-Calangute-Candolim-Sinquerim stretch and Anjuna in Bardez, and in Salcete and Mormugao on the north and central coasts of Goa.

Impacts of Recreational Activities

Recreational facilities affecting the coastal environment are generally, but not limited to, those related to upscale tourist activities. These are:

- *Swimming pools:* The water for this is invariably drawn from subsurface aquifers. The withdrawal of large amounts of ground water in a limited area can be detrimental to the water table of the region, particularly since it is a source of drinking water. Additionally, some parties owning wells with a good underground stream of fresh water sell their water at Rs.100 (US$2.5) per 500 litre tank to fill these swimming pools. Consequently, the ground-water levels in some coastal areas is decreasing and is frequently accompanied with salt water intrusions. The manifestation of sea water intrusions in the form of salt water in wells along the coastal belt from Chapora to Aguada has been observed in coastal aquifer studies.
- *Water sports:* Motor boats used in shallow coastal waters continuously disturb the habitats of endangered species and other marine life. Moreover, they tend to degrade water quality by the discharge of oil and grease.
- *Beach driving:* Tourists regularly drive on the beaches during low tide. Concrete ramps have even been

constructed to take the vehicles on the beaches such as at Palolem.

- *Beach accommodations:* In the initial states of tourism in Goa, beach shacks became popular due to their small numbers, economical rates and simple decor; however, after several decades, these structures crowd the shorelines without any comfortable space among them, and they lack ecofriendly toilet facilities and proper refuse collection, all of which often result in waste invariably find its place in the coastal waters.
- *Sanitation:* Goa lacks modern treatment and disposal systems for both sewage and garbage. Even the internationally famous beach stretch of Baga-Calangute-Sinquerim, does not have rudimentary toilet facilities. Tourists, locals, shop owners and the hordes of migrant labourers, who are employed by construction companies along the beaches, have no other option than to use the beaches to answer the call of the nature.
- Beach litter: Plastics are among the very serious problems in a number of Goas beaches, and an action plan is urgently needed to mitigate the problem. Both the last mentioned problems could be solved through improved enforcement of regulations and infrastructual improvements.

Impacts of Expanded Transport

Even though tourists in Goa are almost exclusively accommodated in coastal areas, they arrive and depart Goa by some kind of transportation operating in other areas of the state. While the air and sea travel would cause negligible damage to the environment in broad terms, motor vehicles cause air pollution by their uncontrolled exhaust fumes. Also, the alignment of the Konkan Railway has broad reaching environmental impacts. The laying of the tracks for the railway in Goa, especially through wetlands and tidal marshes at Maxem and between Bali and Mayem along with numerous bridges on the Mandovi-Zuari estuarine fronts, has been done without proper hydrodynamic and geomorphological studies. The gigantic embankments, several kilometres long, supporting the rail lines along the lowlands of Goa have lead to substantial alterations in physical, chemical, biological and geomorphological setups. Blocking, diminuting or increasing the tidal flow has resulted in a major redistribution of sediments giving rise to erosion/deposition or deposition/erosion with conspicuous changes in shorelines or near-shore realms.

Mangrove swamps have been destroyed; tidal regimes disrupted; paddy fields flooded, and the embankments are sinking due to soft underlying strata 32. A comprehensive analysis of the environmental impacts of the Konkan Railway alignment is needed to study such questions as the following. Is the salutation taking place in the backwaters and estuarine regions of Canacona in South Goa due to river runoffs carrying haphazardly dumped material from the digging out of the railroad? To what extent has the Konkan Railway Alignment through ecosensitive areas contributed to the environmental degradation of estuarine/coastal areas of Goa? In board terms, factors other than tourism could be responsible for the observations made above, but the contributions of the tourism industry in all these situation should be identified given the criticality of the coastal environment demands.

Tourism Policy

In the wake of the report, Our Common Future, by United Nations Commission on Environment and Development in 1983, India passed its own Environment Protection Act in 1986. This was followed by a Notification in February 1991, inviting the governments of Indias coastal states and union territories to prepare Coastal Zone Management Plans for their respective territories. The much publicized Rio Summit in June 1992, along with Indian environmental norms, started a land race for coastal development regardless of the laws, regulations and conventions in vogue. The land race got started probably because the coastal resource users experienced inertia in the implementation of various legislation on the part of the authorities.

It seems increasingly clear that (i) despite several important pronouncements and regulatory mechanisms in place, local planning does not always adhere to guidelines and regulations and (ii) where it does adhere, planning and development regulations have been observed in the breach. Thus, the Government of Goa, in October 1988, published its Regional Development Plan, anticipating, among other activities, the growth of tourism by 2001 A.D. In this plan, a strategy is outlined:

Location of new beach resorts should be considered not only from point of view of land availability but also from the consideration of beach resource ecology, based on the Environmental Assessment Studies. Further, spreading thinly on all available sandy beach stretches from Tlerekhol/Arambol in the north to Betul/Agonda in the south is not advisable from the standpoint of conservation of resources both natural and man-made.

Instead, it is suggested that beach-head developments at certain selected centres should be encouraged. Despite these admirable commitments toward conservation and the protection of the coastal environment and ecology, the Regional Development Plan for Goa 2001 A.D. does not contain any reference to the no development zone. of 200/500 meters from the high-tide line along the seashores, which had been much debated around the country in the early 1980s; nor does it mention the Environment Protection Act of 1986 of the Government of India. Moreover, the Coastal Zone Management Plans, prepared by the Department of Town and Country Planning of Goa in 1995 and 1996 for approval by the Central Government, actually recommend tourism-related development for almost the entire length of the Goan coastline, barring only a few places, which contradicts the Departments own guidelines.

The current policies and relaxed enforcement thereof have led to the haphazard and uncontrolled growth of townships. Places like Calangute and Candolim in Bardez and Colva in Salcete have become over commercialized and haphazard in their development pattern. These areas have a number of unauthorized constructions, which have paid little heed to local planning rules, infrastructural supports or aesthetics. During the 1980s and the early 1990s, the lure of catering to tourists especially, international tourists and the hope of making rapid profits have led to considerable investment in resorts and apartments. Today there are signs of over investment, this is spreading a price war. When a certain location is to be developed as a prominent tourist area requiring extensive infrastructural and other support services, it gets developed as a small township.

This increases its real estate value manifold, inducing other sectors of the society to set up business and residences in these areas as well. A quick look at the developments along the coasts of Goa and the future plans for it, reveals that:

(i) these follow the ideas submitted in the CZM plan of Goa (which is yet to be formally approved) rather than its Regional Development plan; and,

(ii) the tourists are almost exclusively accommodated along the 105 km stretch of the coastline while little effort has been made to adhere to the regional plans of creating other types of tourism besides beach tourism.

One successful example of regulated tourism development is Seychelles, an island nation in the Indian Ocean. It spared its beaches from concretization and allowed resorts to come almost entirely amongst the coconut groves just behind the sandy stretches, taking care of the coastal marine environment. This policy, unfortunately, is not in place in Goa where constructions are allowed as close to the waterline as possible.

Conclusions

Although tourism is concentrated along the coastal zone in Goa, it has had a number of positive benefits in terms of increased incomes, increased employment, added avenues for upward mobility for locals, increased revenue and increased foreign exchange earnings. However, there are also some socioeconomic and environmental impacts associated with these benefits that need to be highlighted. These impacts have arisen as a result of the trajectory that tourism has followed in Goa and can be summed up as follows:

1. The growth of coastal tourism has been rapid and uncontrolled.
2. The seasonal nature of tourism has led to swings in employment and income most markedly in the small sector and to the unskilled worker.
3. There has been no clear nor firm policy relating to tourism; most decisions have been on a purely ad hoc basis, except for a marked predisposition to upmarket tourism. The policy initiatives that have been introduced are not attentive to local concerns. This has led to some disaffection among locals toward tourists that needs to be studied.

4. There has been a marked spatial concentration of tourism development along the coast, which is leading to heavy demand for resources in these places. Cumulatively, this results in concentration and congestion of population, enormous increase in the density of construction, and related infrastructure and facilities. Consequently, there has been an overall decline in the agricultural sector in the state.
5. It poses major changes in land use, shortages of resources, such as land and water, and damage to coastal aquifers, the sand dune system, and mangrove vegetation.
6. Spawning and breeding grounds have been lost due to anthropogenic activities related to tourism; consequently, fish populations are decreasing and traditional fishing activities are on the decline.
7. The principles of sustainability and the norms related to the conservation of the environment and ecology are generally ignored; the coastal environment is becoming irreversibly degraded as evidenced by the concretization of beaches.

It is clear that there is much to be learned about the impacts of tourism in Goa, and that further planning and development requires information gaps to be filled. More specifically, the following actions are needed:

1. A careful study on the type of tourism that best suits Goa: up-scale, low budget or a combination of the two.
2. Recognition that tourism is a vulnerable industry, subject to the fads of the trade; hence, tourism cannot be allowed to permanently change the face of the coast in the long run.
3. A systematic study of the environmental impacts of tourism, through perhaps, a life cycle analysis, and the valuation of the environment to enable its integration into decision-making.
4. An understanding of the processes that make the Goan coast a preferred tourist destination rather than the hills or the hinterland areas.

5. A monitoring and management system to ensure the effectiveness of coastal and environmental regulations. The development of sustainability markers would be a way to ensure this. Such markers will enable both the industry and government to identify the emerging issues and to facilitate mitigation before problems becomes unmanageable. They can also serve as the basis for monitoring changes in the ecosystem, social and economic spheres.
6. The integration of the principles of coastal environment and ecology into the planning stage of any coastal activity, as preventative rather than remedial measures.
7. An environmental impact assessment and studies of Goas coastal stretches including estuaries and backwaters.
8. Policies which recognize the type of interconnections among tourism, local communities and the environment, to ensure that tourism contributes to a sustainable development agenda.

Impacts of Construction Activities in close Proximity to the Marine Environment

The aim of this paper is to assess the impact of tourism on the environment of Maldives and explore the environmental management practices in the tourism industry of Maldives. First, the emergence, growth and present status of tourism development in the Maldives is outlined. Then the environmental impacts of tourism are discussed. Next, the environmental management practices are outlined. The relevant legislation, institutional structure, tourism planning, standards and controls are also presented.

Tourism Development in the Maldives

The Republic of Maldives is a small island, developing state consisting of 26 coral atolls dominated by the sea and is situated in the Indian Ocean, southwest of India. In total, these atolls contain about 1,190 very small islands of which only 200 are inhabited. The capital of the Maldives is Male., an island by itself, and the Male. International Airport also has an island (Hulhule) to itself. Tourism development in the Maldives is based on the principle of isolation of tourists from the bulk of the indigenous population and the physical configuration of tourism development is an unusual one. In the Maldives, the tourism industry is synonymous with resort islands and each resort occupies a separate island and is totally self-contained. This isolation is practical because of the availability of a large number of uninhabited islands that can be developed into tourist resort islands.

According to a tourist opinion survey in 1991 conducted by the Ministry of Tourism, the main attractions in order of priority are white sandy beaches, opportunities for snorkelling and scuba diving among coral reefs and spectacular marine life, sunny weather, clear lagoons and scenic peaceful environments. The expectation is one of a Robinson Crusoe existence without any problems where the Art of Doing Nothing is practiced in a relaxing atmosphere.

Tourism History

Maldivian tourism entered the international scene only in the early 1970s. Tourism commenced with the opening of two resorts in 1972 and about 1,000 tourists visited the islands. Until then the Maldives was virtually unknown to the tourist travel trade. By the late 1970, tour operators, notably from West Germany and Italy, started to feature the islands within their programs and international tourism had become an important source of income for the Maldives. The first decade (1972-1982) in the development of the Maldives tourism industry evolved essentially in an unplanned laissez faire manner. Hulhule Airport was the basic and only gateway entry to the Maldives and the natural hub for tourism development. Thus the first two resorts to be developed were Kurumba and Bandos both on islands in close proximity to Hulhule Airport and Male. In 1973, along with three other resorts, Club Med established itself on Farukolhufushi island, also only 20 minutes by boat from Hulhule Airport.

Tourism in Maldives originated from excursions from Sri Lanka and because of the reputation of Maldives as a diving destination. Tour operators identified the ideal combination of packaging the culturally-orientated product of Sri Lanka with the unique island paradise holiday of the Maldives. During the 1972-1980 period the market changed from the more limited and specialized divers.

Market to the much bigger mainstream market for beach holidays. With the growing importance of the mainstream market for sand, sea and sun holidays, the tour operators found that the market base was sufficient for introducing the Maldives as a separate destination.

With the completion of the runway at Hulhules International Airport in 1981, direct charters from Europe, using wide bodied planes, flew in tourists. The expansion of air travel assisted by various promotional and other concessional fares on scheduled services, together with the rapid growth of charters, has helped the growth and development of the Maldives as a tourist destination. In the beginning the facilities provided for tourists were basic.

The room was furnished with just a bed and the essential cooling fan. Food with no exotic flavours was served by local people with no formal training, and scuba diving and island hopping were the only recreation facilities besides sun bathing and swimming. At present, a diverse range of facilities are offered at different resorts. At the luxurious end of the spectrum, public spaces have expensively tiled finished floors, vast varnished and carved timber frame roofs, elaborate light fittings and plush furniture, impressive reception areas, international cuisine, swimming pools, fountains, piped music and a lush landscape incorporating many ornamental imported species.

Tourism Indicators

Two resorts with a bed capacity of 280 opened in North Male atoll in 1972. By the end of the first decade (1972-1982), 44 resorts became operational and bed capacity rose to just under 4,000. With the spatial policy shift towards opening of Ari Atoll, together with consolidation and upgrading of existing resorts, the next decade (1982-1992) saw the addition of 36 new resorts with over a doubling of bed spaces to reach a total of almost 8,500. By 1995, there were 74 resorts in operation in the Maldives.

During the year of inception of tourism in the Maldives, 1972, only 1097 tourists visited the Maldives. The number of annual tourist arrivals (reaching over 300,000 in 1995) now exceeds the total indigenous population of about 244,000. Europe is the leading generating market followed by the Asian market. Germany and

Italy are the two main suppliers of tourists and in 1994, shared 40 percent of the total tourist arrivals to the Maldives.

In the late 1970s, international tourism became an important source of income for the Maldives. The readiness of the Maldives to develop its tourist sector can only be understood in terms of its very limited economic possibilities, especially the absence of local raw materials to diversify into exports of manufactures. At 17 percent of gross domestic product, which provides over 25 percent of the government revenue and contributes around 60 percent of the country foreign exchange earnings, tourism is the second largest contributor to the economy and it is increasing in importance yearly.

Tourism and the Environment

Tourism depends on environmental quality more than any other activity and a central precept that has been preached in tourism is not to kill the goose that lays the golden eggs. Yet, in general, it is characterized by rapid, short-term development which more often than not damages the very environment the tourists come to enjoy and simply moves off elsewhere.

Without careful attention to the balance between the volume and type of tourist activity, and the sensitivity and carrying capacities of the resources being developed, tourism projects can be not only environmentally harmful but also economically self-defeating. Tourism in the Maldives exists solely due to the physical and geographic features of the coral islands. The beauty of the underwater world at the reefs, clean water in the lagoons, white and pristine sandy beaches, a rich island vegetation and ideal tropical climate which form a virtual paradise that attracts tourists from Europe and Australasia.

Environmental Impacts of Tourism

The first proper evaluation of tourism in the Maldives was carried out in 1983 after 10 years of tourism development. It was revealed that the pollution of the sea with garbage, piles of waste found in the resorts often close to the tourist cottages, the picking of corals, the use of spearguns were features present that did not fit into the tourists image of the Maldives. In 1991, after almost two decades of tourism development in the Maldives, the perception of impacts has changed. According to the present perceptions, the islands offer uncommon visual beauty unspoiled by human settlement, virtually unsurpassed marine environment and the strongest of all, unspoiled, under populated tiny tropical islands replete with natural beauty and abundant sea life.

The Environmental Protocol prepared in 1992 by the Ministry of Planning and Environment to determine the carrying capacity constraints in the tourism sector concluded that the natural resources of the Maldives are in a sufficiently pristine state, and of such high aesthetic quality, that a period exists in which environmental deterioration can occur without an adverse effect on tourism. However, concern was expressed that the duration of this period cannot be predicted and with increasing environmental pressures, rising environmental sensitivity, and without compensatory environmental management, adverse effects may be felt sooner than later.

According to a survey carried-out in August 1995 involving the management of 47 resorts, beach erosion was identified to be the major existing environmental problem facing the resorts. The highly dynamic Maldivian beaches erode and build in response to wave action associated with storms, the tidal cycle, and the monsoons. The results of a survey carried out in 1992 showed that 12.8 percent of the total shoreline of 32 resorts surveyed consists of seawalls and groynes and is not sandy. The same survey also showed that 12 of the 32 resorts surveyed (38 percent) had offshore breakwaters to protect the beach. The maintenance of natural beach is of paramount importance to attract clients to the resorts and the construction of artificial structures designed to control and limit beach erosion are not only unsightly but also expensive. Rubbish on beach is the next environmental problem identified by the resort management. Rubbish on beach mainly results from waste dumped at sea irresponsibly by neighbouring resorts and inhabited islands that get washed ashore onto islands with the current and to some extent from the messy habits of certain tourists. The resort management is quite emotive on this issue as this is one issue that will reflect very badly on the image of the resort environment.

Solid Waste

Solid waste disposal is one of the most obvious impacts of tourist resort operation and one of the easiest environmental management problems to deal with and thus has been addressed in a number of reports on tourism development in the Maldives. The pollution of the sea with garbage and piles of waste found in the resorts often close to the tourist cottages were identified in 1983 among features that was not aesthetically pleasing. In 1985 the Department of Tourism reported that the disposal of non-biodegradable waste was then a serious problem and that there was need for education to increase environmental awareness, and for the use of recycling technology. In the new Tourism Master Plan solid waste is identified as a major issue for resort islands and it is stated that at current tourism levels, problems are probably more aesthetic than environmental.

The plan also points out that while solid waste itself may not currently pose a serious environmental threat, its impact in conjunction (e.g., synergistically) with the effects of other human activities should be considered.

Sewage Disposal

In 1980 only two resorts were reported as discharging saltwater flushed toilets to the open sea. In a survey of methods of sewage disposal reported from 34 resorts in 1992, 23 resorts disposed sewage into the ground while 11 discharged sewage to the sea.

A survey in 1993 revealed that at 67 percent of tourist resorts sewage effluent is piped into septic tanks, and the untreated sludge is dealt with by natural processes and soil absorption. At 33 percent of the resorts analysed, septic tanks and sea outfalls were the reported practices. Measures to protect the environment in cases of direct sewage discharge include the siting of outfall pipes 100m from the island and 30m below mean sea level.

Sewage disposal has both health implications and environmental consequences. Aquifer contamination by faecal coliform bacteria or the contamination of bathing waters could give rise to health problems. Since a very small percentage of resorts pump sewage into the sea and even so, these resorts have a very small population it might be concluded that the current levels of sewage emission into the coastal waters of the resorts do not pose very serious problems to human health.

The capacity constraints survey carried out in 1992 showed that the sewage discharges from resorts are relatively small and the observed effects were limited. Even though the volume of waste matter disposed is quite small, nutrients from sewage could build up over time, especially if the process of discharge is not managed well. However, volumes of water and rates of water exchange are large and in view of the productive fisheries, the atolls are probably already subject to relatively high nutrient input from upwellings as oceanic currents hit them.

Ground-water

There is an increasing move away from using ground-water as a resource in tourist resorts. Drinking water in tourist resort comes from rainwater which is collected on roofs and stored in large tanks and is now supplemented by desalinated water and imported bottled mineral water. There has also been a move away from the system in which ground-water was used for showering and flushing toilets to one in which saltwater is used for flushing with the wastewater pumped out to sea and desalinated water used for showering. Ground-water quality deterioration could be caused through increasing abstraction of ground-water which depletes the already thin freshwater lends; salt water intrusion into the freshwater aquifer; and contamination of ground-water from sewage discharges. In addition to sewage, ground-water can also be contaminated through the use of contaminated soils; the excessive use of fertilizers; the use of pesticides; and inappropriate solid and liquid waste disposal.

An analysis of ground-water quality and pollution in tourist resorts, based on the results of Maldives Water and Sanitation Authority Surveys and consultants opinions showed that ground-water quality in the resorts is deteriorating. However, the capacity constraints study in 1992 concluded that whilst there is some evidence that ground-water quality has deteriorated on some resorts through tourism, the deterioration is not significant and is unlikely to be irreversible. The study also suggested a number of factors mitigating any possible deterioration and they are:

1. The sources of pollution are relatively benign though more and more pesticides are being used and rubbish buried on islands.
2. High rainfall backed up by evidence that salinity vary widely on many of the islands between the wet and dry

season indicates that flushing rates, and oxidation, of contaminants are likely to be rapid.

3. Before upgrading, resorts traditionally used ground-water flushing for toilets and for showering, this minimizes the historic loss of ground-water.
4. The contaminant adsorption properties of coralline soils are generally extremely limited.

One advantage of this is that any contaminants should be flushed out eventually. This is good for the state of the ground-water but not so good for adjacent lagoon waters.

Coral Reefs

On tourist resort islands reef damage has been caused by scuba divers, and by snorkelers and bathers walking out across the reef flat. The greatest threat at present almost certainly arises from snorkelers and bathers, from both inadvertent breakage and deliberate removal of coral and coral fauna for souvenirs. A study at Kurumba Village has assessed the effects of snorkelers on the reef flat/crest at depths up to about 1.5 m. Results indicate breakage of 18 percent of all Arcopora corals/month. Hence most or all coral colonies of this genus stand to get broken each year, suggesting a significant effect from snorkelers.

The present evidence on reef degradation from sewage in the Maldives is inconclusive. The Environment Protocol reported that none of the 32 resorts surveyed in 1992, and none of the 70 dive base operators on 41 resorts, identified sewage as a problem causing reef deterioration. Direct and indirect damage to reefs is also caused by divers and tourists. demands. However, the greatest impact to reefs in the Maldives has originated from coral mining for construction purposes.

Island Vegetation

The image of a palm fringed sandy beach and lush tropical vegetation is integral to the perception of, and satisfaction, with Maldives as a tourist designation. At present there is no requirement to survey and consider the vegetation of an island as part of the planning approval process prior to resort development. In the construction process trees and shrubs are cut down and coastal vegetation is removed. Exotic ornamental and fast growing species are imported to replace the vegetation removed and for new resort gardens. The introduction of exotic species not only reduces the ability of the island to recover to its natural state but also the exotic species may overcome local ones directly or through the introduction of pests.

There is also the matter of maintaining the natural perception of the island for marketing purposes. Whilst the palm is the most important vegetation feature on an island, there are local plants that have historic and cultural importance and so have marketing value which imported exotics do not have.

Soil and fertilizer have largely been imported to improve the growth prospects of exotic imports. These imports are very much on trial and error basis and there is little doubt that many soils and a variety of fertilizers have been tried. This process detracts from efforts to use local vegetation which is already adapted to local conditions, and so should not have to be sustained artificially. Imports may also introduce soil associated pests and diseases for which local plants have limited resistance.

Environmental Management

National Legislation: The Department of Tourism and Foreign Investment was organized in 1978 and made responsible for supervision, coordination and maintaining standards of tourist services in the country. To develop and regulate tourism, and simultaneously to strengthen the institutional framework for administering and monitoring the industry, this department was renamed the Department of Tourism in November 1982 and made solely responsible for tourism management. In 1984, the Tourism Advisory Board was established as a consultative body affiliated to the tourism authority.

The tourism sector was given elevated status in 1988 with the establishment of the Ministry of Tourism, according to the designating law 3/68 J under 1/69 J as at 1993, to provide ways to develop the tourism industry in the Maldives, to plan methods of income generation through tourism, to provide guidelines, and to administer the industry. The Ministry of Planning and Environment was established in 1988. This Ministry is responsible for the formulation of policies on environment, environmental guidance to other development sectors, the implementation of environmental impact assessment and the designation of protected areas.

Policy and Planning

During the first decade of tourism development, there was no specifically planned development; rather, tourism took place according to individual private sector initiatives in locations that offered market advantages principally related to the access opportunities offered by Hulhule Airport. This essentially informal development managed to generate almost 3,500 bed spaces of international quality and the industry was achieving enviable occupancy rates of up to 80 percent in the high season. The first formal initiative to plan, in an integrated way, the future development of the tourism industry in the Maldives, came when the Department of Tourism and Foreign Investment commissioned Dangroup International in November 1980 to carry out a Maldives Tourism Development Plan. This long-range (10 years), tourism development plan was prepared for the Maldives in May 1983 and some, but not all, of its recommendations were considered feasible for implementation.

The tourism plan provided some ideas for development. However, to date, most of the tourism planning and management has resulted from government initiatives, based on its evaluation of the best forms and standards of development. Many of the governments present approaches and standards have evolved through the monitoring of the earlier phases of development to determine what is most suitable. Approaches and standards have been refined and some abandoned based on the experience gained from previous types of development.

By government policy, the resorts are located on uninhabited islands, in order to reduce any possible sociocultural impacts. Also most islands are too small to contain both resorts and traditional villages. These islands are owned by the government and it can allocate them for resort use as needed. The resort developer receives a long-term lease and pays an annual rent that is calculated individually for each island. The resorts must supply their own infrastructure of electric power, water supply, sewage and solid waste disposal, boat dock and recreation facilities. They must also provide housing and related facilities for the resort employees. The families of the resort employees remain on their home islands, often some distance away.

The government policy has been to expand tourism for its economic benefits, but in a systematic manner of staged development. In the late 1980s, Kaafu Atoll was considered saturated with resort development. This decision was made within the framework of maintaining high environmental standards for the existing resorts, and retaining sufficient land for village and urban expansion and recreation parks.

All new resort development was then programmed to take place in Alif Atoll, which is accessible by sea and air from the international airport. In parallel the government policy turned to encourage expansion and upgrading of existing resorts to higher standards, including meeting present environmental quality standards. This upgrading was considered necessary to maintain the viability and competitiveness of these resorts and to maintain all tourism development at a reasonably high level, catering to quality tourist markets.

As an inducement to achieve these objectives, resort leases were extended from 10 to 21 years and much of this upgrading has been accomplished. The Third National Development Plan (1991-1993) recommended the development of a ten-year zoning plan (1991-2000).

Under strategies and policies to achieve the main objectives of tourism development, the NDP (1991-1993) included a proposal to assess environmental impacts of resort developments and operations, and further strengthen measures taken to protect and conserve the environment and natural setting for tourism, and to adopt remedial measures on environmental degradation. The issues that are examined in the new Tourism Master Plan draft include new markets, priority markets, air travel and other transportation issues, tourism infrastructure development, legal aspects, human resource development, gender situation, sociocultural aspects and environmental impacts.

Environmental Impact Assessment

The Environmental Protection and Preservation Act of Maldives (4/93) provided the basic framework for the Environmental Impact Assessment (EIA) process in the Maldives and under Article 5 (1) of the Act, an impact assessment study shall be submitted to the Ministry of Planning, Human Resources and Environment (MPHRE) before implementing any activity that may have an impact on the environment. According to the EIA guidelines issued by MPHRE all new resort developments require an EIA study before approval for development can be made.

Carrying Capacity Limits

As an important basis for deciding the number of rooms and extent of resort facility development allowed on each resort island, the government has established carrying capacity standards. These are based on several factors. The cutting of trees is controlled so that the natural appearance and facade of the island are maintained and no buildings are allowed to appear above the tree tops. The maximum area of the island to be occupied by buildings is 20 percent, with two story buildings allowed to conserve land area if there is sufficient vegetation to conceal these buildings from the ocean view. To preserve the tourists perceptions and image of beach orientation, all guest rooms should be facing the beach, with a minimum of 5 meters of linear beach available in front of each room. Only 68 percent of the beach length can be allocated to guest rooms as 20 percent has to be allocated to public use and 12 percent left as open space. Construction on reef flat and lagoon are discouraged; however, as over water bungalows are very popular among tourists, they are permitted provided that equal open space is left on the land for each building developed on the lagoon.

Architectural and Design Controls

The design of resort buildings is controlled so that they are well integrated into the island environment, take advantage of the tropical climate and use local building materials to the extent possible, such as thatch roofs. Previously many buildings were constructed from coral mined from the reefs. However, the use of coral is now restricted and use of imported materials is now encouraged, although these are expensive by local standards. Coral and sand mining from resorts and their house reefs is strictly prohibited. Hard engineering solutions for dynamic coastlines are discouraged and construction of solid jetties and groynes are controlled. Design of boat piers and jetties should be in such a way that they do not obstruct the original flow of currents or disrupt the wave climate within the lagoon.

Biodiversity Conservation

To protect and preserve marine biodiversity a number of measures have been prescribed. Spear, poison and dynamite fishing are strictly prohibited. Net and trap fishing are controlled and confined to certain areas. Removal of shells, juvenile lobsters and lobsters ready to lay eggs are strictly prohibited.

The catching of turtles is strictly prohibited and trade in all turtle products is banned. The commercial exploitation and export of a number of other species is also banned. Resort operators also voluntarily prohibit the catching of reef fish from the house reef or tourist resorts. Fifteen important dive sites have been declared as protected areas in 1994, where fishing, anchoring, removal of coral and other destructive activities are prohibited.

The Ministry of Tourism recognizes the importance of vegetation in maintaining the natural beauty of the islands and there are a number of regulations which aim to secure this resource. These include a limit of 20 percent of the islands for building, the requirement that no buildings be put up that disrupt the natural facade of the island, that there be a minimum setback limit of 5 meters from the vegetation line of the island, and that no buildings should appear above the tree tops.

Waste Disposal

According to the regulations issued by the Ministry of Tourism, garbage from tourist resorts should be disposed off in a manner that would not cause any damage to the environment. All garbage disposed into the sea should be done as far away into the sea as necessary in order to ensure that it does not get washed onto any islands with the current.

Tourist resorts are required to have incinerators and compactors adequate in size to burn all flammable materials and crush all the cans respectively. Those who lack these facilities are not allowed to operate. Plastic or polythene bags should not be thrown into the sea and such material should be burnt. Those who contravene these regulations are subject to fines and penalties. Two airlines have joined in the effort to keep Maldives clean by arranging for waste to be carried back to Europe. Under this program all tourists who fly in to the Maldives in these airlines are given a bag and asked to bring to the airport, all the waste they produce during their stay in the Maldives when they depart. The airlines carry the waste to the original destination for recycling free of charge.

Under sewage and excreta disposal the tourism book of regulation specifies that the sewage system should be prepared such that pollution of water supplies, beaches and other areas are prevented; nuisance, ugly sights, and unpleasant odors do not occur, human wastes do not come into contact with people, animal and food; and breeding of flies and mosquitoes will be prevented.

Tourism in the Maldives began in 1972 and it then evoke the image of a lost paradise. The tourism industry of the Maldives is dependent entirely on environmental quality and since it established itself in the tourism market it has maintained its strong position in a rapidly growing market. A few critics in the 1980s proclaimed that environmental pollution had begun to rear its ugly head in the Maldives. However, the natural resources of the Maldives are still in a sufficiently pristine state and of very high aesthetic quality and environmental concerns are few. Environmentally unsound practices in solid waste and sewage disposal pose the most serious threat from tourism to the delicately balanced coral reef ecosystem of the Maldives. Though solid waste is a cause of environmental concern, at current level it is more of an aesthetic problem. In the past the portion of waste and garbage which could not be burned was dumped into the sea. This practice is now prohibited by law and waste incinerators and crushers have to be used in all resorts. Sewage effluent is discharged into the sea by the resorts. However, their discharges from resorts are very small and the evidence on reef degradation from sewage discharges is inconclusive. Some of the resorts are turning to the latest technology in sewage treatment using UV radiation to produce virtually pure water. The Maldives has developed a very suitable form of tourism, appropriate for the small island environment. The present form of tourism development has not generated any serious environmental impacts. This has been accomplished through careful management. The government has developed appropriate policies, legislation and plans and instituted mechanisms to apply strict standards and regulations.

5

Learning Curves on Environment

The quality of the environment, both natural and man-made, is essential to tourism. However, tourism's relationship with the environment is complex. It involves many activities that can have adverse environmental effects. Many of these impacts are linked with the construction of general infrastructure such as roads and airports, and of tourism facilities, including resorts, hotels, restaurants, shops, golf courses and marinas. The negative impacts of tourism development can gradually destroy the environmental resources on which it depends.

On the other hand, tourism has the potential to create beneficial effects on the environment by contributing to environmental protection and conservation. It is a way to raise awareness of environmental values and it can serve as a tool to finance protection of natural areas and increase their economic importance.

Tourism's Three Main Impact Areas

Negative impacts from tourism occur when the level of visitor use is greater than the environment's ability to cope with this use within the acceptable limits of change. Uncontrolled conventional tourism poses potential threats to many natural areas around the world. It can put enormous pressure on an area and lead to impacts such as soil erosion, increased pollution, discharges into the sea, natural habitat loss, increased pressure on endangered species and heightened vulnerability to forest fires. It often puts a strain on water resources, and it can force local populations to compete for the use of critical resources.

Depletion of Natural Resources

Tourism development can put pressure on natural resources when it increases consumption in areas where resources are already scarce.

Water Resources

Water, and especially fresh water, is one of the most critical natural resources. The tourism industry generally overuses water resources for hotels, swimming pools, golf courses and personal use of water by tourists. This can result in water shortages and degradation of water supplies, as well as generating a greater volume of waste water. In dryer regions like the Mediterranean, the issue of water scarcity is of particular concern. Because of the hot climate and the tendency of tourists to consume more water when on holiday than they do at home, the amount used can run up to 440 litres a day. This is almost double what the inhabitants of an average Spanish city use.

Golf course maintenance can also deplete fresh water resources. In recent years golf tourism has increased in popularity and the number of golf courses has grown rapidly. Golf courses require an enormous amount of water every day and, as with other causes of excessive extraction of water, this can result in water scarcity. If the water comes from wells, over pumping can cause saline intrusion into ground-water. Golf resorts are more and more often situated in or near protected areas or areas where resources are limited, exacerbating their impacts.

Local Resources

Tourism can create great pressure on local resources like energy, food, and other raw materials that may already be in short supply. Greater extraction and transport of these resources exacerbates the physical impacts associated with their exploitation. Because of the seasonal character of the industry, many destinations have ten times more inhabitants in the high season as in the low season. A high demand is placed upon these resources to meet the high expectations tourists often have.

Land Degradation

Important land resources include minerals, fossil fuels, fertile soil, forests, wetland and wildlife. Increased construction of tourism and recreational facilities has increased the pressure on these resources and on scenic landscapes. Direct impact on natural resources, both renewable and nonrenewable, in the provision of tourist facilities can be caused by the use of land for accommodation and other infrastructure provision, and the use of building materials. Forests often suffer negative impacts of tourism in the form of deforestation caused by fuel wood collection and land clearing. For example, one trekking tourist in Nepal-and area already suffering the effects of deforestation-can use four to five kilograms of wood a day.

Pollution

Tourism can cause the same forms of pollution as any other industry: air emissions, noise, solid waste and littering, releases of sewage, oil and chemicals, even architectural/visual pollution.

Air Pollution and Noise

Transport by air, road, and rail is continuously increasing in response to the rising number reported that the number of international air passengers worldwide rose from 88 million in 1972 to 344 million in 1994. One consequence of this increase in air transport is that tourism now accounts for more than 60% of air travel and is therefore responsible for an important share of air emissions. One study estimated that a single transatlantic return flight emits almost half the CO_2 emissions produced by all other sources consumed by an average person yearly.

Transport emissions and emissions from energy production and use are linked to acid rain, global warming and photochemical pollution. Air pollution from tourist transportation has impacts on the global level, especially from carbon dioxide (CO_2) emissions related to transportation energy use.

And it can contribute to severe local air pollution. Some of these impacts are quite specific to tourist activities. For example, especially in very hot or cold countries, tour buses often leave their motors running for hours while the tourists go out for an excursion because they want to return to a comfortably air-conditioned bus.

Noise pollution from airplanes, cars, and buses, as well as recreational vehicles such as snowmobiles and jet skis, is an ever-growing problem of modern life. In addition to causing annoyance, stress, and even hearing loss for it humans, it causes distress to wildlife, especially in sensitive areas. For instance, noise generated by snowmobiles can cause animals to alter their natural activity patterns.

Solid Waste and Littering

In areas with high concentrations of tourist activities and appealing natural attractions, waste disposal is a serious problem and improper disposal can be a major despoiler of the natural environment-rivers, scenic areas, and roadsides. For example, cruise ships in the Caribbean are estimated to produce more than 70,000 tons of waste each year. Today some cruise lines are actively working to reduce waste-related impacts. Solid waste and littering can degrade the physical appearance of the water and shoreline and cause the death of marine animals. In mountain areas, trekking tourists generate a great deal of waste. Tourists on expedition leave behind their garbage, oxygen cylinders and even camping equipment. Such practices degrade the environment with all the detritus typical of the developed world, in remote areas that have few garbage collection or disposal facilities. Some trails in the Peruvian Andes and in Nepal frequently visited by tourists have been nicknamed "Coca-Cola trail" and "Toilet paper trail".

Sewage

Construction of hotels, recreation and other facilities often leads to increased sewage pollution. Wastewater has polluted seas and lakes surrounding tourist attractions, damaging the flora and fauna. Sewage runoff causes serious damage to coral reefs because it stimulates the growth of algae, which cover the filter-feeding corals, hindering their ability to survive. Changes in salinity and salutation can have wide-ranging impacts on coastal environments. And sewage pollution can threaten the health of humans and animals.

Aesthetic Pollution

Often tourism fails to integrate its structures with the natural features and indigenous architectural of the destination. Large, dominating resorts of disparate design can look out of place in any natural environment and may clash with the indigenous structural design. A lack of land-use planning and building regulations in many destinations has facilitated sprawling developments along coastlines, valleys and scenic routes. The sprawl includes tourism facilities themselves and supporting infrastructure such as roads, employee housing, parking, service areas, and waste disposal.

Physical Impacts

Attractive landscape sites, such as sandy beaches, lakes, riversides, and mountain tops and slopes, are often transitional zones, characterized by species-rich ecosystems. Typical physical impacts include the degradation of such ecosystems. An ecosystem is a geographic area including all the living organisms (people, plants, animals, and microorganisms), their physical surroundings (such as soil, water, and air), and the natural cycles that sustain them. The ecosystems most threatened with degradation are ecologically fragile areas such as alpine regions, rain forests, wetlands, mangroves, coral reefs and sea grass beds. The threats to and pressures on these ecosystems are often severe because such places are very attractive to both tourists and developers. Physical impacts are caused not only by tourism-related land clearing and construction, but by continuing tourist activities and long-term changes in local economies and ecologies.

Physical Impacts of Tourism Development

Construction activities and infrastructure development: The development of tourism facilities such as accommodation, water supplies, restaurants and recreation facilities can involve sand mining, beach and sand dune erosion, soil erosion and extensive paving. In addition, road and airport construction can lead to land degradation and loss of wildlife habitats and deterioration of scenery. In Yosemite National Park (US), for instance, the number of roads and facilities have been increased to keep pace with the growing visitor numbers and to supply amenities, infrastructure and parking lots for all these tourists. These actions have caused habitat loss in the park and are accompanied by various forms of pollution including air pollution from automobile emissions; the Sierra Club has reported "smog so thick that Yosemite Valley could not be seen from airplanes". This occasional smog is harmful to all species and vegetation inside the Park.

Deforestation and intensified or unsustainable use of land: Construction of ski resort accommodation and facilities frequently requires clearing forested land. Coastal wetlands are often drained and filled due to lack of more suitable sites for construction of tourism facilities and infrastructure. These activities can cause severe disturbance and erosion of the local ecosystem, even destruction in the long term. Marina development of marinas and breakwaters can cause changes in currents and coastlines. Furthermore, extraction of building materials such as sand affects coral reefs, mangroves, and hinterland forests, leading to erosion and destruction of habitats. In the Philippines and the Maldives, dynamiting and mining of coral for resort building materials has damaged fragile coral reefs and depleted the fisheries that sustain local people and attract tourists. Overbuilding and extensive paving of shorelines can result in destruction of habitats and disruption of land-sea connections (such as sea-turtle nesting spots). Coral reefs are especially fragile marine ecosystems and are suffering worldwide from reef-based tourism developments. Evidence suggests a variety of impacts to coral result from shoreline development, increased sediments in the water, trampling by tourists and divers, ship groundings, pollution from sewage, overfishing, and fishing with poisons and explosives that destroy coral habitat.

Physical Impacts from Tourist Activities

Trampling Tourists using the same trail over and over again trample the vegetation and soil, eventually causing damage that can lead to loss of biodiversity and other impacts. Such damage can be even more extensive when visitors frequently stray off established trails.

Trampling impacts on vegetation	Trampling impacts on soil
Breakage and bruising of stems	Loss of organic matter
Reduced plant vigour	Reduction in soil macro porosity
Reduced regeneration	Decrease in air and water permeability
Loss of ground cover	Increase in run off
Change in species composition	Accelerated erosion

Source: University of Idaho

Anchoring and other marine activities In marine areas (around coastal waters, reefs, beach and shoreline, offshore waters, uplands and lagoons) many tourist activities occur in or around fragile ecosystems. Anchoring, snorkelling, sport fishing and scuba diving, yachting, and cruising are some of the activities that can cause direct degradation of marine ecosystems such as coral reefs, and subsequent impacts on coastal protection and fisheries.

Alteration of ecosystems by tourist activities Habitat can be degraded by tourism leisure activities. For example, wildlife viewing can bring about stress for the animals and alter their natural behaviour when tourists come too close. Safaris and wildlife watching activities have a degrading effect on habitat as they often are accompanied by the noise and commotion created by tourists as they chase wild animals in their trucks and aircraft. This puts high pressure on animal habits and behaviours and tends to bring about behavioural changes. In some cases, as in Kenya, it has led to animals becoming so disturbed that at times they neglect their young or fail to mate.

Effects of other Industries on Tourism

Impacts from other industries often have a more dramatic effect on the environment and can seriously affect tourism.

* Oil spills, like the oil tanker disaster that occurred off the Galapagos Islands (Ecuador) in January 2001, can cause severe short-term damage to tourist attractions. In that case, a freight ship loaded with 160,000 gallons of diesel fuel and 80,000 gallons of other petroleum products ran aground on the coast of San Cristobal and spilled nearly all of its load. Unique local marine and land species and the tourism potential of the area were badly affected.
* Agricultural runoff or industrial discharges can cause water pollution and may cause algae blooms like those that occurred in the Adriatic Sea in the early 1990s. In spite of improved control of sewage from tourism developments, the Mediterranean sea floor is increasingly carpeted with these quick-growing invaders, many rising 30 inches or more above anchoring runners. They appear equally adept at colonizing rock, mud, and sand in a virtually continuous swath that can extend from the beach

out to a depth of about 150 feet, smothering coral reefs, fish and other sea flora and fauna in the process.

* Destructive practices such as blast fishing, with poisonous chemicals like cyanide, and muro-aminetting (pounding reefs with weighted bags to scare fish out of crevices) directly destroy corals. They can also destroy a major draw for tourists.

Loss of Biological Diversity

Biological diversity is the term given to the variety of life on Earth and the natural patterns it forms. The effects of loss of biodiversity:

* It threatens our food supplies, opportunities for recreation and tourism, and sources of wood, medicines and energy.
* It interferes with essential ecological functions such as species balance, soil formation, and greenhouse gas absorption.
* It reduces the productivity of ecosystems, thereby shrinking nature's basket of goods and services, from which we constantly draw.
* It destabilizes ecosystems and weakens their ability to deal with natural disasters such as floods, droughts, and hurricanes, and with human-caused stresses, such as pollution and climate change.

Tourism, especially nature tourism, is closely linked to biodiversity and the attractions created by a rich and varied environment.

It can also cause loss of biodiversity when land and resources are strained by excessive use, and when impacts on vegetation, wildlife, mountain, marine and coastal environments and water resources exceed the carrying capacity. This loss of biodiversity in fact means loss of tourism potential.

Introduction of Exotic Species

Tourists and suppliers-often unwittingly-can bring in species (insects, wild and cultivated plants and diseases) that are not native to the local environment and that can cause enormous disruption and even destruction of ecosystems.

Depletion of the Ozone Layer

The ozone layer, which is situated in the upper atmosphere (or stratosphere) at an altitude of 12-50 kilometres, protects life on earth by absorbing the harmful wavelengths of the sun's ultraviolet (UV) radiation, which in high doses is dangerous to humans and animals. For instance, one of the reasons scientists have put forward for the global decrease of amphibian populations is increased exposure to UV radiation. Ozone depleting substances (ODSs) such as CFCs (chlorofluorocarbon) and halons have contributed to the destruction of this layer. The tourism industry may be part of the problem; direct impacts start with the construction of new developments and continue during daily management and operations. Refrigerators, air conditioners and propellants in aerosol spray cans, amongst others, contain ODSs and are widely used in the hotel and tourism industry. Emissions from jet aircraft are also a significant source of ODSs. According to Tourism Concern, scientists predict that by 2015 half of the annual destruction of the ozone layer will be caused by air travel.

UNEP's OzonAction Programme works with governments and industries, including the tourism industry, to phase out ODSs and find safer alternatives. UNEP has developed extensive information and guidance on how many types of businesses can eliminate ODSs and contribute to preservation of the ozone layer. For further reading see the publication How the Hotel and Tourism Industry can Protect the Ozone Layer.

Climate Change

Climate scientists now generally agree that the Earth's surface temperatures have risen steadily in recent years because of an increase in the so-called greenhouse gases in the atmosphere, which trap heat from the sun. One of the most significant of these gases is carbon dioxide (CO_2), which is generated when fossil fuels, such as coal, oil and natural gas are burned (e.g. in industry, electricity generation, and automobiles) and when there are changes in land use, such as deforestation. In the long run, the accumulation of CO_2 and other greenhouse gases in the atmosphere can cause global climate change-a process that may already be occurring.

Global tourism is closely linked to climate change. Tourism involves the movement of people from their homes to other destinations and accounts for about 50% of traffic movements; rapidly expanding air traffic contributes about 2.5% of the production of CO_2. Tourism is thus a significant contributor to the increasing concentrations of greenhouse gases in the atmosphere.

Air travel itself is a major contributor to the greenhouse effect. Passenger jets are the fastest growing source of greenhouse gas emissions. The number of international travellers is expected to increase from 594 million in 1996 to 1.6 billion by 2020, adding greatly to the problem unless steps are taken to reduce emissions. For more information on the relationship between energy and the environment, see UNEP's Energy Programme, which provides information and publications on energy efficiency and alternative energy sources to reduce the environmental impacts of energy use and of transportation.

How Global Environmental Impacts Affect Tourism

Natural Disasters

Catastrophes like floods, earthquakes, wildfires, volcanoes, avalanches, drought and diseases can have a serious effect on inbound and domestic tourism and thus on local tourism industries. The outbreak of the foot and mouth disease epidemic in England earlier this year (2001), for instance, has severely affected Great Britain's inbound tourism market. A BHA/Barclays Hospitality Business Trends Survey found that 75% of hotels in England, 81% in Scotland and 85% in Wales continued to be affected by the foot and mouth outbreak, and over 60% forecast a decline in business in the June-September 2001 period.

Climate Change

Tourism not only contributes to climate change, but is affected by it as well. Climate change is likely to increase the severity and frequency of storms and severe weather events, which can have disastrous effects on tourism in the affected regions. Some of the other impacts that the world risks as a result of global warming are drought, diseases and heat waves.

These negative impacts can keep tourists away from the holiday destinations. Global warming may cause:

* Less snowfall at ski resorts, meaning a shorter skiing seasons in the Alpine region. In already hot areas like Asia

and the Mediterranean, tourists will stay away because of immense heat, and out of fear of diseases and water shortages.

* Harm to vulnerable ecosystems such as rainforests and coral reefs because of rising temperatures and less rainfall. A major risk to coral reefs is bleaching, which occurs when coral is stressed by temperature increases, high or low levels of salinity, lower water quality, and an increase in suspended sediments. These conditions cause the zooxanthallae (the singlecelled algae which forms the colours within the coral) to leave the coral. Without the algae, the coral appears white, or "bleached"-and rapidly dies. The Great Barrier Reef, which supports a US$ 640 million tourism industry, has been experiencing coral bleaching events for the last 20 years.
* Rising sea levels, the result of melting glaciers and polar ice. Higher sea levels will threaten coastal and marine areas with widespread floods in low-lying countries and island states, increasing the loss of coastal land. Beaches and islands that are major tourism attractions may be the first areas to be affected.
* Increased events of extreme weather, such as tornadoes, hurricanes and typhoons. These are already becoming more prevalent in tourist areas in the Caribbean and South East Asia. Hurricane Mitch in 1998, for instance, heavily affected tourism in the Caribbean. Wind damage, storm waves, heavy rains and flooding caused major losses in the local tourism sector.

How Tourism can Contribute to Environmental Conservation

The tourism industry can contribute to conservation through:

Financial Contributions

* ***Direct financial contributions:*** Tourism can contribute directly to the conservation of sensitive areas and habitat. Revenue from park-entrance fees and similar sources can be allocated specifically to pay for the protection and management of environmentally sensitive areas. Special

fees for park operations or conservation activities can be collected from tourists or tour operators.

* *Contributions to government revenues:* Some governments collect money in more far-reaching and indirect ways that are not linked to specific parks or conservation areas. User fees, income taxes, on sales or rental of recreation equipment, and license fees for activities such as hunting and fishing can provide governments with the funds needed to manage natural resources. Such funds can be used for overall conservation programs and activities, such as park ranger salaries and park maintenance.

For Costa Rica, for example, tourism represents 72% of national monetary reserves, generates 140,000 jobs and produces 8.4% of the gross domestic product. The country has 25% of its territory classified under some category of conservation management. In 1999, protected areas welcomed 866,083 national and foreign tourists, who generated about US$ 2.5 million in admission fees and payment of services.

Improved Environmental Management and Planning

Sound environmental management of tourism facilities and especially hotels can increase the benefits to natural areas. But this requires careful planning for controlled development, based on analysis of the environmental resources of the area. Planning helps to make choices between conflicting uses, or to find ways to make them compatible. By planning early for tourism development, damaging and expensive mistakes can be prevented, avoiding the gradual deterioration of environmental assets significant to tourism.

Cleaner production techniques can be important tools for planning and operating tourism facilities in a way that minimizes their environmental impacts.

For example, green building (using energy-efficient and non-polluting construction materials, sewage systems and energy sources) is an increasingly important way for the tourism industry to decrease its impact on the environment. And because waste treatment and disposal are often major, long-term environmental problems in the tourism industry, pollution prevention and waste minimization techniques are especially important for the tourism industry. A guide to sources of information on cleaner production (free) is available here.

Environmental Awareness Raising

Tourism has the potential to increase public appreciation of the environment and to spread awareness of environmental problems when it brings people into closer contact with nature and the environment. This confrontation may heighten awareness of the value of nature and lead to environmentally conscious behaviour and activities to preserve the environment.

For instance, Honduran schoolchildren from the capital city of Tegucigalpa are routinely taken to visit La Tigra cloud forest visitor centre, funded in part by ecotourist dollars, to learn about the intricacies of the rainforest.

If it is to be sustainable in the long run, tourism must incorporate the principles and practices of sustainable consumption. Sustainable consumption includes building consumer demand for products that have been made using cleaner production techniques, and for services-including tourism services-that are provided in a way that minimizes environmental impacts.

The tourism industry can play a key role in providing environmental information and raising awareness among tourists of the environmental consequences of their actions. Tourists and tourism-related businesses consume an enormous quantity of goods and services; moving them toward using those that are produced and provided in an environmentally sustainable way, from cradle to grave, could have an enormous positive impact on the planet's environment.

Protection and Preservation

Tourism can significantly contribute to environmental protection, conservation and restoration of biological diversity and sustainable use of natural resources. Because of their attractiveness, pristine sites and natural areas are identified as valuable and the need to keep the attraction alive can lead to creation of national parks and wildlife parks. In Hawaii, new laws and regulations have been enacted to preserve the Hawaiian rainforest and to protect native species. The coral reefs around the islands and the marine life that depend on them for survival are also protected. Hawaii now has become an international centre for research on ecological systems-and the promotion and preservation of the islands' tourism industry was the main motivation for these actions.

Grupo Punta Cana, a resort in the Dominican Republic, offers an example of how luxury tourism development and conservation can be combined. The high-end resort was established with the goal of catering to luxury-class tourists while respecting the natural habitat of Punta Cana.

The developers have set aside 10,000 hectares (24,700 acres) of land as a nature reserve and native fruit tree garden. The Punta Cana Nature Reserve includes 11 fresh water springs surrounded by a subtropical forest where many species of unusual Caribbean flora and fauna live in their natural state. Guests can explore a "nature path" leading from the beach through mangroves, lagoons of fresh water springs and dozens of species of Caribbean bird and plant life. The Punta Cana Ecological Foundation has begun reforesting some parts of the reserve that had been stripped of their native mahogany and other trees in the past.

Other environmentally protective policies have been put into effect at the resort, such as programs to protect the offshore barrier reefs and the recycling of wastewater for use in irrigating the grounds. The fairways of the resort's new golf course were planted with a hybrid grass that can be irrigated with sea water The grass also requires less than half the usual amounts of fertilizer and pesticides. The resort has also established a biodiversity laboratory run by Cornell University.

Tourism has had a positive effect on wildlife preservation and protection efforts, notably in Africa but also in South America, Asia, Australia, and the South Pacific. Numerous animal and plant species have already become extinct or may become extinct soon. Many countries have therefore established wildlife reserves and enacted strict laws protecting the animals that draw nature-loving tourists. As a result of these measures, several endangered species have begun to thrive again.

Alternative Employment

Tourism can provide an alternative to development scenarios that may have greater environmental impacts. The Eco-escuela de

Espanol, a Spanish language school created in 1996 as part of a Conservation International project in the Guatemalan village of San Andres, is an example.

The community-owned school, located in the Maya Biosphere Reserve, combines individual language courses with home stay opportunities and community-led ecotours. It receives around 1,800 tourists yearly, mostly from the US and Europe, and employs almost 100 residents, of whom around 60% were previously engaged in mostly illegal timber extraction, hunting and *milpas*, or slash-and-burn agriculture.

Careful monitoring in 2000 has shown that, among the families benefiting from the business, the majority has significantly reduced hunting practices, and the number and extension of "slash-and-burn" agricultural plots. Furthermore, as most families in the village benefit directly or indirectly from the school, community-managed private reserves have been established, and social pressure against hunting has increased.

Regulatory Measures

Regulatory measures help offset negative impacts; for instance, controls on the number of tourist activities and movement of visitors within protected areas can limit impacts on the ecosystem and help maintain the integrity and vitality of the site. Such limits can also reduce the negative impacts on resources.

Limits should be established after an in-depth analysis of the maximum sustainable visitor capacity. This strategy is being used in the Galapagos Islands, where the number of ships allowed to cruise this remote archipelago is limited, and only designated islands can be visited, ensuring visitors have little impact on the sensitive environment and animal habitats.

The Social Impacts of Tourism

Today, tourism is one of the largest and dynamically developing sectors of external economic activities. Its high growth and development rates, considerable volumes of foreign currency inflows, infrastructure development, and introduction of new management and educational experience actively affect various sectors of economy, which positively contribute to the social and economic development of the country as a whole.

Most highly developed western countries, such as Switzerland, Austria, and France have accumulated a big deal of their social and economic welfare on profits from tourism. According to recent statistics, tourism provides about 10% of the world's income and employs almost one tenth of the world's work force.

All considered, tourism's actual and potential economic impact is astounding. Many people emphasize the positive aspects of tourism as a source of foreign exchange, a way to balance foreign trade, an "industry without chimney" — in short, manna from heaven. But there are also a number of other positive and negative sides of tourism's economic boom for local communities, which not always considered by advocates of tourism perspectives. Therefore in this paper I will consider the main social and environment impacts of tourism at the country level.

The Positive and Negative Social and Environmental Impacts of Tourism

Socially tourism has a great influence on the host societies. Tourism can be both a source of international amity, peace and understanding and a destroyer and corrupter of indigenous cultures, a source of ecological destruction, an assault of people's privacy, dignity, and authenticity. Here are possible positive effects of tourism:

- Developing positive attitudes towards each other.
- Learning about each other's culture and customs.
- Reducing negative perceptions and stereotypes.
- Developing friendships.
- Developing pride, appreciation, understanding, respect, and tolerance for each other's culture.
- Increasing self-esteem of hosts and tourists.
- Psychological satisfaction with interaction.

So, social contacts between tourists and local people may result in mutual appreciation, understanding, tolerance, awareness, learning, family bonding respect, and liking. Residents are educated about the outside world without leaving their homes, while their visitors significantly learn about a distinctive culture. Local communities are benefited through contribution by tourism to the improvement of the social infrastructure like schools, libraries, health care institutions, internet cafes, and so on. Besides, if local culture is the base for attracting tourists to the region, it helps to preserve the local traditions and handicrafts which maybe were on the link of the extinction.

For example in Uzbekistan, particularly in such famous regions as Samarqand, Buhara, and Horezm tourists contribute significantly to the preservation of traditional handcrafting wood carving, hammered copper work, handmade silk and carpets, and of course to preservation and maintenance of architectural and historical monuments. Since Uzbekistan proclaimed its independence in 1991 many museums and monuments were renovated or opened to promote the national culture and traditions. Growing interest in this culture makes the local people proud of their way of life.

On the other side tourism can increase tension, hostility, and suspicion. Claims of tourism as a vital force for peace are exaggerated. Indeed there is little evidence that tourism is drawing the world together. In this context economic and social impacts on the local community depend on how much of the incomes generated by tourists go to the host communities.

In most all-inclusive package tours more than 80% of travellers' fees go to the airlines, hotels and other international companies, not to local businessmen and workers. On the other hand large hotel chain restaurants often import food to satisfy foreign visitors and rarely employ local staff for senior management positions, preventing local farmers and workers from reaping the benefit of their presence.

Tourism has the power to affect cultural change. Successful development of a resource can lead to numerous negative impacts. Among these are overdevelopment, assimilation, conflict, and artificial reconstruction.

While presenting a culture to tourists may help preserve the culture, it can also dilute or even destroy it. The point is to promote tourism in the region so that it would both give incomes and create respect for the local tradition and culture. There are also both negative and positive impacts of tourism on the local ecology. Tourism often grows into mass-tourism. It leads to the over consumption, pollution, and lack of resources.

However, from the ecological point of view tourism is often more acceptable and preferable than any other industrial production, as it is environmentally friendlier. The problem is that it is not easy to change the traditional way of life of the local communities. It often creates pseudo conflicts.

Undoubtedly in some regions or countries the alternative industries are even more harmful to the environment than tourism. Besides that in many countries of Asia and the Pacific, for example in Cook Islands, Samoa and others, tourism is the main source of income or the friendliest to the environment. It is at least better than chopping down the forests or destroying coral reefs.

Conclusion

Thus, the preceding paragraphs show that the impact of tourism on local communities can be both positive and negative, whether it comes to economic, social, or environmental effects. It depends to which extent tourism is developed in a particular region. Every region has its bearing capacity, that is to say the limit of the incoming influence that does not harm the host community.

If we overcome that limit negative impacts of tourism will follow. Here is a figure which shows the dynamics between people, resources, and tourism in successful tourism: each makes a positive contribution to the others. All the three elements in this model are in co-interaction. Local communities use the natural resources but they also protect them. Tourists come to enjoy the nature and get knowledge about it, but they also can pollute and destroy it, or on the other side help to protect it by drawing attention to unique natural resources in the area. Local communities affect tourists by giving them knowledge of their culture and way of life.

Tourists' impact on the local populations can be first of all economic by generating income, developing resources, sharing knowledge and experience, etc. Whenever we develop a new tourist destination we should always bear in mind this co-interaction. In order to decrease the negative effects on local societies we can check the following points when arranging a tourism activity in a region or taking part in it (Fennell1999, lecture notes):

* Are local§ people involved in the tourism industry as employees?

* Does the§ organization cooperate with the local businesses?
* Does it have a§ respectful attitude to the local culture?
* Is there§ respect to nature and how is it protected?
* How much§ economic benefit will the local population get from tourism?
* Are tour§ operators concerned about ecological hotels, transport, and restaurants?

We can see it is a great challenge to make a profitable business running tourism in an area without some negative effect to the local communities. It is possible for the tourism industry to cooperate with other industries and bring benefits to both the tourism organizations and local businesses. The first step to achieve it is to understand the needs and desires of both the host community and the tourists.

Economic and Social Impacts

The economic and social impacts of tourism are a big subject that cannot be covered thoroughly here. They should be examined in detail for any large tourism development project. Economically, tourism can create jobs for local people and bring money into the country. However many tourists like their comforts from home, and it is often necessary to import a large part of their requirements, so that much of the money may leave the country again to pay for these imports. If the resorts and hotels have been financed by overseas investors, they will also want to export their profits.

The developers may want the government to improve the airport, roads and other infrastructure, and possibly to provide tax breaks and other financial advantages, which cost the country money. The remaining benefit to an island country from some kinds of tourism development may thus be small indeed. Other kinds of tourist facilities provided by villages or financed locally may be economically more interesting. The social impacts of tourism may also be important. Most jobs for local people in the tourist industry are as servants, house maids, waiters, gardeners and other menial work that may give people a sense of inferiority.

At the same time the tourists come from other societies with different values and lifestyles, and because they have come seeking pleasure, they may spend large amounts of money and behave in ways that even they would not accept at home. Local people seeing the tourist example may want to live and behave the same way. Tourists may also, out of ignorance or carelessness, fail to respect local customs and moral values. These and other social effects may be among the most important long-term impacts of tourism development.

Negative Social Aspects of Tourism

Tourism can undoubtedly bring benefits to an area protecting pristine habitats and conserving cultures and wildlife in some of the world's poorest countries and revitalising regions within developed nations where traditional industries have declined, but it often comes at a cost.

This effect is, of course, most keenly felt in the developing world where the stark juxtaposition of affluent consumerism with subsistence lifestyles jars most noticeably. As a holiday-maker it is impossible to avoid the simple truth that the loose change lying forgotten in your bag would feed many of the local people for the best part of a week.

If you notice their poverty, how can they fail to notice your wealth? The more well-attuned your social awareness, the more difficult it is to ignore that tourism is essentially rooted in this inequality. However, there are more problems than simply forcing people to come face to face with that particular reality.

Assimilating Values

It is not simply the disparity of economic influence which can affect tourist areas. Other factors such as the collapse of traditional lifestyles, values and moralities can also be influenced and eroded by contact with travellers from different lands. This issue is, however, a difficult one. As the age-old adage tells us "travel broadens the mind" and this is often taken to mean that by going to other countries and experiencing their ways, we become more open and accepting of doing things differently ourselves.

The problem is that this is, inevitably, a two-way street; if we are open to learn from the meetings we have with other cultures and societies on our travels, why should they be any the slower to assimilate some of our values? There will always be an element of the "grass always being greener" – but does that make a particular view any the more or less valid? In truth, the answer has to be "no" and in as much as from our perspective "they" remind "us" of what we have turned our backs on in the material west, then perhaps, at least for some, we may represent their aspirations.

In the west, social values are often more fluid and ill-defined, beyond the most broad of consensus; this model does not fit well alongside a more structured and traditional society and for those who do embrace the alien culture – however slightly – life can be difficult. One outcome is mounting dissatisfaction and disaffection; the other is the gradual disintegration of a way of life which in many cases was the reason tourists came in the first place.

Practical Issues

Some of the negative effects of tourism are much less philosophical. In many areas, crime increases dramatically during the tourist season, falling back to more usual levels when the visitors have all gone home. Although much of this will be targeted at the supposed easy pickings of the tourists themselves, it is not without its repercussions on the local population and the police and consular authorities on the ground.

In some places, the price of many staple foods and other essential items can be hiked up considerably to maximise the catch of tourist dollars, but this artificial inflation can often catch local people too – who often can least afford it.

In addition, in countries which are rich in wildlife and natural beauty, although initiatives to bring in tourists often contribute to parts of the local economy, by no means everyone benefits. It is also one of eco-tourism's greatest ironies that attempts to safeguard the environment can also make life worse for indigenous people, particularly if vast swathes of their traditional lands become part of a protected reserve.

There is a well established principle in science that you often alter the thing you observe just by the act of observing it. In many ways, tourism is no different– it is impossible to visit "untouched" lands without leaving your touch upon them, somehow. With many of the world's most beautiful and fragile ecosystems inhabited by some of the poorest people, it is inevitable that tourism throws the often conflicting environmental, economic and social forces into sharp relief. Much of the damage is unintentional; even if we try to live up to the responsible traveller's mantra of taking nothing but photographs and leaving nothing but footprints, sometimes the footprints we leave will be deeper than we think.

Tourism: Yesterday, Today and Tomorrow

Tourism, the act of paying money to go from one place to another to see different and unique sights, has been a fact of civilized life since approximately the 12th century. Of course, back in those days it was basically the upper, classes that had the time, the money, and the interest in travelling from one spot to another.

The word "travel" by the way comes from the medieval English word "travail" which means suffering great hardship, and that is a very good description of travel in its earliest days. Much has been written about the journeys of Marco Polo, who until recently was considered the world's first tourist.

Celebrated in books, movies, musicals and television specials in several countries, Marco Polo is today a hero in Italy and in China:

> *Venice named its airport after a beloved native son. There's the Marco Polo bridge outside Beijing, and no tourist to the Chinese capital in the 1980s was ever allowed to miss the Marco Polo Carpet Shop at the Temple of Heaven. Across Asia, in tributaries of the storied Old Silk Road that linked West and East, Polo's name beckons modern travellers to restaurants, hotels and souvenir shops.*

Now the question of whether Marco Polo actually did his famous travels has come up for hot dispute after a British Librarian, Frances Wood, published a small book called Did Marco Polo go to China?

In that, she uses vast research to cast doubts freedom to explore on their own (all for the investment of a little time, patience and gasoline). The advent of air travel in the 1930's heralded the true beginnings of what is called "tourism" today. Today's Travel for the Masses Data from the American Society of Travel Agents (ASTA) suggests that at any given moment of any given day, more than 2 million people around the world are in the process of travelling from one place to another.

Indeed, depending on whose figures one believes, the "tourism" industry worldwide can be said to range from $80 billion to $200 billion per year. Of course, these figures on the low side represent direct travel expenses (airfare, car rentals, train and bus travel, cruise ships, and so on) while the higher figures represent the addition of hotels, restaurants, entertainment, and "attendant revenue flows" into the local economies. At a summit meeting of congressional representatives and tourism industry leaders, the importance of tourism to the American economy was emphasized. There it was stated that "for many years, the United States was second only to France as the world's top tourist destination.

Environmental Impacts of Tourism Facilities

Tourism development usually starts with the construction of hotels, resorts and other places for tourists to stay. In addition there may be restaurants, night clubs, and recreation facilities such as golf courses, tennis courts, swimming pools, and marinas. These facilities require a lot of space, and land is usually scarce on an island.

Land and resources used for tourism are not available for other uses; developers may even want to keep local people away from beaches, reefs and lagoon areas reserved for tourists only. Whenever possible, tourism developers prefer to build on the coast, where the hotel will front on a beach and perhaps a coral reef, yet the coast is the most fragile and vulnerable area on an island, with the greatest conflicts between uses.

The construction of these facilities can have the same kinds of impacts as any other construction projects, such as soil erosion, changes in water runoff, and damage to natural environments. If the resort is on the coast, the plans frequently call for changes in the coastline, such as the creation or improvement of a beach, the construction of an artificial island, or the dredging of a harbour or building of a dock for tour boats to use to pick up and leave off the tourists.

These changes may upset normal coastal processes and be very difficult to maintain. Coastal hotel sites themselves are often vulnerable to storm damage, erosion and other problems because of their exposed location. Tourist developments also require resources that may be scarce on an island. Water may be in short supply, yet tourist use of water is usually much greater per person than among the local population. Tourists require large quantities of high quality food; if it cannot be produced locally, it will have to be imported.

The sewage from large hotels can be a source of pollution if it is not treated and disposed of carefully. Most hotel projects include waste water treatment plants, but these can be difficult to maintain in the islands and need to be monitored regularly. Tourist facilities also produce large amounts of solid waste which can add to the existing solid waste disposal problems on many islands.

Infrastructure Requirements

Any major tourist development requires a good airport where large jets can bring tourists from overseas countries. Visits by tour ships may require improved docking facilities. Roads may have to be built to resort sites, or improved for tour buses. Water and electricity supplies may have to be increased.

All these kinds of infrastructure require investments which must be added on to the direct cost of a tourism project. Building roads, airports and docks can have major environmental impacts which are beyond the scope of this unit. Their overall effects, however, may be positive as well as negative. Such facilities benefit local people as well as tourists, reducing the isolation of remote areas and increasing the convenience of travel within the country and overseas. Tourism development can thus support useful expenditures that could not be justified for the local people alone.

Damage from Tourist Use

Tourists are often unaware of how fragile some island environments are. They may trample vegetation and thus cause erosion, or disturb birds and wildlife. They may leave their rubbish behind, littering the environment. They are apt to break corals as the walk or swim over the reef. Even anchoring in a fragile reef area can result in significant damage to corals.

Tourists love to collect corals, shells and other pretty objects as souvenirs, but too much collecting can damage a reef or other site. Fishing is sport for a tourist, but it may take away resources needed as food in nearby villages. Where a few tourists may do little damage, thousands of them can be a disaster. Think of the difference between one tourist breaking off a piece of coral, and hundreds of tourists each taking a piece of coral; a reef could quickly be stripped of its corals and shells. Areas subject to heavy tourist pressure should be protected from damaging activities.

Laws may be needed to protect wildlife and to control collecting. The increasing demand for curios such as stuffed turtles, turtle shell jewellery, mounted butterflies, and traditional objects made with rare bird feathers or animal skins can threaten rare species with extinction. The manufacture and sale of such objects should be prohibited or strictly controlled. Coral, shells for handicrafts or collectors, and local trees used for carving can also be wiped out locally or reduced to low levels when too much is used to supply the tourist trade.

Planning Tourism Development

One major question to be answered in planning tourism development is what scale of tourism is appropriate for the local environment and culture. Every place has a carrying capacity that cannot be exceeded without bringing about serious changes or even the collapse of important resources or systems.

While some small-scale tourism can be fit in almost anywhere, large scale tourism can cause major problems if it is not planned very carefully. The number of tourists an area can absorb should be decided before tourism development goes to far, because there always will be pressures for bigger and bigger developments. The appropriate scale of tourism may be determined by the most limited resource, such as water or coastal land, or by the desire to prevent serious social or cultural impacts. How many people, for instance, can a community receive comfortably as visitors, or how would it feel to be outnumbered by the tourists on your own island?

Comprehensive Planning for Tourism

Unlike most development projects that only involve a specific site or area, tourism frequently depends to some extent on an entire country or island. It is therefore in the interest of the tourist industry to see that the overall planning of the country's development includes the requirements of tourism. As more governments begin environmental planning and make physical plans (including town plans, master plans and coastal zone plans), it is essential that these plans include the sites of particular scenic or recreational potential.

The coastlines, vistas, swimming beaches, waterfalls, mountains and lagoons that tourists visit and photograph are capital assets just like hotels, but they are generally not owned by the tourism interests that benefit from them. Only careful comprehensive planning, and often the understanding and support of the traditional owners, can protect these resources from degradation and destruction.

Planning helps in making choices between conflicting uses, or in finding ways to make them compatible. It should aim to locate unsightly or polluting activities, like industrial areas, fuel storage depots, rubbish dumps, etc., where they will not destroy the beauty of a town or coastline or conflict with tourist sites. In many island towns, there are already too many cases where urban pollution is making tourist beaches unsightly or unsafe. Planning early for tourism development can help to avoid damaging and expensive errors and also to prevent the gradual erosion of environmental values significant to tourism. Improvements that help tourism, like better transportation, tree planting, restoration of historic sites, urban beautification and cleanliness, also improve the environment for the local population. Tourism development can help to stimulate general community improvement.

6

Innovation in Eco-tourism

Angling Eco-tourism: Issues, Guidelines and Experience from Kamchatka

Recreational fishing is an important component of the tourism industry and an important component of regional economies around the world. When angling tourists reach threatened freshwater ecosystems, however, there is a risk of degrading the very fishery and landscapes that attracted them, thwarting long-term economic development prospects and reducing biodiversity. Following the emergence of catch-andrelease recreational fishing, we believe that angling can be legitimately considered a form of Eco-tourism that contributes positively to conservation, science, and local or regional economic development. With successful angling Eco-tourism projects, anglers and local populations can become viable constituencies for conservation. We describe the angler-sponsored research programme of the Kamchatka Steelhead Project as one case study where many aspects of a successful Eco-tourism project were present. We then propose guidelines for future angling Eco-tourism projects and address opportunities and obstacles to the continued development of angling Eco-tourism.

In the United States, over 34 million people participated in recreational angling and 29.4 million recreational fishing licenses were issued in 2001 (American Sportfishing Association, 2004; USFWS, 2002). The revenues from fishing licenses support fish and wildlife management agencies at all levels of government, and the expenditures from recreational fishing contribute to local and regional economies, especially in regions where fisheries have been preserved in pristine or near-pristine conditions. Recreational fishing in Alaska is a $1 billion per year industry, more than $500million of which comes in direct in-state expenditures, including money spent on guides, supplies, accommodations and provisions. More than 11,000 Alaskans are employed to support the recreational fishing industry, many of them in regions that are otherwise job-poor (American Sportfishing Association, 2003). The value of these expenditures is multiplied as funds ripple through regional economies.

Reviews of recreational fishing tourism tend to focus on the economic impact of anglers travelling from one location to another in search of quality angling experiences (Ditton et al., 2002). Other analyses, however, have argued that a fish caught by a recreational angler may be worth 40 times more to the economy than the same fish caught as part of a commercial harvest (Hayden, 2000). The 1994 value to British Columbia, Canada (consumer, worker and business surplus, plus government revenue) of its 431,000 commercially-caught chinook in that year has been calculated at CDN$8.2 million, while the value from 239,000 recreationally-caught fish has been calculated at CDN$96.5 million (Gislason, 2001). Well-regulated recreational fishing is an economically viable use of a natural resource that can be both lucrative and sustainable for local communities and ecosystems.

Despite its attractiveness as a vehicle for economic development and sustainability, recreational fishing ventures in vulnerable ecosystems like those of Alaska pose potentially serious ecological risks. Shortsighted choices made by tourism promoters and regulatory agencies in terms of lodging and transportation options, energy and resource use, visitor quotas, and fishing techniques can degrade fisheries and stress the ecological resources of water bodies. Practiced recklessly, recreational fishing can lead to overfishing just as commercial fishing can. In the United States, for example, the recreational fishing sector is responsible for 23% of landings of 'species of concern' (Coleman et al., 2004).

Promoting a sustainable model for angling Eco-tourism is in the interest of natural resource managers, environmentalists, tourism promotion agencies, and local communities. In parts of the world, recreational fishing may be the primary tourism attraction and, if pursued as Eco-tourism, could form a vital component of sustainable development. To date, the literature has not examined the acceptable forms of angling Eco-tourism and only one regional Eco-tourism certification body has issued guidelines (Nature's Best, Sweden). It would be wise to address and discuss the issues in a comprehensive way rather than wait for Eco-tourism certification bodies or entrepreneurs to take the lead.

Angling as Eco-tourism

Perhaps the two fundamental attractions of Eco-tourism are that it can contribute positively both to conservation efforts and to local economies (Honey, 1999). While angling tourism holds these potentials, the literature has not clarified the status of angling tourism in regards to Eco-tourism. The concept of Eco-tourism encompasses three primary dimensions: a focus on nature, sustainable management, and environmental education (Blamey, 2001). These aspects position Eco-tourism primarily as a subset of nature tourism and entirely as a subset of sustainable tourism (Weaver, 2001).

Traditionally, the limit to viewing angling as a form of Eco-tourism has focused on the character of its environmental impacts without engaging with the question of whether or not those impacts are sustainable over the long term. Fishing is typically viewed as a consumptive activity that provides products – though the status of catch and release fishing is uncertain – and the implicit argument is that non-consumptive activities, which provide experiences, have lower impacts and therefore should uniquely qualify as Eco-tourism (Weaver, 2001).

There are problems with using the consumptive/non-consumptive dichotomy to define Eco-tourism, however, since all tourism involves consumption on some level. Virtually all forms of tourism burn fossil fuels in transportation, produce cumulative impacts from visitor footprints, and use resources to produce souvenirs (Weaver, 2001). It would be more appropriate to place tourism activities along a continuum that examines the particular impacts of each activity in detail and acknowledges that most tourism activities provide both products and experiences (Vaske et al., 1982). It is likely that most capture fishing would fall closer to the consumptive side of this continuum, while catch and release fishing would lie nearer to the middle.

Other, similar criteria have also been proposed as essential points for Eco-tourism. Duffus and Dearden (1990) draw a line by examining the mindset of the participant and excluding activities where the goal is to remove an organism from the natural world. Fennell (2000) has argued for a 'moral principle' to be included in definitions of Eco-tourism that would identify activities 'founded upon respect for plants and animals'. These two subjective metrics, however, are problematic criteria for defining Eco-tourism due to their emphasis on process and intent rather than performance. If defined solely by process, Eco-tourism may look good on paper and yet still irreparably harm the environment, as has been seen in the attempts to certify Eco-tourism ventures (Honey & Rome, 2001) or in case studies of failed Eco-tourism ventures. Performance on the ground must be the defining criteria of Eco-tourism.

The major definitions of Eco-tourism, including those of Ceballos-Lascura'in, The Eco-tourism Society, the Eco-tourism Association of Australia, the National Eco-tourism Strategy of Australia, and Tickell (all quoted in Blamey, 2001), support this view by placing emphasis on sustainability and minimal impact rather than non-consumption per se. For example, The Eco-tourism Society's definition is 'responsible travel to natural areas which conserves the environment and improves the well-being of local people' (1991). The National Eco-tourism Strategy of Australia mentions that Eco-tourism is 'managed to be ecologically sustainable', which involves an 'appropriate return to the local community and long-term conservation of the resource' (Allcock et al., 1994). Honey (1999) argues that, while generally nonconsumptive, Eco-tourism can include consumptive activities such as hunting if they are 'sustainable industries based on renewable resources'. Recreational fishing can be a sustainable industry when pursued responsibly. Without ignoring the poor status of overfished species, there exist many fish populations around the world that are healthy and can support smallscale extraction in ways that will not diminish future population health. For the purposes of angling Eco-tourism, the emergence and widespread acceptance of catch-and-release recreational fishing has created an unprecedented opportunity. Valuable sport fisheries in both saltwater and freshwater have recently been converted primarily to catch-and-release. By regulation, the most accessible and popular wild steelhead fisheries in British Columbia are managed on a catch-and-release basis (Hooton, 2002a).

Other advances in angler ethics also contribute to the potential sustainability of recreational fishing. The National Marine Fisheries Service Code of Angling Ethics, developed with the participation of both angling groups and conservationists, specifies limiting catch to the desired species and size and using techniques that minimise harm to fish when releasing them (NMFS, 1999).

These approaches include many techniques. Fly hooks, for example, typically catch in the periphery of a fish's jaws or mouth and produce less damage than the deeper hookings of lures and, in particular, bait. Post-release mortality rates in steelhead fisheries in British Columbia, Canada, range from 10% for bait fishing and 3% for lures to 1% for fly-fishing (Hooton, 2002b). Reduced exposure to air (under 30 seconds for), handling with wet hands, and reduced 'playing' with a fish are also thought to decrease mortality rates in catch and release fishing (Catch and Release Foundation, 2001; Hooton, 2002b). Avoiding the use of non-native species as live bait and unwashed fishing gear in multiple waters can lower the risk of disease and invasive species being introduced into a river.

More generally, several practices can reduce angler 'efficiency' (catch per unit effort), including the avoidance of bait, fishing from shore rather than boats, flyfishing rather than spincasting, and using barbless hooks. For example, the probability of capture in flyfishing may be as low as one-fifth that of bait fishing. By reducing the number of fish caught per angler, a river's carrying capacity can support a larger number of fishermen, thereby providing a greater economic opportunity for the region. With healthy populations and moderate levels of fishing, the inevitable impacts on fish populations may be minimal and sustainable for the natural ecosystems in which a recreational fishing Eco-tourism operation occurs.

Beyond environmental sustainability, however, Eco-tourism's concept of sustainable management includes economic and social considerations. Minimising negative impacts is an identifying aspect of sustainable tourism, while Eco-tourism is additionally expected to contribute positively to conservation and local economies.

With this in mind, recreational fishing Eco-tourism presents particular opportunities to enhance conservation activities and local communities through new and alternative revenue streams. Fishing permits, a concept with which anglers are familiar, provide a straightforward method to raise funds for conservation or economic development, while park fees are an alternative method. The intensely local experience of fishing in a given water body has the potential to convince tourists to make direct donations for local conservation efforts if such channels are readily available. These donations can be facilitated and encouraged by travel operations.

Similar to many other forms of Eco-tourism, recreational fishing trips are often guided. Properly trained, these guides and other staff can be hired from local communities. Products and services for the fishing operation can be procured locally to maximise local economic impact. Where the infrastructure or capacity to provide tourism services and products locally does not exist, tourism operators can assist in developing these capabilities.

In Costa Rica, tourists practicing catch and release angling for billfish spent $17.8 million in the 1993–1994 season (Ditton & Grimes, 1995). British Columbia's Skeena River steelhead fishery, also managed on a catch and relase basis, is worth at least $1.9 million per year. The Togiak National Wildlife Refuge in Alaska provides more than 50 jobs and contributes more than $1.5 million to the local economy. Properly managed and practiced, recreational fishing Eco-tourism has a great potential to contribute positively to conservation and local development efforts while engaging in a sustainable activity. Implementing Eco-tourism on the ground, however, may be a complex task.

Case Study: Kamchatka Steelhead Project

Kamchatka is a 1250 km peninsula in the far east of the Russian Federation, bordered to the east by the Pacific Ocean and to the west by the Sea of Okhotsk. Economic development on this remote peninsula has been sparse due to historical isolation of the region under the Soviet Union, and large areas of the peninsula have been left relatively wild. Poaching is widespread, however, in part due to high unemployment rates, and constitutes a major threat to the health of certain salmon runs. Oil and gas development, which would pose a serious threat to salmon habitat, is being considered as an economic development strategy. There are few plans for the sustainable use of regional renewable resources, and Eco-tourism has been called the 'best opportunity for an environmentally sustainable industry employing a broad range of local people' (Newell, 2004). In the early to mid-1990s, however, tourism infrastructure was either scarce or non-existent.

From 1994–2003, a partnership between the Wild Salmon Centre (Portland, Oregon, USA), and the Ichthyology Department of Moscow State University (Moscow, Russia) operated an angler-sponsored scientific research programme on the Kamchatka peninsula. The Flathead Lake Biological Station of the University of Montana (Missoula, Montana, USA) also joined this effort in later years.

The angler-sponsored programme was designed to fund scientific expeditions and was one of the pioneers in bringing paying foreigners to the peninsula. Before its transfer in 2002 to an independent non-profit, the angler-sponsor programme was part of the Kamchatka Steelhead Project (KSP), a 20-year research effort dedicated to the study and conservation of Kamchatka's Oncorhynchus (parasalmo) mykiss – both the anadromous steelhead (syomga) and resident rainbow trout (mikizha) life histories. The steelhead and other salmonids of Kamchatka are unique for their large sizes, healthy populations, and wide range of life histories. Some individual river systems in Kamchatka host as many as six species of Pacific salmon, plus grayling, varieties of trout, and three species of char. In total, the rivers of Kamchatka are believed to serve as the spawning grounds for as much as one-quarter of Pacific salmon stocks. Numerous human communities rely upon these healthy salmon stocks, as do half of the global population of Steller's sea eagles, the world's largest population of brown bears, and 1800 Steller's sea lions.

Participants in the programme included scientists from the United States and Russia and conservation-minded anglers from the United States and elsewhere. Anglers supported the conservation mission both by funding the scientific research and by directly assisting in the collection of biological samples through catch and release fly-fishing. This is a method shown to have low post-release mortality in steelhead. After an angler caught a fish, the angler and researchers collected data on length, girth, weight, sex, scales (to determine life history), and tissue samples for genetic and protein analysis. Individual fish were tagged to track migrations and determine population structure.

The logistics of bringing visitors to Kamchatka were, and remain, complex, but can provide many opportunities for economic benefits to accrue at the regional and local levels, if properly planned. Anglers flew on Magadan Air, a regionally-owned airline for whom the programme was a major client. Anglers typically spent one night during the trip in a hotel in Petropavlosk-Kamchatskiy, the capital of Kamchatka. Due to the remoteness of the region, Russian helicopters were used extensively for transport to and from fishing lodges. The camps and lodges were small in scale and were Russian-owned. Local outfitters ran the trips in Kamchatka and cooks were hired locally, while guides came from Russia and the United States.

As local guides' language and service skills did not meet client expectations, the programme began to train guides from a pool of current students and graduates of the English language faculty of a local university. These efforts built critical local capacity for tourism. However, guide training did not emphasise natural history and guides typically placed little emphasis on education while in the field. From 1994–2003, more than 600 angler-sponsors participated in expeditions supporting the Kamchatka Steelhead Project. At the programme's peak in 2002, an estimated $650,000 in one year was contributed to the economy of the Kamchatka Peninsula through expenditures on local outfitters, helicopter transportation, and field expenses (Klimenko, 2004). Trip costs were high, making this a relatively elite activity, but such expenses may be unavoidable in areas of the world where travel and logistical costs are significant. High accessibility costs are also undoubtedly a key factor in the health of the studied steelhead populations.

The programme's major scientific advances include the discovery of five distinct life histories of O. mykiss in Western Kamchatka and the observation of anadromous O. mykiss parents producing resident rainbow trout offspring, and vice versa. Scientific papers were published from this project in the Journal of Ichthyology and other leading Russian and international journals. In addition, the presence of anglers and scientists on remote salmon-rich rivers during the spawning season caused reductions in illegal poaching for caviar, the primary threat to these salmon populations.

Environmental impacts of the programme included the heavy reliance on air travel, a necessity given the landscape but also an energy-intensive mode of travel. Lodge construction involved the installation of helicopter pads and other landscape modifications. Power at the lodges was produced with diesel generators, the fuel for which also had to be flown in. The project conducted feasibility studies into renewable sources of energy, including wind, solar and micro-hydro, but was not able to implement any of these proposals due to high costs.

Overall, however, environmental impacts would be considered low, primarily due to the small size of the angling and research operations and the efforts made to spread trips out over the fishing season and over the length of the river. On the healthy rivers where the trips occurred, mortality due to catch and release fly-fishing was not a significant factor. In the rare cases of direct steelhead mortality, the fish were taken for full laboratory analyses as part of the expedition's mortality take quota, issued by the Federal Ministry of Natural Resources. Cultural impacts were also low or non-existent, though in this case a key factor was the isolation of tourists in wilderness areas.

Kamchatka Steelhead Project's angler-sponsored research programme offers one case study of a partnership between conservation groups, research teams, anglers, and local organisations that may serve as a valuable model for future angling Eco-tourism operations. Such operations would need to more fully implement educational and interpretive aspects to be considered Eco-tourism, however. While the Kamchatka project model may not be appropriate in all contexts, it demonstrates angling with a strong conservation science orientation, firm standards for environmental protection, partnerships between diverse groups, and progress towards sustainable development and local community involvement. The project produced tangible benefits to conservation through discouragement of poaching activities, increased knowledge about salmon and steelhead biology, donations to a conservation non-profit, support for local economic development through outfitter payments, and increased local and worldwide visibility for the threats facing a globally-important ecosystem. Potential future donors to Kamchatka conservation efforts were also identified.

With this case study as an innovative example, angling Eco-tourism has to potential to make a viable contribution to both regional economic development and social and environmental sustainability.

Guidelines for Angling Eco-tourism

To assist in the development of new Eco-tourism ventures and to evaluate operations marketed as Eco-tourism, many certification and eco-labelling programmes have been developed over the past decades, including over 250 voluntary initiatives around the world.

In referring to codes of conduct, a similar concept, Issaverdis (2001) commented that these initiatives can 'play a part in the overall continuum of developing industry professionalism and can be a useful means of introducing standards to sectors of the tourism industry'.

All such efforts must be based on firm standards and guidelines, but to date, angling Eco-tourism standards do not exist in the literature and the only Eco-tourism body to issue angling Eco-tourism certification criteria – in Swedish – is Nature's Best (The Swedish Eco-tourism Association and The Swedish Travel and Tourism Council, 2002a). Given the vast numbers of angling tourists, standards are a pressing concern.

Any guidelines should flow naturally from the definitions of Eco-tourism. Greater direction, however, can be found in expanded descriptions such as Honey's (1999) eight characteristics of Eco-tourism: (1) involves travel to natural sites; (2) minimises impact; (3) builds environmental awareness; (4) provides direct financial benefits for conservation; (5) provides financial benefits and empowerment for local communities; (6) respects local culture; (7) is sensitive to the host country's political environment and social climate; and (8) supports human rights and international labour agreements. A comparable example is the six overarching criteria of the successful Nature's Best Eco-tourism certification programme in Sweden: (1) respect the limitations of the destination – minimise negative impact in nature and culture; (2) support the local economy; (3) make all the company's operations environmentally sustainable; (4) contribute actively to conservation; (5) promote the joy of discovery, knowledge and respect; and (6) quality and safety all the way through (The Swedish Eco-tourism Association and The Swedish Travel and Tourism Council, 2002a).

Out of the above and other examples, we distilled the following six primary areas that guidelines should address in describing angling Eco-tourism.

Nature Experience

While many recreational fishing tourism operations will focus on catching large fish and/or many fish, an Eco-tourism operation needs to take a broader perspective and view the fish within the complex ecosystem needed for their survival. By building clients' appreciation for the beauty and complexity of these ecosystems through direct fishing experiences, Eco-tourism can enlist their support for place-based conservation efforts. Client expectations, impressions, and lessons are shaped from the moment they choose an Eco-tourism programme, and therefore Eco-tourism operations need to have clear objectives from their first interaction with potential clients (Gruin & Rogers, 2004).

Location

Tourism operations are centered around direct experiences and appreciation of fresh or salt water ecosystems and their native fish.

Marketing

Trips are advertised and sold to clients explicitly as angling Eco-tourism trips or as angling Eco-tourism components in broader tourism packages.

Education and Interpretation

Education is a central aspect of many Eco-tourism definitions due to its power to build an 'intellectual, emotional and even spiritual connection between people and places' (Weiler & Ham, 2001). In all interactions, operators should accurately describe the ecosystem in which anglers will be fishing as well as the cultures of surrounding areas.

Education can occur through direct interactions between clients and guides, as well as through reading materials, maps, and poster boards. Fish are important components of many aquatic ecosystems and anglers should be informed of the many processes that contribute to a healthy ecosystem – salmon for example support terrestrial ecosystems by carrying marine nutrients upstream during their spawning migrations (Cederholm et al., 1999).

In order to build future stewards, clients should be informed of the major threats to ecosystems and cultures, the conservation efforts being conducted in the area, and what they can do to help these efforts. As fishing guides will likely be a client's primary contact in an angling Eco-tourism operation, guide training is a critical aspect of a high-quality experience.

Training pertinent to the broader goals of Eco-tourism will be especially important in the angling Eco-tourism sector, since guides will likely come from a recreational fishing background where the traditional focus is typically more tightly restricted to catching numerous large fish.

Knowledge Sharing

Tourism operators share their knowledge of local ecosystems and cultures, and the knowledge of other competent bodies, with customers before and during operations in order to build awareness, respect, and a sense of stewardship.

Guide Training

Guides are trained in the natural history of the area, local cultures, and sustainable tour operating techniques.

Environmentally-sustainable Operations

It is important to understand whether a particular water body is appropriate for angling Eco-tourism and to know the level of angling that the ecosystem can support sustainably. The case study demonstrated how consultation with independent biologists and non-governmental conservation groups can help in finding answers to these questions. Government biologists can also provide assistance.

We suggest setting overall fish mortality limits for the tourism sector in order to avoid 'tragedy of the commons' situations where cumulative impacts from individuals add together to far exceed an ecosystem's carrying capacity. For ease of application, limits should be set by species and water basin – or other appropriate stock definitions – and businesses should coordinate with other tour operators in the area to remain within those limits. Fish mortality is the sum of all killed fish as well as expected mortalities from released fish given relevant mortality rates.

Tour operators and regulatory agencies also need to recognise the cumulative impacts of visitors and limit overall numbers to what the ecosystem can withstand without adverse effects (Honey, 1999). In recreational fisheries more intensively used than those in the case study, an effective regulatory, compliance, and enforcement regime may be necessary to ensure that angling and other activities are sustainably managed. A limited entry fishery may be necessary, whether imposed by the government through the issuance of permits or self-enforced among tour operators in the region. These tactics limit impact on the fishery and, when enforced through permits, generate revenue for management agencies.

Both the case study and the earlier discussion of recreational fishing as a sustainable activity provided examples of angling techniques that can be employed in angling Eco-tourism. As one of possibly a variety of techniques, catch and release flyfishing provides a proven method to ensure broad angling opportunities while limiting harm to hooked fish. More generally, several practices were discussed that can reduce angler efficiency, harm to released fish, and the spread of disease and invasive species. Locally applicable laws and guidelines should also be followed as a minimum but often not sufficient step towards sustainable operations (The Swedish Eco-tourism Association and The Swedish Travel and Tourism Council, 2002b) Implementing all of these techniques may require extensive angler education. More generally, angling Eco-tourism operations, as for all Eco-tourism operations, need to conduct their general operations in an environmentally sustainable manner with minimal negative impact (Blamey, 2001). The infrastructure required for recreational fishing operations typically includes lodges, transportation, and, at times, remote field camps. Minimising impacts may require the use of four-stroke rather than two-stroke engines on motorboats, energy efficiency and energy conservation in lodging, renewable energy generation, recycling plans, and the use of environmentally-friendly alternatives to conventional fuels and chemicals.

Planning Businesses and management agencies know the status of fish populations in their region of operation and the threats to these populations. Businesses operate within biological limits so that impacts from recreational fishing Eco-tourism will be minimal and sustainable given other pressures on the populations.

Angling Practices

All fish are caught and handled usingmethods that limit fish injury and mortality to minimal and sustainable levels. Anglers abide by applicable fisheries laws and regulations.

General Operations

All aspects of the Eco-tourism operation are conducted so as to minimise the consumption of natural resources and reduce the production of waste and pollution.

Respect for Local Cultures

For indigenous and local cultures around the world, fishing has played important subsistence, economic, and cultural roles. The annual migrations of salmon, for example, have structured societies from the Ainu in Japan to the Tlingit in Alaska (Roche & McHutchison, 1998). Cultural aspects may provide a rich way to connect angler tourists to the traditions of an area or to learn about sustainable use. By the same token, tourism operations need to respect traditional customs surrounding fish and local community needs for fish resources. In Alaska, many native and non-native households continue to rely on locally available food for 'essential economic, nutritional, cultural and social benefits' (Kelso, 1982). The complexities involved in cultural matters will require careful cooperation between tour operators and local or indigenous communities. The most effective dialogues will likely begin early in the Eco-tourism planning process.

Interaction with Cultures

Operators and clients are respectful of local and indigenous traditions and needs regarding fish, land, and other resources.

Angling Eco-tourism in Kamchatka

Contribution to Conservation, Monitoring, and Research

The Eco-tourism concept includes the need to actively support conservation efforts (Blamey, 2001; Honey, 1999). This can occur through fees, business donations, and client donations, as well through participation in rehabilitation projects or scientific monitoring (Blamey, 2001).

As many recreational anglers are used to buying fishing permits, fees may be a particularly applicable method for governments or resource management agencies to raise funds for conservation. The case study showed, however, that the tour operator is probably not the appropriate actor to levy these fees. A more productive example for tour operator contributions may be a formula whereby businesses donate a percentage of yearly profits to conservation programmes (Alaska Wildland Adventures, 2004). This strategy requires strong partnerships with local conservation groups. The case study showed how this can occur when such groups are included in planning from the outset. In most parts of the world, a large opportunity also exists for angling Eco-tourism to participate directly in fisheries monitoring and research. Even in the United States, where a large agency structure supports fisheries data collection, information on recreational fisheries and fish populations are lacking (Donofrio, 2004). Throughout Far Eastern Russia, where the case study was located, scientific work is only just beginning to examine salmon distribution and population trends in many river basins (Augerot, in press). By enlisting angling Eco-tourism operations as partners in ecosystem monitoring, conservation efforts can gain access to more of the information they need to accomplish their goals.

Given the decentralised nature of tour operators, it seems unlikely that an appropriate data collection protocol will be developed or data aggregated in meaningful ways without cooperation between tour operators and scientists in the academic, non-governmental, or governmental sector. Preferably, all angling Eco-tourism operators in an area would participate in the same program using common standards, metrics, and data reporting formats. Data collection will likely include keeping accurate and thorough records of the size, weight, sex, and species of the fish caught and reporting data to the appropriate groups. These catch statistics are also important for evaluating an operation's environmental impacts (The Swedish Eco-tourism Association and The Swedish Travel and Tourism Council, 2002b).

Conservation

Tour operators support local conservation efforts through donations and cooperation and as well as by informing anglers about conservation organisations.

Monitoring and Research

Tour operators and guides work in cooperation with academic researchers, conservation groups, and/or government scientists to monitor and research fish populations and other environmental indicators. Accurate catch statistics are maintained.

Contribution to Local Economies

Eco-tourism can contribute to local economies in many ways, including foreign exchange earnings, employment, infrastructure development, longterm economic stability, and economic diversification (Blamey, 2001).

Preferential purchasing of local goods and services along with opportunities for residents to directly market crafts and other products to visitors can also play a part of these efforts. In the case study, Eco-tourism provided an alternative source of employment for communities that were turning to destructive practices such as poaching. Eco-tourism can thus provide a strong economic incentive for resource protection (Blamey, 2001). By demonstrating the economic value of a sustainably used resource, Eco-tourism can lead local communities to value healthy ecosystems and waters rich with fish (The Swedish Eco-tourism Association and The Swedish Travel and Tourism Council, 2002b).

Ideally, Eco-tourism must also contribute to the transfer of economic and political control to the local scale, a difficult and time-consuming process (Honey, 1999). In the case study, small steps were made in this direction by training guides locally. Local and/or indigenous involvement in Eco-tourism operations and planning is an important component of building capacity and sustainable development.

Local Residents

Significant economic benefits from angling Eco-tourism operations accrue to local residents in a manner that builds local support for resource protection.

Opportunities and Challenges for Angling Eco-tourism

As both recreational fishing and tourism expand in economically and ecologically important fisheries worldwide, the need to define angling Eco-tourism grows more pressing. It is necessary to set a high standard that recognises the need to conserve ecosystems and sets limits on the overall impact of anglers. In addition to promoting conservation and benefiting local economies, that high standard will add value for environmentally-conscious tourism operators and recreational fishing guides by enabling them to selectively market their services to discriminating customers and charge premium prices on the basis of a fishery's environmental attributes.

Despite these promising opportunities, there are challenges looming in the near future. Should the term 'angling Eco-tourism' or 'recreational fishing Eco-tourism' enter into common usage, it is likely that many tour operators and recreational fishing guides will use it in promotional material. Many of them will be sincere and diligent in their desire to minimise environmental impacts and promote conservation, but some will not.

As the vernacular of environmentalism has grown more prevalent, the number of travellers on ecotours has increased, but the conservation missions, ecological integrity of nature sites, and environmental education components have all been diminished (Honey, 1999). Travel industry 'greenwashing' of conventional tourism has devalued the market worth of Eco-tourism organisations and sustainably managed tour companies, crowding some out of the market.

In certain pristine and hitherto-remote regions, Eco-tourism has even served as a Trojan horse – attracting sustainable levels of tourism at first, before conventional mass tourism operations respond to growing demand (Butler, 1990).

Predictably, the environmental and social infrastructure of a region can be quickly stressed and degraded by increased numbers of visitors. Kamchatka is not currently subject to these demands, but some recreational fisheries of Alaska and British Columbia already suffer from overfishing and habitat degradation. Examples of degradation include erosion on riverbanks, noise pollution from motorboats, and improper disposal of human waste.

At the same time, regions wishing to use angling Eco-tourism as a form of economic development need to understand the limitations on the market for world-class angling tourism on the scale enjoyed by areas like Alaska. A clear attraction needs to be present, such as the steelhead in Kamchatka or the giant king salmon of the Kenai River in Alaska. When logistics are more complex or when tourists must travel larger distances for fishing, the cost of transportation will limit the potential tourism market to wealthier individuals. Certain regions may want to focus on local angling Eco-tourism markets, rather than trying to compete at the international scale. Regardless of the scale, angling Eco-tourism should almost always be considered in the context of a broader Eco-tourism development strategy that includes a diversity of Eco-tourism forms such as wildlife watching, photographic expeditions, adventure trips, agritourism, and ethnotourism.

For angling Eco-tourism to avoid the pitfalls encountered by other Eco-tourism ventures, conservation groups, fisheries regulatory agencies, local communities, and tourism operators must cooperate early and operate in good faith. They cannot expect the problems and possible contradictions of angling Eco-tourism to be solved from the outside. While certification bodies provide general Eco-tourism guidelines, the specifics of angling Eco-tourism remain largely ignored. For angling Eco-tourism to mature from a vague, looselyapplied concept to a thoughtfully implemented practice, carefully formulated standards and guidelines will be needed. As angling tourism expands, it brings with it not only great opportunities, but threats to sensitive and ecologically valuable fisheries worldwide. In the case study we present, anglers played an active role in advancing the scientific understanding of the salmonid fisheries of Kamchatka. Not only did the lowimpact angling fund the activity of fisheries conservation groups, but it directly contributed to data-gathering and environmental monitoring of the fishery. This study is only one of many possible examples, however, and more work is needed to examine fully the various challenges and opportunities presented by angling Eco-tourism.

To provide better clarity to the angling Eco-tourism concept, we propose guidelines for this activity designed specifically to minimise environmental impacts, generate support for local economic development, and contribute directly to conservation. Our specific principles are applicable in a range of ecosystems and emphasise the need for cooperation between stakeholders.

While angling Eco-tourism is an exciting and highly promising venture, it faces threats and challenges discussed above, particularly the danger of 'greenwashing' and the use of the Eco-tourism label to promote conventional, unsustainable angling tourism. For angling Eco-tourism to succeed, there is a pressing need to set high standards and coordinate the actions of all stakeholders. All parties will play integral roles in making angling Eco-tourism a valid and vital tool for science, conservation and sustainable development.

Angling in India

The Indian Himalayas are an ideal for sport fishing. Anglers from all over the world come to the Indian rivers to try and hook the Himalayan Rainbow trout or the mighty Mahaseer. Good fishing is possible in the north of the country on the Ganga, Kali rivers for mahseer and on the Tirthan, Tons and Sainj rivers for trout. In the east of the country, rivers like the Kameng, Teesta, Brahmaputra etc. provide excellent angling opportunities.

India with its dozens of rivers and thousands of streams, offers vast opportunities for fishing and angling. Whether you're a first time angler or an expert angler,-India's waters, both fresh and salt, can be a pleasant surprise for you. The country has an estimated 50,000 km of waters-rivers, streams, and lakes included-and an additional 3,000 km of coastline. There's definitely a lot of scope for some satisfying angling in India. Major rivers like the Ganga and its tributaries, the Yamuna, the Brahmaputra, the Mahanadi, the Krishna and the Kaveri are home to a wide spectrum of fish, including mahseer, rohu, katli, and trout. The coastal waters caressing the shorelines of India harbour marine fish like-mackerel, marlin and sea bass.

In India, most major cities lie along the rivers, as a result finding a fishing zone is generally not a problem. In addition to this, most states have well-organised Departments of Fisheries, where special breeding areas assure that there's always a gene pool of local and exotic fish. Fish sanctuaries and breeding grounds in Jammu and Kashmir, Himachal Pradesh, Uttar Pradesh and other states through which major rivers flow, conserve a vast stock of fish which are specially bred for re-stocking rivers.

Licenses and Permits

Fishing licenses are mandatory for all anglers. Go to the concerned official before you throw your line into the water, or else you will be penalised for not having the fishing license. In most cases, fishing licenses are not issued during the monsoon (when most fish species breed); in addition, most licenses are issued for only a specified stretch of water.

Furthermore, there are conditions that all fish caught must be released into the water, and anglers are restricted to catch a specified number of fish per day you can get the license from the Fisheries Department of the state where you have come for angling.

Foreigners, who are head towards the Lakshadweep or Andaman & Nicobar Islands for fishing & angling, will need a permit from the Ministry of Home Affairs in New Delhi-or an authorised official in the state. The same applies to certain areas of Himachal Pradesh, Jammu and Kashmir and other border states.

Things to Bring

The basic fishing equipment required includes rods, lines, hooks, reel, flies, spinners, spoons and bait-in the form of worms, paste or other lure. Light, waterproof clothing-brown or green in colour-is essential, as are waterproof shoes or light sandals which can easily be slipped off to drain out sand or water. Sunscreen, a light hat and dark glasses are necessary, and during the winter make sure you're well clad with sufficient woollens and a macintosh. Some travel agencies and tour operators in India provides everything from equipment and experienced guides to boarding, lodging and transportation to the anglers.

Some Best Zones for Anglers

The main river expanse suitable for angling are in the lower Himalayas, the Satpuras, and the Aravalis, all of which have rivers teeming with a broad range of fishes. India's rivers acquire about 31 species of freshwater fish which are of interest to anglers; these include trout (brown and rainbow trout, both introduced species); murrel, catfish and cyprinids.

Agritourism

Agritourism, as it is defined most broadly, involves any agriculturally-based operation or activity that brings visitors to a farm or ranch. Agritourism has different definitions in different parts of the world, and sometimes refers specifically to farm stays, as in Italy. Elsewhere, agritourism includes a wide variety of activities, including buying produce direct from a farm stand, navigating a corn maze, picking fruit, feeding animals, or staying at a B&B on a farm. Agritourism is a form of niche tourism that is considered a growth industry in many parts of the world, including Australia, Canada, the United States, and the Philippines. Agritourism overlaps with geotourism, Eco-tourism, and culinary tourism. Other terms associated with agritourism are "agritainment", "value added products," "farm direct marketing", and "sustainable agriculture".

Agritourism in the United States

Agritourism is widespread in America. Agritourists can choose from a wide range of activities that include picking fruits and vegetables, riding horses, tasting honey, learning about wine and cheesemaking, or shopping in farm gift shops and farm stands for local and regional produce or hand-crafted gifts.

According the USDA, Cooperative State, Education and Extension Service, "Tourism is becoming increasingly important to the U.S. economy. A conservative estimate from the Federal Reserve Board in Kansas, based on 2000 data, shows that basic travel and tourism industries accounted for 3.6 percent of all U.S. employment. Even more telling, data from the Travel Industry Association of America indicate that 1 out of every 18 people in the U.S. has a job directly resulting from travel expenditures."

Through the Small Farm Centre at the University of California, "Agricultural tourism or agritourism, is one alternative for improving the incomes and potential economic viability of small farms and rural communities. Some forms of agritourism enterprises are well developed in California, including fairs and festivals. Other possibilities still offer potential for development." The UC Small Farm Centre has developed a California Agritourism Database that "provides visitors and potential entrepreneurs with information about existing agritourism locations throughout the state." In Western North Carolina, the organization HandMade in America is using agritourism to develop their local economy and craft trades, and to educate visitors about agriculture practices. On the web site, *Hand Made in America,* they look at agritourism as a "... niche market [that] not only assists communities with solutions to help diversify their economic base, but it also helps our regional urban centres and increasingly suburban populations to understand the important role that farming and rural life plays in our history, by highlighting the need for it in our contemporary society. Agri-tourism projects reinforce the need to support local growers and sources and allow the visitor to experience what it is to be part of the land..."

The publication *Promoting Tourism in Rural America* explains the need for planning and marketing your rural community and weighing the pros and cons of tourism. According to the publication, local citizen participation is helpful and should be included in starting any kind of a tourism program. Citizen participation in planning tourism can contribute to buliding a successful program that enhances the community.

Additional websites that promote and publicize agritourism in the United States include Rural Bounty, founded by agritourism consultant Jane Eckert, Sleep in the Hay, a nationwide directory of farm stays, and Farm Stay USA, a blog that profiles farm stays and tracks agritourism news.

Reasons for Popularity

People have become more interested in how their food is produced. They want to meet farmers and processers and talk with them about what goes into food production. For many people who visit farms, especially children, the visit marks the first time they see the source of their food, be it a dairy cow, an ear of corn growing in the field, or an apple they can pick right off the tree.

Agritourism was featured in the satirical NBC television comedy series *The Office* in the episode entitled "Money" from season . The character Dwight Schrute lives on a beet farm, and in this episode reveals that he has opened a B&B in his farmhouse. The characters Jim and Pam proceed to visit the farm, where they choose the "irrigation" themed room. They choose to participate in various farm activities, including plowing the fields, making wine from beets, and watching a table making demonstration. In the episode, Dwight explains that Trip Advisor is the lifeblood of the agritourism industry. The episode portrayed agritourism in a somewhat unappealing light, as Dwight's beet farm and rural lifestyle are often objects of ridicule on the show. Still, the episode brought the concept of agritourism to the show's many viewers.

Dude Ranches

Dude (or guest) ranches offer tourists the chance to work on cattle ranches, and sometimes participate in cattle drives. The fact sheet, *Promoting the Farm and Ranch Recreation Business*, gives farmers and ranchers information on marketing and developing strategies to win tourism dollars. Dude ranches are common in the United States and Australian Outback.

Eco-tourism

'Eco-tourism' (also known as ecological tourism) is responsible travel to fragile, pristine, and usually protected areas that strives to be low impact and (often) small scale. It purports to educate the traveller; provide funds for conservation; directly benefit the economic development and political empowerment of local communities; and foster respect for different cultures and for human rights. Eco tourism is held as important by those who participate in it so that future generations may experience aspects of the environment relatively untouched by human intervention. Most serious studies of Eco-tourism including several university programs now use this as the working definition.

Eco-tourism appeals to ecologically and socially conscious individuals. Generally speaking, it focuses on volunteering, personal growth and environmental responsibility. It typically involves travel to destinations where flora, fauna, and cultural heritage are the primary attractions. One of the goals of Eco-tourism is to offer tourists insight into the impact of human beings on the environment, and to foster a greater appreciation of our natural habitats.

Responsible Eco-tourism includes programs that minimize the negative aspects of conventional tourism on the environment and enhance the cultural integrity of local people. Therefore, in addition to evaluating environmental and cultural factors, an integral part of Eco-tourism is the promotion of recycling, energy efficiency, water conservation, and creation of economic opportunities for local communities.

Criteria

Eco-tourism is a form of tourism that involves traveling to tranquil and unpolluted natural areas. According to the definition and principles of Eco-tourism established by The International Eco-tourism Society (TIES) in 1990, Eco-tourism is "Responsible travel to natural areas that conserves the environment and improves the well-being of local people." (TIES, 1990). Martha Honey, expands on the TIES definition by describing the seven characteristics of Eco-tourism, which are:

- Involves travel to natural destinations.
- Minimizes impact.
- Builds environmental awareness.
- Provides direct financial benefits for conservation.
- Provides financial benefits and empowerment for local people.
- Respects local culture.
- Supports human rights and democratic movements.

Ideally, Eco-tourism should satisfy several criteria, such as:

- conservation of biological diversity and cultural diversity through ecosystem protection
- promotion of sustainable use of biodiversity, by providing jobs to local populations
- sharing of socioeconomic benefits with local communities and indigenous peoples by having their informed consent and participation in the management of Eco-tourism enterprises
- tourism to unspoiled natural resources, with minimal impact on the environment being a primary concern.
- minimization of tourism's own environmental impact
- affordability and lack of waste in the form of luxury
- local culture, flora and fauna being the main attractions.

For many countries, Eco-tourism is not simply a marginal activity to finance protection of the environment, but is a major industry of the national economy. For example, in Costa Rica, Ecuador, Nepal, Kenya, Madagascar and Antarctica, Eco-tourism represents a significant portion of the gross domestic product and economic activity. The concept of Eco-tourism is widely misunderstood and in practice is often used as a marketing tool to promote tourism that is related to nature. This is an especially frequent malpractice in the realm of Jungle tourism. Critics claim that these greenwashing practices, carried out in the name of Eco-tourism, often consist of placing a hotel in a splendid landscape, to the detriment of the ecosystem. According to them, Eco-tourism must above all sensitize people to the beauty and the fragility of nature. They condemn some operators as greenwashing their operations: using the labels of "green" and "eco-friendly", while behaving in environmentally irresponsible ways. Although academics disagree about who can be classified as an ecotourist and there is little statistical data, some estimate that more than five million ecotourists-the majority of the ecotourist population-come from the United States, with many others from Western Europe, Canada and Australia. Currently, there are various moves to create national and international Eco-tourism accreditation programs, although the process is also controversial. National Eco-tourism certification programs have been put in place in countries such as Costa Rica, Australia, Kenya and Sweden.

Eco-tourism, responsible tourism, jungle tourism, and sustainable development have become prevalent concepts since the late 1980s, and Eco-tourism has experienced arguably the fastest growth of all sub-sectors in the tourism industry. The popularity represents a change in tourist perceptions, increased environmental awareness, and a desire to explore natural environments. At times, such changes become as much a statement affirming one's social identity, educational sophistication, and disposable income as it has about preserving the Amazon rainforest or the Caribbean reef for posterity.

Criticisms

Definitional Problems and Greenwashing

To approach an understanding of the problem, a clear definition must delineate what is, and is not, Eco-tourism. Ideally, Eco-tourism satisfies several general criteria, including the conservation of biological diversity and cultural diversity through ecosystem protection, promotion of sustainable use of biodiversity, share of social-economic benefits with local communities through informed consent and participation, increase in environmental and cultural knowledge, affordability and reduced waste, and minimization of its own environmental impact. In such ways, it contributes to the long term benefits to both the environment and local communities.

However, in the continuum of tourism activities that stretch from conventional tourism to Eco-tourism proper, there has been a lot of contention to the limit at which biodiversity preservation, local social-economic benefits, and environmental impact can be considered "Eco-tourism". For this reason, environmentalists, special interest groups, and governments define Eco-tourism differently. Environmental organizations have generally insisted that Eco-tourism is nature-based, sustainably managed, conservation supporting, and environmentally educated. The tourist industry and governments, however, focus more on the product aspect, treating Eco-tourism as equivalent to any sort of tourism based in nature. As a further complication, many terms are used under the rubric of Eco-tourism. Nature tourism, low impact tourism, green tourism, bio-tourism, ecologically responsible tourism, and others have been used in literature and marketing, although they are not necessary synonymous with Eco-tourism.

The problems associated with defining Eco-tourism have led to confusion among tourists and academics alike. Definitional problems are also subject of considerable public controversy and concern because of green washing, a trend towards the commercialization of tourism schemes disguised as sustainable, nature based, and environmentally friendly Eco-tourism. According to McLaren, these schemes are environmentally destructive, economically exploitative, and culturally insensitive at its worst. They are also morally disconcerting because they mislead tourists and manipulate their concerns for the environment. Despite objections, green washing continues to grow unabated. The Nature's Sacred Paradise, a theme park in Quintana Roo, Mexico, is responsible for displacing local Mayan communities and illegally keeping endangered species in captivity to attract visitors. The development and success of such large scale, energy intensive, and ecologically unsustainable schemes are a testament to the tremendous profits associated with being labeled as Eco-tourism.

Negative Impact of Tourism

Eco-tourism has become one of the fastest-growing sectors of the tourism industry, growing annually by 10-15% worldwide (Miller, 2007). One definition of Eco-tourism is "the practice of low-impact, educational, ecologically and culturally sensitive travel that benefits local communities and host countries" (Honey, 1999). Many of the Eco-tourism projects are not meeting these standards. Even if some of the guidelines are being executed, the local communities are still facing other negative impacts. South Africa is one of the countries that are reaping significant economic benefits from Eco-tourism, but negative effects-including forcing people to leave their homes, gross violations of fundamental rights, and environmental hazards-far outweigh the medium-term economic benefits (Miller, 2007). A tremendous amount of money is being spent and human resources continue to be used for Eco-tourism despite unsuccessful outcomes, and even more money is put into public relation campaigns to dilute the effects of criticism. Eco-tourism channels resources away from other projects that could contribute more sustainable and realistic solutions to pressing social and environmental problems. "The money tourism can generate often ties parks and managements to Eco-tourism" (Walpole et al. 2001). But there is a tension in this relationship because Eco-tourism often causes conflict and changes in land-use rights, fails to deliver promises of community-level benefits, damages environments, and has plenty of other social impacts. Indeed many argue repeatedly that Eco-tourism is neither ecologically nor socially beneficial, yet it persists as a strategy for conservation and development (West, 2006). While several studies are being done on ways to improve the Eco-tourism structure, some argue that these examples provide rationale for stopping it altogether.

The Eco-tourism system exercises tremendous financial and political influence. The evidence above shows that a strong case exists for restraining such activities in certain locations. Funding could be used for field studies aimed at finding alternative solutions to tourism and the diverse problems Africa faces in result of urbanization, industrialization, and the over exploitation of agriculture (Kamuaro, 2007). At the local level, Eco-tourism has become a source of conflict over control of land, resources, and tourism profits. In this case, Eco-tourism has harmed the environment and local people, and has led to conflicts over profit distribution. In a perfect world more efforts would be made towards educating tourists of the environmental and social effects of their travels. Very few regulations or laws stand in place as boundaries for the investors in Eco-tourism. These should be implemented to prohibit the promotion of unsustainable Eco-tourism projects and materials which project false images of destinations, demeaning local and indigenous cultures.

Direct Environmental Impacts

Eco-tourism operations occasionally fail to live up to conservation ideals. It is sometimes overlooked that Eco-tourism is a highly consumer-centered activity, and that environmental conservation is a means to further economic growth.

Although Eco-tourism is intended for small groups, even a modest increase in population, however temporary, puts extra pressure on the local environment and necessitates the development of additional infrastructure and amenities. The construction of water treatment plants, sanitation facilities, and lodges come with the exploitation of non-renewable energy sources and the utilization of already limited local resources. The conversion of natural land to such tourist infrastructure is implicated in deforestation and habitat deterioration of butterflies in Mexico and squirrel monkeys in Costa Rica. In other cases, the environment suffers because local communities are unable to meet the infrastructure demands of Eco-tourism. The lack of adequate sanitation facilities in many East African parks results in the disposal of campsite sewage in rivers, contaminating the wildlife, livestock, and people who draw drinking water from it.

Aside from environmental degradation with tourist infrastructure, population pressures from Eco-tourism also leaves behind garbage and pollution associated with the Western lifestyle. Although ecotourists claim to be educationally sophisticated and environmentally concerned, they rarely understand the ecological consequences of their visits and how their day-to-day activities append physical impacts on the environment. As one scientist observes, they "rarely acknowledge how the meals they eat, the toilets they flush, the water they drink, and so on, are all part of broader regional economic and ecological systems they are helping to reconfigure with their very activities." Nor do ecotourists recognize the great consumption of non-renewable energy required to arrive at their destination, which is typically more remote than conventional tourism destinations. For instance, an exotic journey to a place 10,000 kilometers away consumes about 700 litres of fuel per person.

Eco-tourism activities are, in of itself, issues in environmental impact because they disturb fauna and flora. Ecotourists believe that because they are only taking pictures and leaving footprints, they keep Eco-tourism sites pristine, but even harmless sounding activities such as a nature hike can be ecologically destructive. In the Annapurna Circuit in Nepal, ecotourists have worn down the marked trails and created alternate routes, contributing to soil impaction, erosion, and plant damage. Where the Eco-tourism activity involves wildlife viewing, it can scare away animals, disrupt their feeding and nesting sites, or acclimate them to the presence of people. In Kenya, wildlife-observer disruption drives cheetahs off their reserves, increasing the risk of inbreeding and further endangering the species.

Environmental Hazards

Unfortunately, industrialization, urbanization, and unsustainable agriculture practices have all had serious effects on the environment. Eco-tourism is now also playing a role in this depletion. While the term Eco-tourism may sound relatively benign, one of its most serious impacts is its consumption of virgin territories (Kamuaro, 2007). These invasions often include deforestation, disruption of ecological life systems and various forms of pollution, all of which contribute to environmental degradation.

The number of motor vehicles crossing the park increases as tour drivers search for rare species. The number of roads has disrupted the grass cover which has serious effects on plant and animal species. These areas also have a higher rate of disturbances and invasive species because of all the traffic moving off the beaten path into new undiscovered areas (Kamuaro, 2007). Eco-tourism also has an effect on species through the value placed on them. "Certain species have gone from being little known or valued by local people to being highly valued commodities. The commodification of plants may erase their social value and lead to overproduction within protected areas. Local people and their images can also be turned into commodities" (West, 2006). Kamuaro brings up a relatively obvious contradiction, any commercial venture into unspoiled, pristine land with or without the "eco" prefix as a contradiction in terms. To generate revenue you have to have a high number of traffic, tourists, which inevitably means a higher pressure on the environment.

Local People

Most forms of Eco-tourism are owned by foreign investors and corporations that provide few benefits to local communities. An overwhelming majority of profits are put into the pockets of investors instead of reinvestment into the local economy or environmental protection. The limited numbers of local people who are employed in the economy enter at its lowest level, and are unable to live in tourist areas because of meager wages and a two market system.

In some cases, the resentment by local people results in environmental degradation. As a highly publicized case, the Masai nomads in Kenya killed wildlife in national parks to show aversion to unfair compensation terms and displacement from traditional lands. The lack of economic opportunities for local people also constrains them to degrade the environment as a means of sustenance. The presence of affluent ecotourists encourage the development of destructive markets in wildlife souvenirs, such as the sale of coral trinkets on tropical islands and animal products in Asia, contributing to illegal harvesting and poaching from the environment. In Suriname, sea turtle reserves use a large portion of their budget to guard against these destructive activities.

Displacement of People

One of the most powerful examples of communities being moved in order to create a park is the story of the Masai. About 70% of national parks and game reserves in East Africa are on Masai land (Kamuaro, 2007). The first undesirable impact of tourism was that of the extent of land lost from the Masai culture. Local and national governments took advantage of the Masai's ignorance on the situation and robbed them of huge chunks of grazing land, putting to risk their only socioeconomic livelihood. In Kenya the Masai also have not gained any economic benefits. Despite the loss of their land, employment favours better educated workers. Furthermore the investors in this area are not local and have not put profits back into local economy. In some cases game reserves can be created without informing or consulting local people, who come to find out about the situation when an eviction notice is delivered (Kamuaro, 2007). Another source of resentment is the manipulation of the local people by their government. "Eco-tourism works to create simplistic images of local people and their uses and understandings of their surroundings. Through the lens of these simplified images, officials direct policies and projects towards the local people and the local people are blamed if the projects fail" (West, 2006). Clearly tourism as a trade is not empowering the local people who make it rich and satisfying. Instead Eco-tourism exploits and depletes, particularly in African Masai tribes. It has to be reoriented if it is to be useful to local communities and to become sustainable (Kamuaro, 2007).

Bibliography

Carl H. : *Internet Distribution of European Travel and Tourism Services,* Research Centre of Bornholm, Denmark, 1999.

Craig Zacker : *Networking: The Complete Reference,* Tata McGraw-Hill, Delhi, 2007.

Cukier, J. : *Tourism Employment in Bali: Trends and Implications,* London: Thompson, 1996.

Daniel Minoli : *A Networking Approach to Grid Computing,* Wiley, Delhi, 2010.

Digumarti Bhaskara Rao: *International Meetings on Human Rights,* Discovery, 2001.

Donald E. : *Public Personnel Management: Contexts and Strategies,* Upper Saddle River, NJ: Prentice Hall, 1998.

Donald M.: *Customer Service in the Hospitality and Tourism Industry,* Englewood Cliffs, Prentice Hall, 1994.

Douglas C: *Practical Tourism Forecasting,* Oxford, Butterworth Heinemann, 1996.

Eberts, Marjorie: *Careers in Travel, Tourism, and Hospitality,* Lincolnwood, VGM Career Horizons, 1997.

Eckel, Peter J.: *College & University Foodservice Management Standards,* Westport, AVI Pub. Company, 1985.

Elio, C.: *The Hospitality Law Desk Reference,* Miami, Southern Beverage Journal, 1994.

Foster, Douglas: *Travel and Tourism Management,* London, Macmillan Educational, 1985.

Fowler, Peter: *Heritage and Tourism: In the Global Village,* London, Retailed, 1993.

Ghimire, Krishna: *The Native Tourist*: Mass Tourism within Developing Regions, London, Earthscan, 2001.

Gopalkrishnan: *Brand Alliances : New Models of Networking*, ICFAI, 2007.

Graham M S: *Language of Tourism*, The, Wallingford, CAB International, 1996.

Harish Kapadia: *Meeting the Mountains*, Indus, Delhi, 1998.

Her Majesty's : *Higher Education in the Polytechnics and Colleges, Hotel, Catering and Tourism Management*, London, DES, 1992.

Holloway, C. : *Learning and Earning: Reassessing the Aims and Purposes of a Tourism Degree*, Developments in the European Tourism Curriculum, Tilberg, 1998.

Ireland, Lewis: *Quality Management for Projects and Programs*, Upper Darby, PMI, 1991.

Jennings, Gayle: *Tourism Research*, Chichester, Wiley, 2001.

Karski, A: *Urban Tourism* - A Key to Urban Regeneration?, 1990.

Klein, S. : *Information & Communication Technologies in Tourism*, Springer-Verlag, Wien-New York, 2000.

Kotler, Philip: *Marketing for Hospitality and Tourism*: New Jersey, Prentice-Hall, 1998.

Labarge, Margaret Wade: *Medieval Travellers: The Rich and Restless*, London, Hamish Hamilton, 1982.

Larkham, P J: *Building a New Heritage: Tourism, Culture & Identity in the New Europe*, London, Routledge,1994.

Laws, E. : *The ATTT Tourism Education Handbook*, London, Tourism Society, 1997.

Maitland, R: *Tourism Destinations, London*, Hodder and Stoughton, 1997.

Medlik, S. : *Tourism, Past, Present and Future*, London, Heinemann, 1981.

Negi, K.S. : *A Textbook of Hotel Management*, Wisdom Press, Delhi, 2011.

Norman G.: *Hotel, Restaurant, and Travel Law: A Preventive Approach*, Albany, Delmar Publishers, 1993.

Pearce, Douglas: *Tourism Today: A Geographical Analysis*, Harlow, Longman, 1995.

Peter J.: *College & University Foodservice Management Standards*, Westport, AVI Pub. Company, 1985.

□□□